Cultural Intelligence

Youth, Family, and Culture Series

Chap Clark, series editor

The Youth, Family, and Culture series examines the broad categories involved in studying and caring for the needs of the young and is dedicated to the preparation and vocational strengthening of those who are committed to the spiritual development of adolescents.

Cultural Intelligence

Improving Your CQ to Engage
Our Multicultural World

David A. Livermore

Baker Academic
a division of Baker Publishing Group
Grand Rapids, Michigan

Published by Baker Academic
a division of Baker Publishing Group
P.O. Box 6287, Grand Rapids, MI 49516-6287
www.bakeracademic.com

Printed in the United States of America

Library of Congress Cataloging-in-Publication Data
Livermore, David A., 1967–
    Cultural intelligence : improving your CQ to engage our multicultural world youth, family, and culture / David A. Livermore.
        p.   cm.
    Includes bibliographical references and index.
    ISBN 978-0-8010-3589-0 (pbk.)
    1. Christianity and culture. I. Title.
BR115.C8L58 2009
261—dc22   2008045365

contents

series preface

In many ways, youth ministry has come of age. No longer seen as "a stepping-stone to real ministry in the church," especially in North America, youth ministry is now seen as a viable career option. Over the last few decades a wide range of professional resources, conferences, periodicals, and books have been developed on this topic. Most Christian colleges and seminaries now offer a variety of courses—if not degree programs—in youth ministry. Youth ministry has all it needs to continue to push the church to care about and serve the needs of the young in God's name, except for one thing: we have a long way to go to develop a rich, broad, and diverse conversation that frames, defines, and grounds our missional call.

There is good news, of course. There is a professional organization, Association of Youth Ministry Educators, that sponsors an annual conference and publishes a solid emerging journal. Several thoughtful books have helped to shape the discipline's future. There are also now two major publishers who have academic lines dedicated to furthering the field of youth ministry. We have made great progress, but we must all work together to continue deepening our understanding of what youth ministry should be.

The purpose of Baker Academic's Youth, Family, and Culture series is to raise the level of dialogue concerning how we think about, teach, and live out youth ministry. As a branch of practical theology, academic youth ministry must move beyond a primarily skills-based focus to a theologically driven expression of a contextualized commitment of the local church to a targeted population. James Fowler defines practical theology as "theological reflection and construction arising out of and giving guidance to a community of faith in the *praxis* of its mission. Practical theology is critical and constructive reflection leading to ongoing modification and development of the ways the church shapes its life to be in partnership with God's work in the world.[1] And as Scott Cormode reminds us, we must not shirk our calling, but "must strive to nurture leaders that are faithful. . . . Schools must prepare leaders to translate this faithfulness into effective action."[2] This is precisely what those of us who are called to engage the church in theological reflection of contemporary youth and family issues must do—develop a practical theology that takes seriously the reality of the context we are in, regardless of how and where it takes us. This is the future of youth and family ministry in the church.

Dave Livermore's *Cultural Intelligence* is the second book in the Youth, Family, and Culture series. Dr. Livermore brings a vital and helpful correction to how we think about cross-cultural ministry and relationships, issues highly relevant to individuals involved in youth ministry, missions, and church ministry. His book is thoroughly theological and at the same time eminently practical. Thus, this volume is an example of a practical theology of youth and family ministry. May this book spur on our much-needed conversation of what it means to be in youth ministry, now and in the future.

Chap Clark
Fuller Theological Seminary
May 2008

acknowledgments

To Andrew and Lynn Rudd, for a priceless friendship made richer because of our shared journey through fundamentalism.

To Steve and Jen Argue, for the taste of heaven I get from the countless ways our lives, families, and ministry intersect.

To my colleagues and students at Grand Rapids Theological Seminary, for the ways you supportively stretch me in thinking about what culturally intelligent service looks like for our learning community.

To Bob Hosack and Chap Clark, for a professional relationship built upon shared concerns and friendship and for making this topic a publishing priority.

To Linda, Emily, and Grace, for loving me like no one else does, despite my manic moments of writing and traveling. You've shared every moment of this book with me. I love you.

introduction

What do you do when you encounter someone who isn't like you? How do you feel? What goes on inside you? How do you relate to him or her? These are the kinds of questions we want to explore in this book. Few things are more basic to life than expressing love and respect for people who look, think, believe, act, and see differently than we do. We want to adapt to the barrage of cultures around us while still remaining true to ourselves. We want to let the world change us so that we can be part of changing the world. And we want to move from the *desire* to love across the chasm of cultural difference to the *ability* to express our love for people of difference. Relating lovingly to our fellow human beings is central to what it means to be human. And when it comes down to it, Christian ministry at its core is interacting with all kinds of people in ways that give them glimpses of Jesus in us.

The billions of us sharing planet Earth together have so much in common. We're all born. We all die. We're all created in the image of God. We eat, sleep, persevere, and care for our young. We long for meaning and purpose, and we develop societies with those around us.

But the way we go about the many things we have in common is deeply rooted in our unique personalities and cultures. So although we have so much in common, we have as much or more about us that's different. Asian. European. Tattooed. Clean-cut. Male. Female. Old. Young. Pentecostal. Emergent. Republican. Democrat. Suburban. Rural. Urban. These points of difference are where we find both our greatest challenges and our greatest discoveries. And as the world becomes increasingly more connected and accessible, the number of encounters we have with those who are culturally different are growing daily. Most of us are more comfortable with people like ourselves. But seeking out and loving people of difference is a far greater challenge. Therefore, learning how to reach across the chasm of cultural difference with love and respect is becoming an essential competency for today's ministry leader.

Why This Book?

There are several helpful resources available on cross-cultural ministry. Many of these have informed my own thinking and practice. However, research has shown that a significant number of missional initiatives continue to fail because of cultural differences.[1] Whether it is Bruce Wilkinson's failed attempts at saving AIDS orphans in Swaziland,[2] well-intentioned short-term missionaries who end up hindering the work of local churches,[3] or the ways churches unknowingly perpetuate racism in their local communities,[4] something has to change. With the growing opportunities for multicultural interactions at home and abroad, the question of how ministry leaders and their organizations can effectively minister in culturally diverse situations is a critical and challenging problem. This problem cannot be addressed by simple lists of cultural taboos that sometimes appear in books on cross-cultural interaction. On the other hand, some books on contextualization are so complex and cerebral that ministry leaders are tempted to toss them aside as little more than ivory-tower rhetoric. This book attempts to bridge the gap between theory and practice.

The most helpful resources about cross-cultural ministry that have been distributed by Christian publishers are oriented primarily toward missionaries.[5] I've often wished more pastors and parachurch leaders would read these books as well because there is much to be learned from them for the work of ministry leaders who never move abroad. But ministry leaders at home often overlook such books. This book draws from some of the most helpful material written for the missionary audience and applies it to ministry leaders working in rural, urban, and suburban contexts at home. And I hope the book serves as a helpful addition to the resources needed by ministry leaders living and serving abroad as missionaries or in other capacities of service.

The primary distinction of this book is that it uses an approach to cross-cultural interaction that stems from inward transformation rather than from information or, worse yet, from artificial political correctness. Our goal is not simply to learn more about different cultures, nor is it just to become better at "navigating cultural differences." *We must actually become more multicultural people so that we might better express love cross-culturally.* Avoiding ethnic slurs and having a Latino celebration is a start—but to stop there is a superficial approach at best.

Most of the resources addressing cross-cultural communication and behavior emphasize what we need to know (information) and how we need to act (behavior). Clearly those are important priorities for cross-cultural interaction, but they aren't enough. Often we learn about another culture we intend to visit, but as soon as we visit and encounter dissonance, we abort the knowledge we gained and resort to what's comfortable. Furthermore, two individuals can go through the same cross-cultural training and perform very differently when they actually engage in cross-cultural relationships. Transformation from within is what is needed most.

As a result, *Cultural Intelligence: Improving Your CQ to Engage Our Multicultural World* takes a different approach. This book draws from the emerging domain of cultural intelligence to take us on an inward journey while simultaneously reaching across the chasm of cultural difference. A cultural intelligence quotient (CQ) measures the ability to effectively reach across the chasm of cultural difference in ways that are loving and respectful. It is a measurement and a metaframework that draws from a variety of disciplines. Although cultural intelligence includes having information about different cultures and what they value, it begins with understanding ourselves. This book is as much about discovering ourselves and understanding the cultures of which we're a part as it is about understanding others. As we widen our view to include what's going on within us, we will be able to interact more lovingly with our ethnically different neighbors and the indigenous workers with whom we partner across the ocean. That's our destination in this journey—learning how to effectively express love for people unlike us.

Book Organization

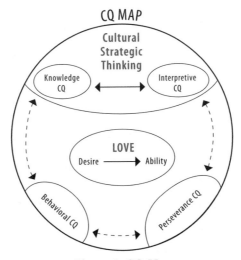

Figure 1. CQ Map

Cultural intelligence consists of four different factors, knowledge CQ, interpretive CQ, perseverance CQ, and behavioral CQ, all of which overlap in a variety of ways (see fig. 1). These four factors are incorporated into the organization of the book.

The first part of the book, "Love: CQ Overview," includes three chapters that provide an overview of cultural intelligence as the pathway toward more authentically expressing our love for the Other. In these chapters, I will consider why CQ matters from three different vantage points: in light of the realities of twenty-first-century ministry, from a theological perspective, and as compared to the many other theories of intercultural competency. These vantage points provide the backdrop for an understanding of why ministry leaders from Kansas to Timbuktu must be committed to growing in cultural intelligence as a way to effectively serve and lead. Love is the primary reason cultural intelligence is an essential competency in the life of twenty-first-century ministry leaders.

The second part of the book, "Understand: Knowledge CQ," covers the seminal material related to the first factor of cultural intelligence: knowledge. Knowledge, or cognitive, CQ measures one's understanding of cross-cultural issues and differences. It is the aspect most often emphasized when dealing with issues of cultural difference. This part begins with a chapter about American culture as a way for American readers to begin their inward journey as it relates to cultural awareness. This part also covers the important elements of a general cross-cultural understanding, including understanding the notion of culture itself, its application to a variety of cultural domains, and the relevance of language and cultural values to knowledge CQ.

The next part of the book, "Go Deep: Interpretive CQ," is devoted to interpretive, or metacognitive, CQ. Interpretive CQ is the degree to which we're mindful and aware when we interact cross-culturally. This is the dimension of cultural intelligence that appears to be most lacking in the performance of many American ministry leaders. Yet interpretive CQ is the key process linking the understanding gained in knowledge CQ with the actual ability to apply it to how we behave. The chapters in this part move through the integral aspects of interpretive CQ, beginning with the importance of becoming mindful and aware, then examining some of the ways we actually think about the world and how that affects the way we do ministry. This part concludes by looking at a model to assist in nurturing interpretive CQ in ourselves and others.

The final part, "Express: Perseverance and Behavioral CQ," while entirely dependent on the understanding and interpretations that come from knowledge and interpretive CQ, moves us toward actually applying cultural intelligence to our service and relationships. Both of the final two factors of cultural intelligence—perseverance and behavioral—are covered in this part because they're the dimensions of cultural intelligence that most explicitly influence how we live out these ideas.

Adapting our message, our curriculum, and our programs is one thing. But adapting ourselves is the far greater challenge. That's the issue we're most interested in pursuing in this journey together—What does it look like to contextualize ourselves to the various cultures where we find ourselves in any given week? What do we do when we encounter the Other and how do we react to him or her? By "Other" I simply mean those not like us. The Other is a concept developed by the German philosopher Hegel that has been popularized as a way of referring to those different from us. The markers of difference can be racial, geographic, ethnic, economic, or ideological. When thinking of "us" as compared to "them," the "them" is what we mean by the Other. This term can sound pejorative, but it need not be as long as we keep in view that all of us are created in the image of God. Throughout this journey toward more effectively expressing love to the Other, we'll explore the significance of seeing both ourselves and the Other as expressions of who God is. Consistent with its use throughout intercultural studies, the term "Other" is used throughout this book to refer to those coming from a different cultural context, be it a socioethnic culture, an organizational culture, or a generational culture.[6]

We encounter the Other in various ways, all day long, and the Other encounters us. Clearly we can't become experts about every culture we encounter. There are more than five thousand distinct cultural groups in the world. Add to those the many subcultural contexts that exist among various age groups and organizations and the number of distinct cultures in which we minister becomes impossible to quantify. But how might we grow in cultural intelligence so that we can better reflect the love of Jesus in what we say and do as we encounter people who see the world differently than we do, whatever their cultural context? How do we become more multicultural people while still remaining true to who God made us to be? These are the driving questions behind this book.

Rather than simply dump a lot of information on you, I want to invite you into a shared journey using the fascinating pathway of cultural intelligence. I'll share information and examples from my own research and the research of others (see appendix C for research methodology), but along the way we'll stop to reflect on some of the implications for us personally and for the ministries of which we're a part. The goal isn't cultural intelligence in and of itself. Instead, cultural intelligence is the pathway for moving us along in the journey from the desire to love the Other to the ability to express that love in ways that are meaningful and respectful.

Overviews and summaries are provided throughout the book to connect one part to another. Some readers may find these helpful in seeing how all the pieces fit together, while others may find them unnecessary or redundant. I encourage you to engage with the transitional material at whatever level is helpful for your own journey through the book. Appendix A contains a glossary that defines some of the important terms used throughout the book. Grab a journal and keep it nearby as you read. Consider the questions that are posed along the way. And find some peers who will jump into this reading journey with you. Discuss what you encounter on these pages and, more importantly, what you see when looking deep within yourself.

To love, seek to understand, go deep, and express: that is the journey ahead of us. Thanks for joining me in the quest to better love the Other and reflect who Jesus is among the various cultural contexts where we lead and serve.

part 1

love: CQ overview

Cultural intelligence: reaching across the chasm of cultural difference in ways that are loving and respectful.

From my journal:

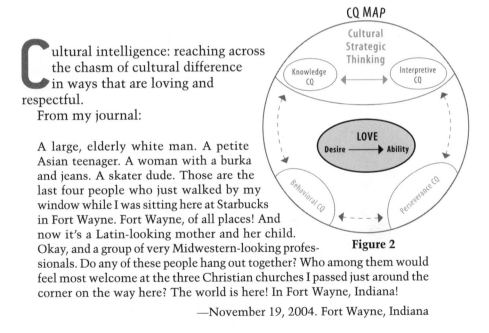

CQ MAP

Figure 2

A large, elderly white man. A petite Asian teenager. A woman with a burka and jeans. A skater dude. Those are the last four people who just walked by my window while I was sitting here at Starbucks in Fort Wayne. Fort Wayne, of all places! And now it's a Latin-looking mother and her child. Okay, and a group of very Midwestern-looking professionals. Do any of these people hang out together? Who among them would feel most welcome at the three Christian churches I passed just around the corner on the way here? The world is here! In Fort Wayne, Indiana!

—November 19, 2004. Fort Wayne, Indiana

Love. That's our destination. We're on a journey from the desire to love the Other[1] to a place where we effectively *express* the love of Jesus to people of difference. Be encouraged. The desire itself, along with the supernatural work of the Holy Spirit, provides the fuel we need to embark on this sojourn.

> Stop and think about what group represents the Other for you. To which culture or subculture do you find it hardest to relate? In what context do the skills that usually come to you naturally feel incredibly awkward and strained? Jot down a few names or examples as we move forward in improving the way we love and serve.

There's something secure and stabilizing about being with people who view the world like us. Laughing together about things we find funny, ranting together about things that tick us off, and sharing an appreciation for some of the same food, art, and perspectives on the world can be the ingredients for building serendipitous memories together. But quite honestly, there's nothing very remarkable about enjoying time with people like ourselves. Everyone fares pretty well there. But to love and appreciate someone who despises the very things we value and vice versa—now that's another story. Yet the real mystery of the gospel lies in how we deal with those relationships of difference.

I can't think of a more scandalous example of friendship than the one shared by Larry Flynt, *Hustler* magazine founder, and Jerry Falwell, the late founder of the fundamentalist Moral Majority. On the day Falwell died, lots of news pundits were brutal with their critiques of his life. But here's what Flynt said: "My mother always told me that no matter how much you dislike a person, when you meet them face-to-face you will find characteristics about them that you like. Jerry Falwell was a perfect example of that. I hated everything he stood for, but after meeting him in person, years after the trial, Jerry Falwell and I became good friends. . . . I always appreciated his sincerity even though I knew what he was selling and he knew what I was selling."[2]

Not to fear. I'm not interested in setting up Falwell or Flynt as examples we're interested in following. But there's something beautiful about Flynt being able to call Falwell a "good friend." And when the gospel comes up close—face-to-face—something mysterious happens. Many fields and disciplines are interested in cultural intelligence. The business world is tapping into the research to become more successful in culturally diverse markets. Government officials are being trained in cultural intelligence to become better at "winning" in foreign settings. And educational institutions want to know how to accomplish learning objectives among students coming from different cultural backgrounds.

But nowhere does cultural intelligence find a better home than in the Christian faith. Sadly, Christendom itself has often created some of the most notable examples of cultural ignorance. Missionaries have gone into foreign lands insisting that locals adopt dress, use music, and build churches that mirror their own. Older generations have shamed younger generations for the use of inappropriate music genres in worship. And it has been noted far too many times that Sunday morning is the most racially divided time of the week in many American cities. Furthermore, some of the greatest controversies entangling many churches and ministries today revolve around the issue of contextualizing the gospel to various cultural contexts—what's up for grabs and what isn't? Throughout this book, we'll explore several realities facing ministry leaders in contextualizing the gospel to culture. We'll examine both positive and negative examples of how many ministry leaders are responding to these challenges. Rather than perpetuating unloving, disrespectful interactions in these varying cultural contexts, the church can lead the way in authentically expressing love across the chasm of cultural difference.

This first part of the book describes the essential role of cultural intelligence for ministry leaders, whatever their ministry context. There's little need for more information on why cultural intelligence is necessary for people serving internationally. But we want primarily to consider how developing cultural intelligence is becoming an increasingly important skill for ministry leaders serving in places close to home. Before immersing ourselves in the cultural intelligence framework, I want to answer the question, why CQ?

Ultimately the answer is "Love." Jesus synthesized all the teaching of the Law around the greatest commandments, "Love God. Love Others" (see Matt. 22:37–39). *Maitri*, a word for love found in the Sanskrit language, is rooted in the idea that compassion and generosity begin with an individual's *desire* to love. But *maitri* is expressed only when one knows how to move from *desire* to *action*. Based on my research, I'm confident most ministry leaders *want* to love the Other. But gaining the *ability* to love the Other and leading others in our ministries to do the same is the journey we're interested in exploring in this book. That's why love is the center of the CQ map (fig. 2), reminding us that our journey is from the *desire* to love the other to the *ability to express* that love in effective ways. Cultural intelligence is a pathway to help us along the journey from desire to action. It's the bridge that helps us more effectively express and embody Christ's unconditional love across the chasm of cultural difference.

Because we want to live out our love for God and others, cultural intelligence is an essential issue for us in the twenty-first century. Chapter 1 addresses the relevance of cultural intelligence in light of the sociological realities of the twenty-first-century world. We examine the multicolored mosaic of the communities where we live and minister as the backdrop for our need for cultural intelligence.

Chapter 2 approaches the topic of cultural intelligence from a theological perspective. How do we ensure that we aren't simply selling out to a politically correct view of tolerance toward different cultures and viewpoints? This chapter examines the essential place this topic has continually occupied in the life of Christians and presents a framework for how God contextualized himself to us through Jesus.

Chapter 3 provides an overview of the cultural intelligence framework and examines some of the many helpful theories and approaches to cultural sensitivity and intercultural competence. This chapter compares cultural intelligence with some of the other theories and posits why cultural intelligence is uniquely suited for the challenges facing twenty-first-century ministry leaders at home and abroad. The chapter also provides a brief overview of the four factors of cultural intelligence, each of which are more thoroughly described later in the book.

The first leg of our journey is an exploration into how cultural intelligence helps us live out the primary command to love. Most of us probably don't need much convincing that love for people is central to the Christian life. Loving and serving the Other has always been at the core of living out our God-given mission, even when the Other may be the "Flynt" to our "Falwell." But today more than ever, we need cultural intelligence in order to authentically and effectively express our love for the people we encounter day in and day out.

1

twenty-first-century CQ

Getting Along in the Flat World

'Ve spent a lot of time over the last few years researching some of the paternalistic, albeit usually unintentional, attitudes reflected in many cross-cultural[1] ministry efforts. The research process has been a bit of a voyeur's dream: going through stacks of journals to read the personal musings of others. I've read the journals of American high school students serving in places such as Mexico, West Virginia, and Kenya. Pastors have allowed me to observe their reflections about their efforts to bridge the racial divides that exist in their communities. Inner-city ministry leaders have shared vulnerable confessions of how it feels to be the recipients of suburbanites' good will. This isn't something I treat lightly. And I've read enough of these that there aren't many reflections that now surprise me. In fact, one of the disappointments has sometimes been the familiarity of what is recorded again and again.

But I was unprepared for the effect that reading one short-term missionary's journal had on me. The observations seemed much like those that I had read before. But this one hit me differently. Here are a few of the excerpts with certain phrases italicized for emphasis:

> **April 10.** The support letters just went out. Now I wait and pray. Lord, I believe you want me to *bring the gospel to these people in the Amazon.* So please provide the monies needed.

June 20. The money has come in. I'm humbled by the generosity of so many people. . . .

June 22. This is our first day in Iquitos. The challenges began as soon as we landed last night. The airport looked like a dilapidated barn. But they sure took baggage security seriously. They wouldn't let us have our bags until they checked the tags. *I guess they have to do that here; otherwise people would probably steal them.*

June 25. Wow! *The Industrial Revolution obviously skipped this place.* . . . The cool thing is everything is so cheap!

June 27. We're staying in one of the missionary's homes for a couple days while they're away. *If we weren't here, the place would probably be robbed.*

June 29. I spoke at one of the churches today. *They don't speak English* so I had to use an interpreter.

July 3. It was a *productive* day. Two souls were saved.

July 4. It's so weird to be here on the Fourth of July. . . . Being here makes me so thankful for our country. *Why did I get the blessing of being born in America?* What if I had been born here instead?

This short-term missionary demonstrates many of the things I've critiqued throughout the years, such as thinking we're "bringing" the gospel to the Amazon, assuming everyone in a developing country is out to rob us, emphasizing others' inability to speak English rather than our inability to speak the local language, and assuming people aren't "blessed" if they are born outside the United States. The problem is, the short-term missionary who wrote these reflections was me! I discovered this journal a few months ago when I had decided to reread all the journals I've kept over the last several years. As I read the musings I wrote during my first missions trip in 1986, I couldn't believe my eyes. How could it be that my own hand wrote some of the very things I've ranted about elsewhere? It quickly reminded me of my own journey through the fascinating domain of cultural intelligence—reaching across the chasm of cultural difference in ways that are loving and respectful. The journey across the chasm of cultural difference begins with a *desire* to love people of difference but must move toward an *ability* to effectively express that love. It's an ongoing journey for all of us, myself included.

I'm still a far cry from the ideal of cultural intelligence. You'll read many more episodes of cultural ignorance from my life in the pages that follow. But I'm on the journey toward more lovingly and respectfully interacting with those unlike me. And so are you. The very fact you're reading a book about cultural intelligence gives me hope about your interest in joining many others who want to strengthen how we live in the Way of Jesus as we interact with people unlike us.

The world is more connected than ever. As a result, cross-cultural interactions are no longer the exclusive domain of seminary-trained missionaries or of official, State Department diplomats. We all find ourselves encountering people from vastly different cultural backgrounds. *As a result, cultural clashes and the ability to lovingly relate to one another are some of the critical issues of our day.*

I think most Americans want to be effective cross-culturally. I've interviewed and talked with thousands of Americans about this issue over the last decade, and for the most part, I have found people who desperately want to defy the "ugly American" image. Yet by and large, Americans continue to fare poorly in effectively crossing cultures in ways that cause the people they encounter to feel loved and respected. Unfortunately, there is little difference between the cross-cultural sensitivity of American Christians and that of Americans in general. Some would suggest that Christians fare even worse, but there's little conclusive evidence to support that opinion. Regardless, if there were ever an area where the Christian church should be leading the way, it is in being a living picture of what it looks like to interact with our fellow human beings from different cultural backgrounds in ways that are collaborative, respectful, and loving.

The following findings are a sampling of the recurring sentiments that emerged from my research on the cultural issues facing many churches and ministries. I've included a finding here only if it appeared with enough frequency to make it a noticeable trend among the subjects sampled.[2]

From locals who received North American short-term missionaries:
We're not a zoo of poverty. So please put away your cameras for a while.

You conclude you're communicating effectively because we're paying attention, when we're actually just intrigued by watching your foreign behavior.

We are not naive and backward. . . . Instead we are your brothers and sisters in Christ.

From ethnic minorities to white evangelical churches:
I'd love to be invited to speak at your church about something other than issues of race.

The crime in our neighborhoods is not purely a matter of work ethic. We need your help in breaking the systems of oppression that continue.

I [don't] need [one] more message to the kids in our community that says, *Guess what? This six-year-old white kid got you a better gift than your schmuck of a father did.*

From various generations in the church:

Don't assume that just because we're old, we have nothing to offer anymore. We've given our sweat, blood, and tears to this church. And now we're just being written off.

Please give us a chance to make the faith our own. We'll make our share of mistakes, but our attempts to rethink the gospel are not simply because we're angry and rebellious.

It really gets me when the pastor greets me every week by saying, "Good morning, young lady. How are you today?" Who is he kidding? Does he really think I'm not well aware that he and I both know I'm an old woman? I'm not ashamed of it, so why is he?

From various organizational cultures:

They need to get rid of all their formal titles around this place. We're all equal parts of the body.

Presbyterians are all caught up with their highbrow theology, but they can't live it out.

Pentecostals get all emotional, but it's hard to find much intellectual substance.

It is unfair to list these statements without more context. Several of them will show up later in the book with further explanation about what the subject was trying to communicate. For now, my point is that there isn't much love experienced or expressed by the thoughts and feelings represented in these comments.

Be encouraged though. If you and the people in your ministry have the desire to love people of difference, you can move toward more effectively expressing that love cross-culturally. These kinds of indicting statements don't have to be the norm in your ministry. Through cultural intelligence, we can move beyond good intentions to actually serving cross-culturally in ways that are truly loving and transforming for everyone involved.

As we begin our journey toward becoming more culturally intelligent leaders, our first step is to explore some of the reasons why cultural intelligence is an essential skill in the twenty-first century. We'll look at the growth of world travel, the multicultural complexities facing those given international work assignments (missionaries, business expatriates, ESL teachers, etc.), and the many cultural groups that exist in our own communities.

One Billion Frequent Fliers

Our growing awareness of catastrophic hurricanes, tsunamis, and terrorist threats seems to have little sway on our urge to travel around the world. Back in 1995, just over 550 million tourist visas were issued around the world. The number has steadily climbed since then with only a slight lapse in worldwide travel after the September 11 attacks on New York and Washington. Today, nearly 1 billion tourist visas are issued annually, and the number keeps rising every year. That means at least one out of every six people in the world travel to other countries each year, and many of the remaining population are hosting the travelers who come. The desire to travel apparently trumps fear of natural or man-made dangers.[3]

Also, softer borders and cheap airfares between European countries have boosted travel throughout Europe. And singles, couples, and families from all kinds of places are packing their bags to scuba dive in the Maldives, mountain climb in Nepal, and watch wildlife in Kenya.

It used to be only the senior-level executives of large multinational corporations like IBM and Coca-Cola who traveled internationally. Today, international flights are filled with start-up entrepreneurs doing business in Mexico, China, and Bosnia. And mid-level managers and salespeople are increasingly traveling abroad for work in the flattened world, a concept popularized by journalist Thomas Friedman in his best-selling book *The World Is Flat*.[4] Friedman argues that the competitive playing fields between industrial and emerging markets are leveling. Regardless of how you feel about Friedman's economics, any ministry leader in the developed world needs to read this book to get a glimpse of how the businesspeople in our ministries are affected by globalization and technology. Business professionals are learning that global activity is essential to survival in the flattened world. As a result, every day people are being faced with a need to interact with others from different cultures in ways that are loving and respectful.

Worldwide travel spills over into other areas as well. Students and teachers in universities are learning and teaching abroad for periods ranging from a couple of weeks to a year or longer. Conferences for all kinds of professional organizations are held in international locations with delegates from many places. And pastors are expected to participate in and lead short-term missions trips.

In fact, much of the worldwide travel by American Christians happens under the umbrella of short-term missions. Nearly one-third of all American high school students participate in some kind of religious cross-cultural experience before they graduate from high school. It's hard to be deemed a legitimate church ministry for youth these days without running a full-fledged, short-term missions program. More than 5.5 million thirteen- to seventeen-year-old Americans have cumulatively gone on more than 11.5 million mission trips. This involves more than 2 million trips a year just for this age bracket.[5] However, few Christian colleges and universities train youth ministry students in skills such as cultural intelligence; therefore, youth leaders are often underequipped to handle the cross-cultural challenges confronting them.

Though short-term missionaries are most often high school and college students, more and more families, adults, and senior citizens are participating as well. According to Princeton sociologist of religion Robert Wuthnow, about 1.6 million American *adult* church members (Protestants and Catholics) participated in short-term missions trips outside the United States during 2005. And an additional unknown number of American Christians traveled within the United States doing similar kinds of work in cross-cultural contexts, such as rebuilding efforts in New Orleans, development work in West Virginia, or evangelistic outreaches in New York City. Most short-term missions trips are two weeks or less, a period that fits well with school holidays or annual vacations. In contrast to the millions of short-term missionaries traveling annually, approximately sixty thousand long-term American missionaries are living overseas.

Though the short-term-missionary phenomenon seems to have the most momentum in the United States and Canada, it has parallel movements in other parts of the world. Christians in the United Kingdom, Australia, South Korea, and Singapore, as well as Russia, Uganda, Guatemala, and other countries are also traveling around the world on short-term missions trips. For example, between January and September 2005, twenty thousand Koreans participated in two-week short-term missions trips to Mongolia, typically in groups of thirty to eighty people at a time.[6]

I am part of a small but growing research community that has been gathering data and assessing the efficacy of short-term missions.[7] The questionable motivation behind many trips, the paternalistic interactions that often occur, and the increasing amounts of money spent are reasons for concern. Many studies raise questions about whether anything positive results from these trips for the local communities that receive the missionaries.[8] Some receiving communities view short-term missions groups as being primarily a way to enlist needed funds. Other missionaries and national pastors report the ways the same people in their neighborhoods "get converted" week after week as one group after another proselytizes them.

Some researchers even question the transformative impact on the participants that the trips are alleged to have. There is no increase in the number of people enlisting in long-term missionary service as a result of their short-term missions experiences. Longitudinal studies examining the prayer lives, giving habits, and evangelistic pursuits of short-term missionaries after they return home find little difference from the missionaries' behaviors before their trips. And in some cases, short-term missions trips perpetuate the ethnocentrism of participants rather than subverting it.[9] Short-term missionaries often travel to Mexico to show love to the locals there for ten days and return home isolated from the Mexicans living in their own communities. Worse yet, some short-term missionaries continue to discriminate against ethnic groups at home while lavishing love and attention on people they encounter abroad.

Much more needs to be understood about the short-term missions phenomenon. But researchers continue to find that the effectiveness of short-term missions is positively related to the participants' personal growth in cultural intelligence.[10] And those leading short-term missions trips need to develop their cultural intelligence and learn how to help other participants do so as well. Cultural intelligence is one of the most important means of making short-term missions an effective tool for mission and formation for everyone involved.

Moving Abroad

In contrast to the relatively new phenomenon of short-term missions, long-term missionaries have been dealing with cross-cultural issues for centuries. And business professionals with overseas assignments have been engaged in cross-cultural encounters for a few decades. But the cross-cultural challenges facing these groups are also growing. It used to be that an American missionary going to work in Brazil typically joined a group of other American missionaries to work in the same culture. There were often numerous Brazilian subcultures about which American missionaries needed to learn, such as urban life in São Paulo and Brasília and the tribal customs of people living along the Amazon. But the focus of missionaries' cross-cultural learning was relatively clear—"How does an American interact with Brazilian culture(s)?"

Today, more often than not, an American missionary goes to a field where he or she joins missionaries from a variety of other places around the world. Given that 50 percent of missionaries today originate from places other than North America and Western Europe, an American missionary working in Azerbaijan may well be joined by Filipino, Brazilian, Swedish, Guatemalan, and Nigerian missionaries. So those missionaries must become people who not only seek to understand the cultural dynamics of working in Azerbaijan but also grasp the dynamics of working with associates from all those various cultures. For several decades, missions agencies have reported that the number one problem experienced by missionaries is getting along with their missionary colleagues. Add a diversity of cultures to an already conflict-laden relationship, and you can understand why cultural intelligence is essential for effective missionary service.

A similar challenge faces business professionals. No longer is a Singaporean who is an international businessperson solely working with Japanese in Tokyo or Americans in Minneapolis. More often than not, Singaporean business leaders on expatriate assignments work with associates from numerous different national backgrounds wherever they go. The number of cultural contexts in which a missionary or a businessperson works on an overseas assignment has become increasingly diverse. Cultural intelligence is uniquely suited to help us and those with whom we serve respond to the barrage of intercultural interactions facing us.

We Aren't in Kansas Anymore, or Are We?

Meanwhile, most of us need cultural intelligence back home in our own communities. Imagine you go to a Saturday morning farmers' market. In front of you is just what you might expect—a fair-skinned farmer wearing coveralls who is selling sweet corn. But to his right is a Vietnamese couple selling long beans and fresh lemongrass. And on the other side of him is a veiled Yemeni woman selling herbs and spices to a Latino guy wearing a "Big Red" jacket. You might guess I'm describing a scene from a farmers' market in New York City, Seattle, or even Chicago. But I'm describing the farmers' market in Lincoln, Nebraska. Lincoln, a city whose natives used to proudly describe it as "the middle of nowhere," is now home to public schools where students represent more than fifty different nationalities, speaking thirty-two different languages as their first language.[11]

While coastal cities like Seattle, Los Angeles, and New York have experienced some of the greatest internationalization in the United States, the colorful additions of Asians, Africans, and Latinos are also moving into neighborhoods throughout the heartland of the country. I live in the small city of Grand Rapids, Michigan. For several decades, this community was predominantly Dutch American. Fifteen years ago, 3 percent of the population here was Hispanic. Today, more than 17 percent of the Grand Rapids population is Hispanic. And the Asian population in Grand Rapids increased 26 percent in the last decade.[12]

Today, one out of every seven Americans[13] is Hispanic. And soon the ratio will be one in four. By 2016, more than one-third of Americans will be people of color. The color shift in the United States is coming not just from Hispanics, however. High schools will soon routinely offer Hindi and Mandarin, as a growing number of Asians become a more significant part of the American population. Neighborhoods, churches, schools, and businesses are all experiencing the shift from a largely monocultural populace to an increasingly diverse one.

Youth ministries don't need to go on a short-term missions trip to encounter different cultures. The percentage of students in American public schools who are considered part of a racial or ethnic minority group nearly doubled between 1972 and 2003, from 22 percent to 42 percent.[14] Even a predominately white youth ministry likely includes students from a variety of racial groups if it is committed to ministering to the youth in its community.

Fair-skinned sixteen-year-olds are bagging groceries alongside Sudanese refugees in small-town grocery stores across the United States. College students attend class with peers from around the world. And American assembly-line workers are sharing the line with Bosnians, Laotians, and Cubans.

Even if you live in one of the rare communities with very little ethnic diversity, cultural differences exist in other ways in nearly every pocket of the United States and in most other places around the world. For example, in addition to socioethnic culture, two other cultural domains we will explore in the journey across the chasm of cultural difference include organizational and generational cultures. Many ministry leaders fail because they don't understand the strong cultural values and assumptions that underlie the behaviors of an organization. Just as in a socioethnic culture, people often behave within these organizations with little self-awareness, oblivious of the values and assumptions driving their behavior. And few issues are challenging the pastors with whom I speak throughout the United States as much as that of how to deal with the passionate differences between the generational cultures within their churches. Music preferences, teaching styles, programmatic emphases, missionary strategies, and hermeneutics are but a few of the areas where cultural intelligence is needed to successfully pastor a congregation filled with people from different cultural backgrounds. The challenges created by the cultural differences among various generational groups can equal some of those created by various socioethnic groups. We'll more fully explore some of the leadership issues involved with these cultural groups in chapter 6.

Throughout the journey of this book, just as in real life, we will move in and out of socioethnic cultures, generational cultures, and organizational cultures. Numerous other cultural contexts exist in our lives as well, including cultures organized by professional careers, gender-oriented cultures, and cultures characterized by sexual preference and socioeconomic difference. There isn't space in this book to legitimately deal with all these varied contexts, but cultural intelligence can be applied to these cultural settings too.

Let's use a youth leader to think about the reasons a twenty-first-century ministry leader needs cultural intelligence. In addition to serving youth from various ethnic backgrounds, a youth worker also deals with the generational divides between the youth, their parents, and the seniors in the church. On top of that, the youth pastor must learn the culture of the particular church and possibly the denomination of which it is a part. Who holds the power, how is conflict handled, and what are the sacred rituals? But then add to these differences the subcultures among the youth themselves, whether they be jocks, goths, rave enthusiasts, techies, or preppies. Increasingly youth base their cultural identity on issues such as sexual preference, social class, and musical genre. And then the youth leader must deal with the upcoming missions trip to Mexico. And the invitation to partner with an urban youth ministry nearby. And the overriding tension felt by youth pastors to engage students with the gospel while struggling to relate the church culture from which they operate to the all-pervasive popular culture and Internet-linked world in which students feel most at home.[15] Get the picture? Cultural intelligence relates to the everyday realities of life in the twenty-first century.

Conclusion

Latinos are eating sushi, and Thais are eating tacos. Danish journalists are exercising their freedom of speech at the expense of respecting the sanctity of Islamic religious figures. As the world becomes more connected than ever, cross-cultural interactions are becoming the critical issue of our day.

Cultural intelligence isn't something needed only by those with a heart for the so-called mission field. It's needed by ministry leaders all across the United States. Eddie Gibbs, senior professor of church growth at Fuller Seminary, writes, "Local church leaders are trained to be teachers and pastors of their flock rather than cross-cultural missionaries to their broader contexts."[16] We must learn to live alongside sincere followers of other faiths, engage in ongoing conversations, and work together on issues of mutual concern while faithfully witnessing to the reign of God.[17] Otherwise, we'll be left behind by this unavoidable new reality.

Maybe by now you're feeling overwhelmed. Our local communities are being broadened to include Hispanics, former refugees, and international students. Our short-term missions trips are taking us to places where we'll encounter another mosaic of ethnicities. And our youth groups might consist of fifteen different subcultures. Do we have to become cultural experts on every one of these groups? Obviously that's impossible. But reaching across the chasm of cultural difference and lovingly relating to those we encounter isn't impossible. In fact, all kinds of everyday ministry leaders are making great strides in more effectively loving and serving the Other.

Picture the kind of people most difficult for you to love. What do they look like? How do they smell? What do they believe? How do they act? If they have flesh and blood, they aren't your enemy. They're fellow human beings. Look at how you encounter the Other, and you get a glimpse into what it means to live as we were created to live.

The flattened world is bringing us more and more encounters with people who aren't like us. We cannot hope to become experts on every cultural context in which we find ourselves. But through cultural intelligence, we can enhance our ability to interact with one another in ways that are respectful, loving, and dignifying. Herein lies the essence of the gospel.

Think about the five to ten different cultural contexts you most regularly encounter. What ethnic cultures are represented in your community and in your work life? Where do you travel and who do you encounter? What organizational cultures do you engage week by week? What generational dynamics do you face among your family and friends? These are the groups we want to relate to in ways that best reflect Jesus.

Recommended Resources

Friedman, Thomas. *The World Is Flat: A Brief History of the Twenty-First Century*. New York: Farrar, Straus, and Giroux, 2005.

Livermore, David. *Serving with Eyes Wide Open: Doing Short-Term Missions with Cultural Intelligence*. Grand Rapids: Baker Academic, 2006.

Pipher, Mary. *The Middle of Everywhere: The World's Refugees Come to Our Town*. New York: Harcourt, 2002.

US Census Bureau, http://www.census.gov/.

first-century CQ

God Speaks "Jesus"

Some might say all this attention to cultural intelligence and contextualizing the gospel is merely selling out to politically correct agendas for diversity and multiculturalism. Are we just going soft on the gospel and worshiping at the idol of culture? Long before it was fashionable to "celebrate diversity," Jesus's incarnation radically embodied the most extreme demonstration of cultural intelligence. He stretched his arms across the ultimate chasm of difference—God and humanity—to *become* the Second Adam. His life and death are what make it possible for us to seriously consider moving beyond the desire to love the Other to actually doing it.

All the sociological realities of the twenty-first century aside for a moment, cultural intelligence is essential for us because it is rooted in a theology of God's incarnation through Jesus. And Jesus is made incarnate today through you and me—the church. Therefore, we cannot fulfill our God-given mission to love others without contextualizing ourselves through a pathway like cultural intelligence. At the same time, many of the values and ideals of the cultures we encounter conflict with the values and ideals of the gospel. In this chapter, we will explore a theology of cultural intelligence as a way to govern how we pursue loving the Other. We'll look at the connection between the incarnation and cultural intelligence, and we'll examine a framework for dealing with some of the tensions that surface in embodying Jesus as we reach across the chasm of cultural difference.

The Incarnation

The author of Hebrews connects the incarnation with a long history of God contextualizing himself to his people in "culturally intelligent" ways. The author writes, "In the past, God spoke to our forefathers . . . at many times and in various ways" (Heb. 1:1). One of the unique things that distinguished Israel's God from other gods was the way he personally communicated with his people in ways they could understand. Whether it was through a pillar of fire, a moving cloud, ten words miraculously written on a stone, a prophet, or a talking jackass, Yahweh communicated to his people using accessible language and symbols.

The letter to the Hebrews continues, "But in these last days, he has spoken to us by his Son" (Heb. 1:2). Very literally, the author's words could be translated, "God has spoken *in* Son." God's language is Jesus. God most clearly communicates who he is through Jesus. Just as many Thai people use the Thai language to communicate with one another, and German people speak in German, God speaks "in Son." The language of God is Jesus.[1] The incarnation is the ultimate form of contextualization, the fullest embodiment of cultural intelligence.

Rather than cultural intelligence conflicting with Christianity or being merely a reflection of politically correct agendas of our day, cultural intelligence is most at home in Christianity. The commitment to express and communicate love in ways the Other can understand is one of the distinctions of our faith compared to many other religions. Many of our friends from other faiths insist that everyone adhering to their religions must learn the language of God. If you're going to follow Islam devoutly, learning Arabic is a high priority. Allah speaks in Arabic, so good Muslims need to learn Arabic. They pray in Arabic, and they read their holy books in Arabic. In contrast, the message of Christianity is, "Whatever *your* language, God speaks it!" Again, this is one of the distinctions of the Christian faith. As a result, *Christianity is the most multicultural faith in the world.* In fairness, Christianity has its own cultural roots that shape how we practice our faith. Our Christian roots are thoroughly Jewish and Greek, which create their own set of challenges and opportunities for how we contextualize the faith. But the fact remains: there are people from more than three thousand different languages and cultural groups who worship Jesus.[2] The good news can become the good news to oppressed and broken people only if it is translated into pictures and experiences they can understand.

For that matter, the multicultural nature of Christianity might be reason to celebrate rather than mourn the fact that there are so many different denominations within the Christian faith. Instead of seeing denominational differences only as divisive, perhaps we should also see them as an expression of the diversity that exists among us as Christians. Generational expressions from chorales and pipe organs to praise bands and bluegrass are all ways in which Jesus speaks the language of people from different cultures.

There is no one right way for the gospel to be expressed. There are many different and meaningful ways for it to be lived out among the Other. *At the same time, clearly not all expressions of the gospel are equally valid.* As we live out the mission of the church, what is up for grabs and what is not? What in the Scriptures is prescriptive for how we must do church in all times and all places, and what is merely descriptive of how a particular group of God's people lived out the gospel in Ephesus, Philippi, or Antioch?

Korean, Spanish, Urdu, Tamil, hip-hop, middle class, old, young, organ, reggae—God "speaks" all these languages through Jesus. God continues to speak in Son; only today the Son is made flesh through the church—the *body* of Christ. So you and I, along with a billion other Christians scattered across the world, are the way God speaks Urdu, middle class, and hip-hop. Together with God's people around the globe, we're tasked with the privilege of becoming living pictures of Jesus to people wherever we go. To merely announce that God *exists* is hardly noteworthy or compelling. "But that God is here right now, and on our side, actively seeking to help us in the way we most need help—this qualifies as news."[3] We get to be the living, breathing messengers of that good news in all the different cultures we encounter.

My interest in the fascinating pathway of cultural intelligence lies in its incarnational basis. It is a way for us to lovingly communicate who Jesus is and what he is about. We have to learn how to *be* the people who become culturally accessible, living messages of Jesus and his love. Embodying Jesus cross-culturally is a messy, complicated process. This is what often splits churches, divides families, and erodes Christian fellowship. So how do we discern which aspects of Christianity are transcendent for all times and all places and which aspects are subject to the changing styles and tastes of culture? We'll respond to the complexities and tensions that come with that question by examining how Jesus related to the cultural realities of his day. Jesus had a unique and climactic mission specific to his role and his own cultural context, so we cannot simply mimic what he did.[4] Yet his life and ministry provide us with direction for how to think about dealing with the tensions that exist between the gospel and culture.

For the remainder of the chapter, I'll explore four polarities that Christ held in tension as he lived out his redemptive mission in first-century Palestine. Look at figure 3 to see the dynamic relationship between these four priorities: kingdom of God, culture, word, and deed.[5] The kingdom of God was central to Jesus's messianic work, and yet he held that in tension with the first-century culture of Palestine. And Christ intersected these priorities by going about his mission in both word (proclamation) and deed (presence). These four polarities give us theological direction for applying cultural intelligence to our twenty-first-century contexts in a way that continues the incarnation of God through us. We'll continue to use this framework throughout the journey of this book to be sure our culturally intelligent love is theologically informed and centered around being the incarnation of Jesus today.

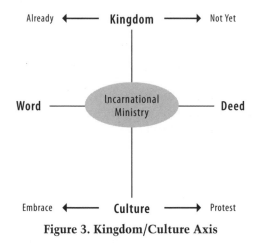

Figure 3. Kingdom/Culture Axis

Kingdom of God

Let's begin thinking about a theology of cultural intelligence by exploring the theological concept of God's reign. "Working for the kingdom, serving the kingdom, and having kingdom-oriented priorities"—these are all phrases that readily flow from our mouths. We speak often of the kingdom. "Kingdom" itself is a cultural metaphor that comes from our Jewish roots as Christians. Kings and kingdoms are not familiar realities for most of us living in the West, but first-century Jewish people had a very real sense of what it meant to live in a kingdom—a place or domain ruled by the king. And the Jews had long anticipated the Messiah coming as the King who would once and for all vindicate them and overthrow the existing kingdoms, usually their enemies.

As Jesus comes to earth, he identifies with the kingdom orientation of the Jewish culture. It is at the forefront of his teaching and conversation. Either directly or indirectly, we continually hear Jesus saying, "What you see on the surface of life is not all there is to life. This Roman kingdom you see is not the kingdom of which you are really a part."

"Instead," Jesus seems to say, "I represent and embody a different kind of kingdom. My kingdom is one where the underdog wins. Mine is one where we subversively overthrow existing kingdoms by turning the other cheek. My kingdom is one that is oriented around the way we were intended to live. It's a place that is missed by really important movers and shakers and sharp religious people. It belongs to children. It looks different from any earthly kingdom you've ever experienced."

When Jesus comes to earth, he enacts and embodies the kingdom of God wherever he goes and in whatever he does. One of the central points of discussion evident in how Jesus describes the kingdom is what theologians call the "already/not yet" tension—that is, the kingdom is *already* present and embodied in Jesus's life and ministry while *not yet* fully present.[6]

On the one hand, as soon as Jesus comes onto the scene in the first-century world, dramatic kingdom sightings begin to spring up all over the place. The days of preparation are over, and Israel's God is now acting as he promised. He heals people and casts out demons. He turns water into wine, he brings about hope, and he replaces shame with grace. Jesus fights for the underdog. The kingdom is more than a promise. Its firstfruits are already appearing.

Israel's God is becoming king in and through the work of Jesus. Jesus says, "The kingdom is at hand. It's here!" He says, "If I drive out demons by the Spirit of God, then the kingdom of God has come upon you" (Matt. 12:28). He declares, "The kingdom of God is within you" (Luke 17:21). The royal power of God is already present in Jesus's words and works (Matt. 12:28) because those who repent already possess the kingdom (Matt. 5:3, 10).

At the same time, Jesus doesn't fully release the power of the kingdom. Evil is still very present in the world, both then and now. Jesus doesn't heal everyone he encounters. He leaves villages with needy people behind, and not all relationships are restored.

So while Jesus says, "The kingdom has come upon you," elsewhere he says, "Repent, for the kingdom of heaven is near." He teaches us to pray, "Your kingdom come." And while in one breath he says, "Blessed are the poor and blessed are the persecuted for theirs *is* the kingdom of heaven," he also says, "Blessed are those who hunger and thirst for righteousness because someday they *will* receive it in full measure" (see Matt. 5:3–9). Therefore, Jesus's work is already present while also moving history forward to the time when all will be made right.

It is fairly easy for us to relate to the already/not yet realities of the kingdom. We all live in this every day. We experience the present realities of the kingdom in our personal lives. We've been rescued from the power of the evil one and from hell. Our lives have meaning, purpose, and significance. We get to enjoy good things in this world. The kingdom's presence is all around us. We get glimpses of peace, love, hope, and the goodness of God in our relationships with one another, in our personal journey with God, and in the beauty around us.

I get glimpses of the kingdom in my everyday life when I linger over an extended meal with friends. I see it when we have one of those days around the house when my daughters interact selflessly with each other or when one of them comes unprompted and apologizes to the other. When I see that, I stop and think, "Thank God! The kingdom is alive in our home!" I experience the kingdom's presence and power in those moments when I pay attention to the Spirit's nudge for me to make a decision that goes against what my vices typically incline me to do. We're already eating from the King's table. It isn't a seven-course meal, but the taste is real.[7]

At the same time, heaven has not yet fully come to reign here. Selfishness, pride, revenge, and insecurity keep rearing their ugly heads in my life. And I often succumb to the same vices over and over again. The news crawl on CNN continues to remind us of the ways death, sickness, injustice, and poverty keep showing up everywhere.

And so we have to forever hold in tension both the present and the future realities of the kingdom. One without the other just isn't possible. If the kingdom is fully future, the church is without power. We might as well huddle with other Christians and isolate ourselves from all those "evil people." If the kingdom is fully present, the church is without hope. After all, why does the evening news sound the way it does if the kingdom is fully present?[8]

What does all this have to do with cultural intelligence and the challenge of contextualizing the gospel? All of life and ministry is to be lived in light of this tension between who we *already* are in Christ and who we *hope* to someday be. We are a colony of the kingdom created to give people pictures of what Jesus's reign looks like and as a testimony of the kingdom that will one day be fully realized. A huge part of the contextualization process is learning to put on kingdom sensors so we can spot where God's reign has sprung forth into our fallen world and where it has not yet come to bear.

The kingdom of God is paramount to Jesus's interaction with his cultural context. Yet it becomes remarkably clear that amid Jesus's ruthless focus on inaugurating the kingdom of God is an equally relentless commitment to doing so in a way that relevantly relates to the world of first-century Palestine. With that in mind, we need to turn our attention to the other end of this axis: culture.

Culture

We must beware of reducing the gospel to a set of cultureless principles. We as Westerners are famous for this. We think we can somehow strip culture from our principles and bullet points and presume they apply equally everywhere. But God's reign is always communicated through the practices of a specific time and place.

Jesus always conveys the kingdom through the medium of culture. As noted in figure 3, the values of culture live in tension with the values of the kingdom. The gospel should not uncritically take on all the values of a cultural context, nor should it ignore them as irrelevant. Jesus turns many of the cultural values of first-century Palestine upside down. Yet Jesus lives as a thoroughly Jewish citizen. Like Jesus, we always live in and among people from particular cultures. There's no such thing as a cultureless gospel. Jesus healed, taught, and preached within a very particular culture.

Jesus's mission is very focused on Israel. As he encounters aspects of his culture that reflect the kingdom's presence (already), he *embraces* them. As he encounters things within his culture that reflect the kingdom's absence (not yet), he *protests* them.[9]

N. T. Wright, one of the foremost contemporary scholars on Jesus, offers a plethora of resources to help us learn how Jesus interacted with the cultural realities of his day. Wright identifies four symbols that shaped Jewish culture: the temple, the land, the Torah, and racial purity.[10] A brief examination of these four symbols sheds light on how Christ lived out the kingdom in light of his culture. We'll look at the significance each symbol had for the Jewish people, consider the ways Jesus embraced this cultural symbol, and consider the ways he protested it.

Temple

The temple was by far the largest religious structure in the first-century world in Palestine, known widely for its wealth and magnitude. In fact, Jerusalem was said to be more like a temple with a city around it than a city with a temple in it. It was the center of religious, social, and political activity for people. It was the epicenter of the entire nation.[11]

Embraced: Jesus regularly goes to the temple. Getting to the temple for Passover is a high priority for him. He throws the money changers out of the temple when they are corrupting its purpose. And he regularly references the temple in his teaching and conversation. These are a few of the ways Jesus embraces the significance of the temple as a Jew.

Protested: Yet Jesus says, "I'm going to destroy the temple and rebuild it in three days" (see John 2:19). He protests the idea that God's presence could be relegated to any physical structure. Far more of his recorded teaching takes place along the roadside and in informal conversations with people than in religious buildings. Just as Jesus embraces the kingdom values present in the temple-dominated life of the Jews, he protests the realities of the temple system that reflect where the kingdom has not yet come.

Land

The land was another integral symbol of first-century Jewish culture. The theme of exile and restoration to the land was and is central to Jewish history and culture. This is an issue where members of the Christian church in other parts of the world can compliment our limited understanding as Westerners. Many of them have a far richer understanding of the symbolism of land to the Jewish people because of its similar symbolism for them. For most of us in the West, land is a commodity meant to be bought and sold. We buy property with an eye toward resale value. But land had sacred and historical value for first-century Jews. The temple was surrounded by land, and Jerusalem was the major focal point of the land of Israel.

Embraced: Jesus embraces the importance of Israel's land. Some commentators suggest his statement, "Render to Caesar what is Caesar's," is his response to being tested about whether he believed the Jewish land should be valued. He acknowledges their land shouldn't be taken from them and that the promised land rightfully belongs to them. Jesus says, "Violent men are taking our land by force." He acknowledges something is desperately amiss (see Matt. 11:12; 13:28; 16:4; Luke 19:44).

Protested: Yet Jesus pushes the Jews beyond merely thinking of the kingdom as a domain limited by geographical and national boundaries. The kingdom, albeit undoubtedly physical in its presence and influence, is not limited by borders. So again, Jesus simultaneously embraces and protests this value of his Jewish culture.

Torah

The temple and the land were regulated by the Torah, the law of Israel. The law formed the covenant charter of all that Israel hoped for. It was their covenantal contract with one another and with God. It is hard to overemphasize just how highly Jesus's peers revered the Torah.

Embraced: Jesus also views the law with great respect. He understands it as the covenant between Yahweh and his people. Jesus studies the Torah, knows it well, and regularly references it in his teaching. The sanctity and extreme importance Jesus gives Torah cannot be overstated.

Protested: Yet Jesus also says that he has come to fulfill the law. And he continually does things that challenge the religious leaders' legalistic interpretations of the law. Jesus tells them they've missed the point of the law. Again, he lives in tension with this sacred value among his people.

Race

Finally, the issue of race was very important to the Jewish people. They felt they had to maintain their ethnic identity at all costs. Racial purity was a driving value for them.

Embraced: As a whole, Jesus seems to embrace the racial identity of the Jews. He is a Jew, and he seems quite content with his Jewish roots. His mission is very focused on the Jewish people. He doesn't dispute that they are the favored people of God.

Protested: But Jesus protests the idea that Jews should discriminate against or even avoid people from other cultures. He makes it a point to travel through Samaria and talks to the woman at the well. He even protests the notion that Rome is ultimately the enemy. The battle isn't merely political or racial; it is cosmic in scope. The enemy is Satan. Jesus suggests that while the Romans and the Greeks may be vehicles of evil and oppression, they themselves are oppressed by Satan.

There are many other ways that Jesus embraces the Jewish culture, including his following the rabbinical model, his observance of their religious festivals, and his selection of twelve men representing the twelve tribes of Israel. But there are as many and perhaps more examples of how he lives in contrast to his culture. He doesn't protest with placards and marches, much less with military force. In fact, it seems he even protests the mainstream approach to protesting. In his kingdom, evil will be defeated not by military victory but by a doubly revolutionary method—turning the other cheek, going the second mile, and taking up the cross. Jesus protests any sense that rich, educated people are the most important people, and instead he honors the poor, the marginalized, and the oppressed. He gives us a living picture of what it means to incarnationally reach across the chasm of difference while fully maintaining the integrity of who he is as God.

The cultural contexts in which we find ourselves are drastically different from Jesus's, but his ministry gives us a glimpse of what it means to live between the tension of God's reign and culture. The tendency throughout the history of the church has been to lean toward one extreme or the other. Fundamentalist movements have often primarily favored the side of protesting anything cultural. The music, books, dress, and artistic expressions of culture are considered bad simply because they didn't originate in the church. On the other hand, some churches work so hard to reflect the culture that they lose whatever distinctiveness the kingdom of God has. This is largely the point that the American evangelical church has reached over the last few decades. There is little difference between the lifestyles, choices, and values of American evangelicals and those of other people living in American culture.[12]

As God's kingdom subjects, we live out the gospel by both embracing and protesting various cultural values just as Jesus did. When we encounter the kingdom's presence, we need to join it and fan it further into flame. As a result of God's grace in all his image bearers, the kingdom's presence is sometimes found in the most surprising places and people. We need to receive and celebrate the presence of kingdom values wherever we find them. On the other hand, as we encounter evil, we need to join God in bringing the kingdom's presence there. These discoveries ought to drive our missional and redemptive priorities.

> Think about the cultural context in which you minister—whether it is the socioethnic culture that is predominant in your community, youth culture, or the culture of your city or region. Consider which aspects of the culture reflect the kingdom. How can you embrace those? And where is the kingdom not yet present in this culture? How can you bring the kingdom to bear upon those realities?

What about those cultural aspects that are not so clearly right or wrong? What about areas that simply differ between one culture and the next? How do we minister in light of those aspects of culture? How do we become conversant in the languages and customs of surrounding cultures so that we can relevantly live out the ethics of the gospel in all those different ways? That is our goal in this pathway of cultural intelligence toward better loving the Other. We want to develop our ability to live out the presence of Jesus in a way that the surrounding cultures can understand while simultaneously developing a kingdom culture that often looks countercultural.[13]

A Word and Deed Gospel

In looking at a theology of cultural intelligence, there is one more aspect of Jesus's approach that bears mentioning here. Jesus lives between the tension of kingdom and culture through both his *words* and his *deeds*. He both proclaims the kingdom in culturally relevant ways and lives out its presence. Consider figure 3 once more to see how these aspects of Jesus's approach fit with a theology of cultural intelligence.

The American church has spent much energy debating the proclamation of the gospel versus the so-called social gospel. Many Christians in other parts of the world find it inconceivable that the gospel could be one without the other. In fairness, the concerns are that, on the one hand, if we merely "preach" the gospel, people may hear a theoretical description of who Jesus is without experiencing any of the realities of who Jesus is. On the other hand, are compassion and service enough?

The gospel must be both proclaimed in word and lived out in deed. N. T. Wright says it this way:

> The gospel is the announcement that Jesus is Lord—Lord of the world, Lord of the cosmos, Lord of the earth, of the ozone layer, of whales and waterfalls, of trees and tortoises. As soon as we get this right we destroy at a stroke the disastrous dichotomy that has existed in people's minds between "preaching the gospel" on the one hand and what used to be called loosely "social action" or "social justice" on the other. Preaching the gospel means announcing Jesus as Lord of the world; and, unless we are prepared to contradict ourselves with every breath we take, we cannot make that announcement without seeking to bring that lordship to bear over every aspect of our world.[14]

Jesus consistently and faithfully announces the presence of God's reign and its implications for life. Again and again he says, "Repent! The kingdom is at hand." His words articulate the realities of what we have just examined: the kingdom of God lived out by real people in real places.

We must faithfully call people to follow Jesus as the best possible way to live. We cannot neglect our responsibility to faithfully announce, *"Repent! The kingdom is at hand."* But we must learn how to explain the message in a language our hearers will understand. Herein lie some of the greatest challenges and opportunities for applying cultural intelligence to our contexts.

How do we communicate the reign of God in this context for these people in this time? That's the driving question for each of us in all the cultural contexts where we interact. The words of the gospel must be expressed in ways that reveal the good news of Jesus. And our words work in tandem with our deeds. Any gospel message that doesn't demonstrate the reign of God over poverty, disease, racism, war, divorce, and financial strain hardly seems like good news.

The "Word become flesh!" Jesus's words were authenticated by his deeds. Though he didn't immediately heal every sick person or restore every broken relationship, his reign brought transformation to every aspect of life. And the integrity with which he lived, the way he healed the sick, and the ways he dealt with the destitute and with religious hypocrites were the central components to his "culturally intelligent" life. His deeds spoke a language that first-century people understood. At the end of the day, the only true defense of the gospel in any culture is the life of the congregation which believes it.[15] Christ both announces (word) and demonstrates (deed) the reign of God in culture. He proclaims and lives out the values of the kingdom in tension with first-century Palestinian values. Living out the Christian gospel in dramatically different cultures is where the rubber meets the road.

The artificial separation of words and deeds by the Western missions movement may be one of the reasons missiologists labeled Rwanda a success story in the early 1990s. By 1990, the gospel had been proclaimed to the vast majority of Rwandans, and as a result, Rwanda was labeled a "reached" nation. Tragically, the 1994 massacres pointedly called into question whether Rwanda was "reached" with the gospel as some had suggested. The kingdom that had been taught didn't seem to have much dominion over the real-life issues of conflict, war, disease, and poverty. The same could be said for many communities in the so-called Bible belt of the United States where racism, violence, and sexual immorality live on alongside the "words" of the gospel.

Jesus's incarnation is at the center of living in tension with announcing and demonstrating God's reign in culture. Our own lives are the most relevant way we can communicate the gospel. Living out the reign of God in response to the realities around us brings the good news up close. Cultural intelligence helps us live out kingdom values through word and deed in a way that effectively expresses love to people in various cultural contexts.

Conclusion

The gospel takes many different forms as it is lived out in various cultures around the world. This makes for a messy, challenging process. Some of the most volatile debates among Christians center around which aspects of Christianity are up for grabs and which are not. It is tempting to pit one form of Christianity against another. The tendency is to see our preference or experience as the one right way to follow Jesus.

We used to live in the suburbs of Chicago. Despite the abundance of churches in the area, we had a very hard time finding a church that we felt connected with our values and priorities. During that time, I was reading a lot of Mark Noll's writings, including his book *The Scandal of the Evangelical Mind*. Given that he was a professor at nearby Wheaton College, I e-mailed him and asked him where *he* went to church. I was hopeful his church might embody some of the ideals expressed in his writing. He enthusiastically recommended his church to us.

The next Sunday we visited Noll's church and loved it. I introduced myself to Dr. Noll and began gushing about how much we loved the church while simultaneously ranting about the endless frustrations we had had with other churches we had visited in the community. After all that, Mark graciously responded, "Isn't it a marvelous wonder that the gospel can take so many different forms and be used by God?" Ouch! I was humbled. My arrogant ranting and raving somehow presumed there should be one, superior way of doing church in suburban Chicago.

God speaks in Son (Heb. 1). The worldwide Christian church is the body of the Son. You and I, together with followers of Jesus in Iraqi churches, hip-hop clubs, and Mongolian villages are the way God continues to speak in Son to those living in those contexts. As we live and speak kingdom values in tension with cultural values, we have the backdrop for culturally intelligent ministry. Few things have caused as much tension for me in my faith than this challenging process of intersecting kingdom values with cultural values. I'll share more of my own journey toward reconciling the universal, exclusive claims of Jesus with the relative, inclusive nature of contextualization and cultural intelligence. This isn't a task that can be figured out in the solitude of library cubicles or solely through books. But when we live closely with people, through incarnational relationships, we learn to hear and speak Jesus in a language the Other can understand.[16]

How do we live out the gospel in this specific place among these people? Cultural intelligence helps us live out the gospel in that way. How do we honor our fellow image bearers with love and respect? That issue is at the crux of cultural intelligence and takes us to the next part of our journey.

Recommended Resources

Bevans, Stephen, and Roger Schroeder. *Constants in Context: A Theology of Mission for Today*. Maryknoll, NY: Orbis, 2004.

The Gospel and Our Culture Network, http://www.gocn.org/main.cfm.

Newbigin, Lesslie. *The Gospel in a Pluralist Society*. Grand Rapids: Eerdmans, 1989.

Volf, Miroslav. *Exclusion and Embrace: A Theological Exploration of Identity, Otherness, and Reconciliation*. Nashville: Abingdon, 1996.

3

CQ 101

The Path to Loving the Other

Why use cultural intelligence as the pathway toward more effectively loving the Other as compared to the many other intercultural theories? There's nothing very new about the topic of crossing cultures. It's a conversation that's been going on for centuries. Missionaries have been at the forefront of cross-cultural work and interaction long before businesses and other sectors of the professional world. From a research perspective, the disciplines of anthropology and sociology have contributed a great deal to the field of intercultural studies. Cultural intelligence itself, however, is a relatively new concept. It is a multidisciplinary approach that draws from anthropology, sociology, and psychology as well as literature from the fields of business, missions, and education. As a result, cultural intelligence is a metamodel, which provides a coherent framework for dealing with the array of issues involved in crossing various cultures—often many cultures at the same time. As already noted, most of us ministering in the twenty-first century are faced with dozens of cultural contexts even in one day of work. So a metamodel is needed to factor in the complexity and breadth of cultures shaping our daily interactions.

Here's how a metamodel such as cultural intelligence helps practically. Most books on how to become more competent cross-culturally focus primarily on different cultural values and how they affect the way you relate to those cultures. For example, there are some helpful books that discuss various cultural values (e.g., individualism vs. collectivism, event time vs. clock time) and how they affect personal life, work, and ministry.[1] Certainly we'll spend some time in this book looking at the importance of understanding cultural values. Other books and training materials for cross-cultural effectiveness place more emphasis on an individual's need to be a humble learner as he or she moves across cultures. These approaches focus more on the personal role of being a learner. But even if I'm a learner, will I know how to translate my learning into loving expressions of friendship and service? Still other books emphasize the practices and taboos of various cultures, such as appropriate gestures, gift-giving protocols, and how to exchange business cards. These kinds of issues are important to our thinking about how we lovingly interact cross-culturally. But the value of these varied emphases is enhanced when wed with a coherent framework for understanding the relation of cultural values with an individual's personal motivation and how to translate that into appropriate cross-cultural behavior.

No two individuals will interact the same way with the values of another culture. We must explore our unique emotional and psychological responses to new situations as well as examine the cultural issues. For example, consider how being an extrovert shapes the way you experience a laid-back culture or the cultural variable of time as compared to the way you would experience it if you were more introverted? My wife, Linda, and I both come from the same basic cultural background. But she welcomes a culture that is less clock oriented, while I find it frustrating. And no two pastors from the United States will have an identical response to a church culture that stresses hierarchical leadership. A coherent framework for understanding the relationship of cultural values to one's personal values and motivation is needed. Personality and cultural dynamics are equally important variables for our understanding.

The cultural intelligence framework synthesizes the findings from these varied approaches to cross-cultural behavior. Cultural intelligence also draws from Howard Gardner's work on multiple intelligences.[2] Gardner, a Harvard professor of cognition and education, argues that the cognitive capacities typically measured by IQ tests are only one form of intelligence. He suggests that each individual manifests varying levels of different intelligences. Similar work is found in the field of social linguistics and multiple literacies.[3]

Don't let the concept of cultural intelligence scare you. Although it is a comprehensive model that accounts for many of the complexities that come with cross-cultural relationships, cultural intelligence itself is not a complicated framework. It provides a useful, coherent approach to account for the internal and external dynamics that occur in cross-cultural interactions. We all know what IQ is—a measurement of our intellectual ability. And in recent years we've heard about EQ, a measurement of how we handle our emotions. Many argue that EQ has far more influence than IQ on how well someone succeeds in life and work. Surely all of us have seen our share of people who have graduated from seminary with honors only to fail miserably in ministry due to an inability to carry on a conversation with another human being. That inability might suggest a low EQ. EQ instruments presume we're familiar with our environment, even if it's a subconscious familiarity. With emotional intelligence, we know how to act and relate to others when we're in our own cultural context.

Cultural intelligence picks up where EQ leaves off by dealing with people and circumstances in unfamiliar contexts. Cultural intelligence measures the ability to move seamlessly in and out of a variety of cultural contexts. That is the ideal. I'm not sure anyone ever does it seamlessly, and in fact, the mistakes we make along the way often provide some of the richest opportunities for growing in cultural intelligence. But developing a repertoire of culturally intelligent thoughts, attitudes, and skills makes us more effective cross-culturally.

There is little we can do to alter our IQ. Criticisms about the validity of IQ tests abound, but it's widely assumed that one's IQ is fixed. Your IQ when you're seven years old is likely to be your IQ when you're thirty-seven and fifty-seven years old. However, cultural intelligence is believed to be malleable. Through interventions like those discussed in this book, we can develop our aptitude for interacting with the Other in ways that are loving and respectful. Surely some people are more naturally gifted for cross-cultural work, just as some individuals are more naturally inclined toward engineering, art, or fixing things around the house. But almost everyone can make progress in becoming more effective cross-culturally. I'll never be the natural that my father-in-law is for repairing just about anything around the house. But I've learned a few skills to get by as a homeowner. Likewise, people who find cross-cultural interactions to be very counterintuitive can still learn a few key strategies for interacting in ways that are loving and respectful. Part of the process requires honestly assessing our natural affinity for cross-cultural service and relationships and then making a commitment to move one step forward in the journey toward more effectively living out our love for the Other.

In summary, cultural intelligence comes from literature in the fields of cross-cultural behavior and multiple intelligences. It is both a measurement and a coherent framework for enhancing our ability to cross the chasm of cultural difference effectively, lovingly, and respectfully. Cultural intelligence consists of four key factors:

1. Knowledge CQ: Understanding cross-cultural issues and differences

2. Interpretive CQ: The degree to which we're mindful and aware when we interact cross-culturally[4]
3. Perseverance CQ: Our level of interest, drive, and motivation to adapt cross-culturally
4. Behavioral CQ: The extent to which we appropriately change our verbal and nonverbal actions when we interact cross-culturally

All four of these factors are interrelated, and one without the other will not only hinder effectiveness but might even be counterproductive to an overall posture of cultural intelligence. The rest of this chapter provides a cursory overview of the four factors of cultural intelligence before more fully examining each of them and their relevance to twenty-first-century ministry. Figure 1 (see p. 13) provides a map of the interrelationship of the four factors of cultural intelligence, with the ultimate goal being expressed love and respect for the Other. It is a map of the journey from a desire to love to actually expressing love for the Other.

Before you go any further, I encourage you to take the CQ assessment found in appendix B or visit http://www.davidlivermore.com. Doing so now will allow you to evaluate your scores in light of what is described in the remainder of the book.

Knowledge CQ

Knowledge CQ, or the more technical term, cognitive CQ, measures our ongoing growth in understanding cross-cultural issues. It refers to our level of understanding about culture and culture's role in shaping behavior and social interactions.

Learning the language of a culture—whether it's studying an ethnic language such as Mandarin or Spanish or understanding the in-house jargon used by a particular denomination—is an essential part of the cultural knowledge needed to effectively serve in cross-cultural contexts. Equally important is an overall understanding of the normative customs followed by people within a particular cultural group. These values may include customs as basic as how men ought to greet women, how a particular church practices holy communion, and the meaning of the color purple in Latin America. It can also include more subtle understandings such as why South Indian food often uses sour milk as an ingredient and the affinity between Episcopalians and Catholics.

Knowledge CQ also involves understanding how people in another cultural context are likely to view us in light of our cultural contexts. Regardless of whether you represent the "average American" (see the next chapter), if you're from the United States, many people from other countries will automatically make assumptions about you. A recent study asked people in a variety of places around the world to share their two pre-dominant images of the United States. The winners: war and *Baywatch*![5] In a post-9/11 era, it takes little guessing to figure out why many people in the world equate the United States with war. And add to the "war against terrorism" the prevalence of military vehicles (i.e., Hummers) used by suburban families to cart groceries and kids around, and you can guess why many people equate our culture with war. As for *Baywatch*, it's the most frequently exported US television program in the world.[6]

You may be an American pacifist who has no clue who David Has-selhoff is. But that doesn't change the fact that many people in the world will see you with a US passport and automatically form assumptions about you that might involve images of war and *Baywatch*. I'm a married American white guy with a PhD who works at an evangelical seminary in the midwestern United States. Talk about an identity loaded with characteristics about which people have preconceived notions. Part of my learning how to adeptly interact with people from various cultural contexts is having some sense of how they may perceive me simply be-cause of the cultural groups of which I'm a part. When speaking to a group of American high school students, I look for ways early on to challenge the assumptions they might have about me as a "seminary guy."

I need to develop both an honest understanding of how my cultural background truly shapes who I am as well as an understanding of ways others might think it shapes me, even if those aren't all legitimate as-sumptions about me. In turn, I need to discern how others' perceptions of my cultural contexts shape the ways they interact with me. This veers closely toward the notion of interpretive CQ—stepping back and interpreting what is happening in a cross-cultural situation. And it is why knowledge CQ and interpretive CQ are so closely linked. They're dependent on each other. We'll return to that idea later.

Knowledge CQ creates the cognitive basis from which to engage in interpretive CQ, the second of the four factors. There's little hope for growing in cultural intelligence without knowledge CQ, but there's almost as little hope for growing in cultural intelligence if knowledge CQ is pursued without the other three factors of cultural intelligence. We'll more fully explore knowledge CQ in part 2 of the book.

Interpretive CQ

Interpretive CQ, or the more technical term, metacognitive CQ, measures our ability to be mindful and aware as we interact with people from dif-ferent cultural contexts. It's one thing to have cognitive understanding about cross-cultural issues. It's another to intuitively understand what occurs in an actual cross-cultural encounter. Interpretive CQ is the ability to accurately make meaning from what we observe. As already noted, interpretive CQ and knowledge CQ are symbiotically dependent on each other. Some measure of cross-cultural understanding is needed to make good interpretations. And becoming more mindful and aware helps increase our understanding about cross-cultural issues.

Because of the seamless connection between these two parts of cultural intelligence—knowledge CQ and interpretive CQ—a great deal of the literature on cultural intelligence deals with these two parts as one, sometimes called "cultural strategic thinking." However, for ministry leaders, there is value in viewing these two related parts separately. If knowledge CQ is the part most emphasized in responding to cross-cultural challenges faced by ministry leaders, interpretive CQ seems to be the part *least* emphasized.

At its core, interpretive CQ calls for a reflective, contemplative mindset, which mitigates against the zealous, activist approach permeating much of American evangelicalism. Thinking and reflection are often disparaged at the expense of "getting things done," and results and action are the lauded ideals.

Interpretive CQ is not thinking just for the sake of thinking. We're not interested in merely philosophizing and somehow believing that a purely cerebral exercise makes us culturally intelligent. The beauty of the cultural intelligence model is that it links thinking and cross-cultural understanding to action. Interpretive CQ is the key linking process between knowledge and action.

Interpretive, or metacognitive, CQ literally means "thinking about thinking." The goal is to look closely at our thoughts and to ask ourselves how we understand new situations. While an example of knowledge CQ might be understanding the offensiveness of showing the bottoms of one's feet while dining in a Thai café, interpretive CQ would be moving into a new cultural context and developing a general understanding of restaurant-related taboos there.[7] Knowledge CQ helps us understand that the Other will have preconceived notions of us (e.g., war and *Baywatch*). Interpretive CQ will help us explore what those preconceptions are and how they affect interaction.

At the crux of interpretive CQ is the effort to make the invisible influence of culture more visible. It starts with being mindful and aware, moves toward making empathetic interpretations, and results in cultural strategic thinking where we "think about thinking" right in the midst of action. We'll look at this progression throughout part 3, but we need to spend a moment now defining "cultural strategic thinking" since that term appears on the CQ map in figure 1 and on the assessment in appendix B.

"Cultural strategic thinking" is a term used by P. Christopher Earley, Soon Ang, and Joo-Seng Tan in their book, *CQ: Developing Cultural Intelligence at Work*, to combine the interdependent factors of knowledge CQ and interpretive CQ into one category. Cultural strategic thinking is the cumulative result of knowledge and interpretive CQ working interdependently. It is having "an *active* and *dynamic* strategy for dealing with the world around" us.[8] Given the impossibility of having a full understanding of all the cultural contexts in which most of us work these days, these CQ experts argue that the development of "cultural thinking" is far more critical than mastering all the nuances of specific cultures. That means, as we understand culture and cultural values, as we become more mindful and aware of what is going on internally and externally in our cross-cultural encounters, and as we learn to empathize with the Other, we then need to focus on developing new hypotheses, options, cues, and goals in cross-cultural encounters. This is cultural strategic thinking.

Part of this kind of strategic thinking involves seeking information to confirm or disconfirm our analysis cross-culturally. Short-term missionaries who view the frequent smiles of people they encounter in underresourced communities are wise to take note of those smiles. But rather than jumping to conclusions about what the smiles mean, the visitors need to critique their underlying assumptions and move toward resolving the dilemma they ought to feel about why it is that so many poor people seem to be smiling at them. They need to test the hypothesis "Lots of poor people are smiling = Poor people are happy."

Likewise, younger leaders who watch the seemingly emotionless worship of older church members need to test a hypothesis such as "Emotionless nonverbals while singing = Older people don't know how to genuinely worship." And older church members who are inclined to write off the worship of the younger church members as little more than emotional hype also need to seek more information before too quickly assuming they have accurately interpreted what is going on in the Other.

We begin to develop our cultural intelligence by continually and dynamically modifying how we interpret the cues and intentions in each cross-cultural situation. Those interpretations will help us plan our interactions accordingly. If I'm going to be working in a place where saving face is a value, then how should I anticipate dealing with a conflict-ridden situation? If I'm presenting a female candidate for the open youth director position in a church that has historically followed conservative, hierarchical roles for men and women, what is the respectful, loving way to do so? We cannot simply use cultural thinking and understanding to politically manipulate those with whom we're working. But when viewed according to the theological framework we developed in chapter 2, we're wise to plan in light of what we intuit about a specific cultural context. We need to draw on our cultural understanding to think about how what we're presenting will be received.

Interpretive CQ is the dimension of cultural intelligence most desperately lacking in the cross-cultural behavior of many American ministry leaders. A large portion of this book, part 3, is devoted to helping us enhance our ability to develop our interpretive CQ.

Perseverance CQ

Perseverance CQ, or motivational CQ, measures our level of interest, drive, and motivation to adapt cross-culturally. Having a good understanding of cross-cultural issues is central, and drawing on that understanding to more reflectively interpret what is occurring in cross-cultural interactions is essential. But at the end of the day, what matters is our ability to personally draw on the cultural strategic thinking that comes from knowledge CQ and interpretive CQ to actually interact in ways that are effective cross-culturally.

Many of us have experienced going through a thorough orientation for a new cultural context only to find ourselves aborting everything we learned because we hit some kind of roadblock. We might know that saving face is more important than direct, "bottom-line" interaction, but that understanding might do little to temper the sheer frustration we feel when trying to confront unresolved conflict.

After spending most of our journey in this book looking at knowledge and interpretive CQ, we'll explore some of the key concerns for persevering through the hard work of cross-cultural ministry. We'll continue to look within ourselves and pay attention to the kinds of things likely to elicit an emotional response from us. This is another one of the important contributions of the cultural intelligence framework that is often lacking in other approaches to cross-cultural competency. You might be an expert in knowing how cultures operate and vary from one another (knowledge CQ). You might journal multiple times a day and come up with some very accurate interpretations of what is occurring in another cultural context (interpretive CQ). But if you can't translate any of your understanding and interpretation into behavior that positions you to communicate and interact effectively, all of your knowledge and interpretive CQ won't make much difference. Or maybe it isn't that you "can't" but that you simply don't want to. Persevering through cross-cultural conflict is tiring.

As you can see, the recurring theme among each of the factors of cultural intelligence is the importance of looking inward. Effective perseverance CQ requires knowing what keeps us going and slows us down. Cultural intelligence relies on understanding what motivates and drives us, and equally important is knowing what drains and depletes our energy. As I come to more clearly understand what drives my emotions, feelings, and behavior, I am better able to tune into the Other more fully.

One of the challenges of perseverance CQ is being honest about the points of resistance we feel with cultural differences and learning when to persevere despite the discomfort and when to respectfully decline. There's nothing wrong with admitting to one's self that eating foods with squishy textures is disconcerting. And there's nothing wrong with admitting that the genre of music written and loved by a different generation doesn't connect with you. But knowledge and interpretive CQ will be needed to discern when I must persevere despite the discomfort it brings me in order to authentically express Jesus to the Other.

Behavioral CQ

Behavioral CQ refers to the actions and words we use as we interact cross-culturally. It refers to the ability to observe, recognize, regulate, adapt, and act appropriately in intercultural meetings. At the end of the day, our cultural intelligence is judged based on how we behave. It isn't enough to be willing to try and persevere. A person growing in cultural intelligence learns what actions are needed to be effective and does them. Behavioral CQ refers to how we behave when we actually find ourselves in the kinds of cross-cultural interactions we've been examining. It measures our ability to appropriately change our verbal and nonverbal actions when we interact cross-culturally.

I might understand that when the seniors group at church complains about the way kids come dressed to church, it's largely a result of the cultural expectations that come from their generation. But my ability to appropriately respond to those criticisms reflects whether I can apply cultural intelligence to that kind of real-life interaction. Or I may accurately interpret why people in Beijing keep giving me "wrong" directions somewhere rather than telling me they don't know. But the impressions I leave with locals as I receive their responses and figure out how to get to my destination is the ultimate challenge. Our "actions, speech, and nonverbal behaviors are what others can observe"[9] and will ultimately communicate our degree of cultural intelligence.

Ironically, we're least likely to see growth in our cross-cultural behavior by working to alter the behaviors themselves. Surely there are some behaviors worth modifying simply to avoid offense, such as reading a business card carefully when it is given to you by a Chinese leader or never handing someone something with your left hand in many Eastern cultures. But the greatest way to get at our behavioral CQ is by paying attention to the preceding three areas. "The illusion of mastering desirable and taboo actions places blinders on Americans and foreigners alike, invites inflexibility, and falls short of equipping them for effective interaction."[10] The very areas we've just reviewed—simultaneously looking within while observing our surroundings in cross-cultural interactions through the lenses of knowledge CQ, interpretive CQ, and perseverance CQ—are the most helpful ways of adjusting our cross-cultural behavior. The degree to which we change internally will be seen in the impressions we leave on others created by our appearance and actions.

Most of our behaviors are habitual. We grow up acting and speaking in a certain way as a reflection of how we've been socialized to see the world. So there's little hope we can deal with our cross-cultural behavior in any kind of sustained way unless we actually become different people. As we think about relating to the Other with love and respect, we have to get beyond behavior modification approaches wherein we *appear* culturally intelligent and respectful and move toward actually *becoming* more multicultural people who genuinely love, respect, and appreciate the Other and his or her differences. Becoming a more multicultural person doesn't imply we can no longer be true to our own cultural backgrounds. We'll discuss that frequently in this journey. But it does mean we have to do more than simply change the way we talk to our other-gender colleagues, and we have to go beyond simply planning a five-week teaching series for our congregation on how to get along with one another. The entire way we view the Other and ourselves may need to be transformed. Cultural intelligence is a transformative model of cross-cultural behavior and leadership rather than a model of behavior modification.

Conclusion

I recently attended a fascinating gathering in Uganda with African pastors from several countries throughout the continent and some American pastors. The conference was structured around some of the parallels between the postmodern context in the West and the postcolonial context in places like Africa and Latin America. There were many rich conversations and points of connection. As I sat with my fellow Americans at this event, much of the conversation focused on the similarities. However, many of my conversations with Africans spoke to the stark differences between our contexts. One sister from Nigeria said, "Surely there's value in looking at some common threads between how the church must reinvent itself in your postmodern context just as we must reinvent ourselves as the church takes on more indigenous flavor in the postcolonial context. But there are more differences than similarities between postcolonial Nigeria and postmodern USA."

The cultural intelligence framework allows for an appreciation of what we have in common with our fellow Christians and other image bearers while placing greater emphasis on the rich, robust things learned by exploring the profound differences. Cultural intelligence is an essential skill for most twenty-first-century ministry leaders. It's necessary for us to embody Jesus among ethnically different people in our neighborhoods. It is what we need when we work with people from different cultural contexts, whether they're across the street or multiple time zones away. Cultural intelligence is needed when planting or pastoring a church in multicultural America, leading a ministry that serves various generational cultures, participating in a short-term missions trip, going overseas to minister long-term, or figuring out the organizational dynamics of the ministry where we serve. Eddie Gibbs, of Fuller Seminary, says that twenty-first-century ministry leaders "need to be trained as cross-cultural missionaries, with a commitment to birthing new and reproducible faith communities, and equipped to function in postmodern, religiously, and socially pluralistic contexts. They need to be able to provide a missional critique of secularization, consumerism, and modernity."[11]

Cultural intelligence draws from a plethora of research and writing about cross-cultural behavior and intelligence. It is a distinctive framework and measurement in that it synthesizes the findings in studies from these varied disciplines and approaches cultural interaction from a transformative model rather than a behavior modification model. As we've seen, it consists of the following four factors:

1. Knowledge CQ: Understanding cross-cultural issues and differences
2. Interpretive CQ: The degree to which we're mindful and aware when we interact cross-culturally
3. Perseverance CQ: Our level of interest, drive, and motivation to adapt cross-culturally
4. Behavioral CQ: The extent to which we appropriately change our verbal and nonverbal actions when we interact cross-culturally

"Not since the first measurements of cultural variation has a construct with so much promise in better understanding cross-cultural interactions been introduced."[12] Cultural intelligence is uniquely suited for the cross-cultural challenges facing ministry leaders today.

Having looked at the CQ map for our journey toward more effectively loving the Other, we'll now hold the magnifying glass over each of these parts of the cultural intelligence pathway. We'll explore the relevance of each of the four factors of cultural intelligence for ministry leadership in the twenty-first century. We will build on the overview in this chapter with much more detail and clarity.

"'Love the Lord your God with all your heart and with all your soul and with all your mind.' This is the first and greatest commandment. And the second is like it: 'Love your neighbor as yourself'" (Matt. 22:37–39). Our destination in this journey is a place where we more effectively live out these commands among those with whom we don't belong. Cultural intelligence is the pathway toward more effectively loving our neighbor, near and far.

Recommended Resources

CQ Profile for Cross-Cultural Ministry, http://grts.cornerstone.edu/resources/glc/cqprofile.

Earley, P. Christopher, Soon Ang, and Joo-Seng Tan. *CQ: Developing Cultural Intelligence at Work*. Stanford, CA: Stanford Business Books, 2006.

Thomas, David, and Kerr Inkson. *Cultural Intelligence: People Skills for Global Business*. San Francisco: Berrett-Koehler, 2004.

part 2

understand: knowledge CQ

From my journal:

I have one more day of teaching this three-day intensive on cultural intelligence. It's a visceral experience to teach this material with four Koreans, three Chinese, four Americans, two Eastern Europeans, and seven Aussies, all in the same classroom. The students have dialogued thoughtfully and passionately. But at mealtimes, almost without fail, the class divides right along ethnic lines. I can't believe it. In a course on CQ no less. I'd think they'd at least fake it. It makes me feel a bit like a failure. I know the material we're covering isn't unimportant, but how do I get them to act on the information we've covered all week in this one simple way, right here!?

—May 19, 2005. Sydney, Australia

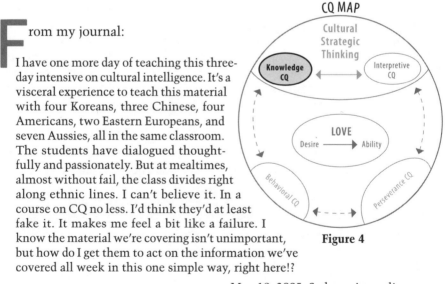

CQ MAP

Figure 4

Understand. That's the next part of following the CQ pathway toward loving the Other. We want to understand how we see the world and how others see us. We want to think about how culture shapes the ways we see, think, act, and love.

Knowledge CQ is the understanding one has about cross-cultural issues and differences. It's understanding *what* culture is and *how* it shapes us. This dimension of cultural intelligence is highly informational. Our goal with knowledge CQ is not to become a master of all the dos and don'ts of every culture we ever encounter. Instead, it is to develop our overall cultural understanding and appreciation for how individuals' beliefs and practices are connected to their cultural backgrounds.

What is your level of knowledge CQ if measured by these indicators?

- Am I fluent in a language other than English?
- Do I know the ways other cultures approach conflict?
- Do I know the different role expectations of men and women in other cultures?
- Do I know the basic cultural values of several other cultures?
- Do I understand the primary ways Christians differ in their beliefs and practices in different cultural settings?[1]

This is the kind of understanding measured when testing knowledge CQ.

Knowledge CQ is the factor that is emphasized most in cross-cultural and diversity-training programs. Education is typically the immediate antidote prescribed for dealing with things like addressing short-term missionaries' offensive behavior, helping parents deal with troubled adolescents, or fending off discrimination in the workplace. The assumption is, *Teach people about these things, and that will take care of the issue.* I'm currently sitting on a committee at our university that's interested in exploring issues of diversity among faculty, staff, and students. The tendency has continually been to move toward training as the primary way to deal with our less than diverse university population. More information often seems to be the default diagnosis. It just isn't that simple.

It is with good reason that we pour a great deal of effort into the educational realities of reaching across cultural differences. Ignorance is surely a major contributing factor to cross-cultural blunders. But the cultural intelligence framework exposes knowledge as only one of four important factors of effective cross-cultural interaction. Cultural knowledge in and of itself is no guarantor of effectiveness. In fact, cross-cultural training without the other aspects of CQ can actually hinder one's effectiveness. A wide-eyed, new pastor who thinks he "knows what Southern Baptist churches are like" or a zealous missionary who has studied the Falawni tribe a bit can know just enough to be dangerous. Education by itself can inoculate us from being true learners.

The answer is not to drop the education and training altogether. Instead, knowledge needs to be combined with contributions from the other three dimensions of cultural intelligence. Educational approaches to cross-cultural interaction must be oriented toward teaching what kinds of questions to ask and what to look for rather than toward teaching people how to become experts at behaving well in another cross-cultural context.

Rather than beginning with a theoretical discussion of cultural understanding, I've begun with an overview of the culture from which many of us come, American culture. Our cultural understanding begins by growing in our awareness of our own cultural heritage. Chapter 4 provides a brief summary of the "American way," a perspective that's needed for anyone connected to the American cultural context in some way.

Chapter 5 looks at the importance of understanding how culture shapes behavior, and we'll work toward an enhanced understanding of culture itself. We'll explore the way culture becomes the nexus between collective human experience and our individual personalities.

Chapter 6 furthers our knowledge CQ by recognizing the presence of culture in three different domains—socioethnic culture, organizational culture, and generational culture. It offers an overview of some implications of applying cultural intelligence to each of these domains.

The final chapters in this part look at the significance of language and cultural values when we interact cross-culturally. There is great value in developing cultural-specific understanding for work that involves ongoing contact with the same culture. But most of our emphasis in this part and throughout the book is on developing a cultural-general understanding that applies to the work and service we do across many varied cultural contexts. Understanding culture and its role in our thoughts and actions is an essential part of the CQ pathway toward loving the Other.

4

the average american

Understanding Our Own Culture

How American are you? Maybe not at all. I hope people from places other than the United States read this book. But I'm guessing many readers will be Americans. Even if you're not an American, don't skip this chapter. It might give you some insight into what's behind how we behave. And more importantly, I hope it will prompt you to spend some time reflecting on your own cultural background and how it shapes the way you think and live.

The first step toward becoming more culturally intelligent is to become more aware of our own cultural identity, which includes the varied cultural domains we're exploring in this book—socioethnic culture, organizational culture, and generational culture. To ignore the reality of one's own cultural identity is just as nonsensical as ignoring that of people in the other cultures with which we interact.[1] We have a universal tendency to think that other people do things for the same reasons we do them. After all, we learned to do what we do by observing others around us. But as we become more aware of our own culture and its values, we're less likely to project our values onto the Other. Understanding our own culture protects us from assuming the actions of the Other mean the same thing as when we act that way.

As we become more aware of the assumptions and values on which our own behavior and thinking rest, we can begin to contrast these assumptions and values with those of the Other. And going through this process with ourselves helps sensitize us to the immense shortcomings of stereotyping others according to cultural norms.

So back to my original question, how American are you? Marketing guru Kevin O'Keefe, in his book *The Average American*,[2] chronicles his search from New Hampshire to Hawaii to find the most average American. He poured over surveys and census data and talked with lots of people in pockets all across the country, trying to find a person who best embodied what it means to be American. Here's a quiz based on O'Keefe's findings to see how American you are:

Are You an Average American?

1. How close is the nearest Wal-Mart to your home?
   a) More than a 20-minute drive
   b) No more than a 20-minute drive
2. Do you believe you are living the "American dream"?
   a) Yes   b) No
3. Are you tolerant of all races?
   a) Yes   b) No
4. Can you name the Three Stooges?
   a) Yes   b) No
5. Can you name the three branches of the federal government?
   a) Yes   b) No
6. Do you prefer smooth or chunky peanut butter?
   a) Smooth   b) Chunky
7. Do you drink the milk in the bowl after the cereal is gone?
   a) Yes   b) No
8. Do you live in a home that's between 10 and 50 years old?
   a) Yes   b) No
9. Do you drink coffee?
   a) Yes   b) No
10. Do you believe sexual education is inappropriate in school?
    a) Yes   b) No

Okay! Start humming the "Star Spangled Banner" and check your answers against those of most Americans surveyed in O'Keefe's study.

Answers:

1—b   2—a   3—a   4—a   5—b   6—a   7—a   8—a   9—a   10—b

How many of your answers agreed with the ones above?
0–3 You march to a different drummer.
4–6 You're somewhere between average and not-so-average.
7–10 You're a full-fledged American!

Try it with a couple friends or family members and see how "American" they are. O'Keefe's book is filled with fascinating stories of Americans he met throughout his study. A few of the other characteristics he cites as descriptive of most Americans include:

Most of us (60 percent) live in the state where we were born.

More than 80 percent of us believe in God and call ourselves "Christians."

And we're generally satisfied with the way things are going in life.

We eat an average of 4.2 meals a week in restaurants or some kind of place where our meals are prepared for us. For many of us, that place is McDonald's, the fast-food restaurant that is within three miles of most American homes. In between trips to the golden arches, we love to snack on peanut butter. Most Americans eat peanut butter at least once a week. Peanut butter is the most common American food, far more common than apple pie. The average American consumes three pounds of *smooth* peanut butter annually.

Most of us earn enough money in thirty-six days to pay for our food consumption for an entire year. As Americans, we're better off financially than 99 percent of the people who have ever lived, including many royalty. Our homes are the largest in the world, and most of us live in the suburbs. Even 40 percent of our nation's poorest live in the burbs. And though we make up only 6 percent of the world's population, we represent 59 percent of the world's wealth.

I live in the city (not the suburbs). I prefer crunchy peanut butter. I can't remember the last time I went to McDonald's. And I was born a couple states away from where I live. Those departures from the "average American" and a whole series of other characteristics about me have often caused me to think of myself as atypical when it comes to being American. Maybe you can relate. But here is what is fascinating about O'Keefe's discovery. The areas where I differ from the majority of other Americans doesn't necessarily mean I'm *not* an "average American." In one sense, there really is no such thing as an "average American."

If you feel as if I'm contradicting myself, bear with me. Those of us who are Americans are strongly shaped by the value of individualism—the right to individual freedom and choices. As a result, most all of us have some idiosyncratic characteristics that set us apart from most other Americans. This is one of the primary theses of O'Keefe's book. An "average American" will have some key points of difference from other "average Americans." We all have something that is not all that average about our lives. And that very uniqueness is part of what it means to be American because of how individualistic we are. Interestingly, the mass-media world has felt the reality of this. The days of true mass marketing are over, and Madison Avenue now talks about niche marketing instead. The last television show a majority of Americans watched was the final episode of *MASH*.[3]

This reality certainly raises some interesting implications for ministries working throughout the United States. It is one of the reasons to celebrate so many varied denominations and expressions of the Christian church. The mosaic of denominational differences with varied church expressions reflects our American culture. It allows God to speak in varied "languages" through his people. And it ought to caution us against mimicking the strategies of the "success stories" of the megachurches running conferences about how to reach the masses in our communities.

So how can we even go about describing a culture as individualistic as American culture, where "difference" is one of the most "common" traits? My reluctance to describe American culture is further exacerbated by thinking about the many subcultures that exist across the American landscape. The variations between the North and the South, the Midwest and the Pacific Northwest, not to mention diaspora groups scattered in every state, generational subcultures, and the many other cultural groupings we're addressing in this book are further reason to be cautious about how broadly we can apply any description of American culture.

These concerns are the very reason I wanted to begin the knowledge CQ part of this book by looking at our own national cultures rather than jumping right in with theoretical concepts about knowledge CQ. Examining how we are like and unlike our national culture makes us better students of how to apply cultural understanding to others.

To what degree do you feel that you mirror the values of your national culture— American or otherwise?

Despite our wide array of individual differences from one another as Americans, there are still some core values that shape the ways most of us think, act, and relate. As I said, I've often thought of myself as not being a very "typical" American. But the longer I study the central values of American life, the more I realize that I'm more American than I may have thought. Few things have made that as clear to me as my travel outside the United States. One of the most valuable things about encountering different cultures when you travel is the mirror it provides for seeing your own culture. Traveling around the world has taught me about many different places and cultures, but it has taught me most about my own cultural background. I've been through the full gamut of emotions in how I've received instruction about my own national culture—from great pride in being an American to utter despair over what it means to be part of this empire. But might I caution us against either extreme? In light of the framework we explored in chapter 2, there are aspects of American culture we should embrace, there are aspects we should protest and redeem, and there are many aspects that are simply "different" from how other cultures live, neither expressly good nor expressly bad.

I'm a first-generation American in my family. My mom was born in Calgary, Alberta, and my dad in Toronto, Ontario (in western and eastern Canada, respectively, for those not up on their Canadian geography). They moved to the United States shortly before I was born. So I'm a full-fledged US citizen. But nearly all my extended family still lives in Canada. Throughout my childhood, we made numerous trips in and out of various places in Canada. I felt sorry for my cousins in Montreal for having to deal with people who spoke only French and for having money that wasn't worth as much. And my cousins called us the flag wavers and the arrogant Americans. With my parents' support, I was proud to quip back that we had something to be proud of and didn't bow to the queen! It was all done in jest, but surely I was growing in my confidence that I was part of the best civilization in the world.

When I first began traveling internationally, my nationalistic pride continued to grow. My journals are filled with reflections wondering why God blessed me to be born in the United States rather than these people who didn't have a choice but to be born in places such as Peruvian villages or Brazilian cities. I often asked the locals if they had ever had a chance to visit the United States, assuming that would, of course, be their dream. And my notions of our place in the world were reinforced by missionaries' requests for me to bring along some goods from home that "these people" just didn't know how to make right (e.g., peanut butter!). Missionaries often alerted me to the many women in Latin America who would try to talk me into marriage so they could gain passage to the land of the free.

As I began to develop trusting friendships with people in other parts of the world and especially as I began to listen more and talk less, my views about the United States began to shift. And for a long time I went to the other extreme. I would deprecate all that was American. For a while this impulse would come and go, but when I was in the throes of my doctoral work, my introductions to people outside the United States began with an apology for being an American. I even looked into getting a Canadian passport so I could claim my Canadian identity rather than the American one. I grimaced at most forms of American patriotism, and Linda persevered through my endless rants about it. I felt the fullness of this love/hate relationship in the days after 9/11. Our family was flying home from Asia on September 11, 2001. We ended up in Calgary,

Alberta, for the rest of the week, ironically my mom's hometown. When we eventually reached Chicago, the entire length of the terminal where we arrived was lined with airport personnel waving flags and cheering on our return to the land of the free. For the first time in quite a while, I felt a tinge of patriotism. But hearing some of the ill-informed commentaries by news pundits and colleagues about the unswaying superiority of the United States caused my patriotism to quickly dissipate. However, I resolved to temper some of my angst regarding my homeland.

Over the last couple of years, I've been growing in my attempts to apply cultural intelligence to my own cultural background. I've been gently challenged by friends in other parts of the world about my tendency to treat my fellow Americans with the same kind of paternalistic arrogance that I accuse them of using with others. One Asian friend said, "But, Dave, might it be that the very things you accuse your fellow citizens of doing in relationship to people from other cultures is the way you're relating to them? *Maybe the Other for you is a less-traveled, less-thoughtful American neighbor!*" Jesus's teaching about missing the beam in one's eye came to mind. I'd love to tell you that I'm now perfectly balanced in seeing my culture for what it is, the good with the bad. No way. It's an ongoing journey.

Now I see this same tendency in some of our seminary students. We sit down for coffee, and they tell me about their aspirations to serve somewhere in the world—anywhere but the United States. They say, "I have no patience for this place!" Sometimes I feel as if they are trying to gain my respect by ranting about all that's "American." Instead, because of my own brokenness in this area, it raises a red flag for me.

Several of the issues explored in the remainder of this book are discussed in light of the American context. But I've devoted this chapter in particular to specifically understanding (knowledge CQ) the threads weaving through our American cloaks. There are a few different ways to approach this task. For example, there are some helpful resources that examine how we as Americans deal with touch, our need for personal space, or learning what our foods say about us. But those kinds of behaviors are indicators of something deeper that drives us. In chapter 8, we'll explore several different cultural values that are used to compare various cultures with one another. That process is another helpful way to understand our national heritage as Americans, but those values have been specifically developed for the purpose of comparing a large number of cultures with one another. Instead, I've organized this chapter around a few core American values. These values have emerged from the work of multiple researchers who have focused specifically on American culture in and of itself. We'll begin by observing how the mantra of American life—"life, liberty, and the pursuit of happiness"—rings as true today as it did a couple of centuries ago. Then we'll look at the ways we resist formality and hierarchy. Next, we'll consider the antihistorical bent found among most Americans, and finally, we'll examine the low level of commitment we often expect in our relationships. Individualism is a thread winding through all these themes. The descriptions included aren't true of all Americans any more than the preferred kind of peanut butter is the same for all Americans. But they are important norms and generalizations that shape our life in the United States of America. For those American readers who, like me, are quick to think, *I'm not an average American*, beware. We might be far more shaped by American culture than we think. Seek to understand yourself and how you're influenced by the American way, or whatever your national culture. This is where our knowledge CQ begins.

Life, Liberty, and the Pursuit of Happiness

Nothing makes for a better American story line than an underdog who triumphs over evil with courage and compassion. This is the American way of life—life, liberty, and the pursuit of happiness. We believe anyone can have it if he or she tries hard enough! The American dream ought to be the "right" of everyone!

Of course, the American dream has become pretty elusive. While a family of four living in the suburbs with a crossover SUV and going to soccer games might be a dream for some, others are far more excited about the urban-chic life of no kids, eating organically, using public transit, and having season tickets to the symphony. I'm unfairly stereotyping, but the American dream includes the idea that no one should tell you what your dream is. That is for you to figure out and pursue.

No one can really define a common American dream these days. But it is as alive as when Thomas Jefferson penned the inalienable rights of Americans—"life, liberty, and the pursuit of happiness." Since our inception as a nation, American citizens have demanded a guarantee of basic freedoms, though it took several decades before women and people of color could even vote. So our actions don't always support our espoused values. But the First Amendment has been our blueprint for personal freedom and the hallmark of an open society. It protects freedom of speech, press, religion, assembly, and petition. It reads: "Congress shall make no law respecting an establishment of religion, or prohibiting the free exercise thereof; or abridging the freedom of speech, or of the press; or the right of the people peaceably to assemble, and to petition the Government for a redress of grievances."[4]

Whether you get your news from FOX, CBS, CNN, or NPR, day after day, you'll hear vigorous debates about how to apply the First Amendment equitably. We debate whether our rights should cover flag burning, hardcore rap and heavy-metal lyrics, tobacco advertising, hate speech, pornography, nude dancing, solicitation, and various forms of symbolic speech. Without the First Amendment, religious minorities could be persecuted, the government might well establish a national religion, protesters could be silenced, the press could not criticize government, and citizens could not mobilize for social change.

Our commitment to protect our personal freedoms is directly connected to being a people who are always searching for something better and for something more fulfilling—happiness. American literary giant John Steinbeck put it this way: We Americans are "restless, a dissatisfied, a searching people. We bridle and buck under failure, and we go mad with dissatisfaction in the face of success. We spend our time searching for security, and hate it when we get it."[5]

This American way of life stems from the cultural value of individualism. We'll look more fully at this value in chapter 8. But we can't talk about the American way without talking about our value of an individual's rights. To be an individualist is to be a self-standing person in a society where all people have a right to their own opinions and can speak for themselves. Taking initiative for one's self is seen as good and expected, and it's assumed that everyone else needs to "mind his own business." We're the most individualistic culture in the world.

My daughter Emily is proud to be an individualist. Emily is in love with dogs like no one I've ever seen. Her bedroom is filled with stuffed dogs. If she had her way, every writing assignment for school would somehow come back to dogs, and she lobbies almost daily for the time when our family will once and for all become dog owners. And in Emily's mind, the bigger the dog the better. In fact, she claims she someday wants at least six German shepherds and six greyhounds.

We recently spent several weeks in Singapore while I was doing some work in the region. Although there were plenty of dogs in the housing estate where we were staying, they were mostly smaller dogs. Emily didn't feel as free to run up and ask permission to pet these dogs as she does when we're home. So one day she asked if we could go to a pet store just so she could get a "dog fix." I agreed and sure enough, we saw lots of dogs for sale. But we also noticed a sign reminding anyone living in public housing—which includes nearly 80 percent of the Singapore population—that each household is allowed one dog of an approved breed. The approved breeds include those such as pugs, shih tzus, and Yorkshire terriers (all little dogs).

Emily was appalled. She ranted, "That's so unfair. What if someone like me lived here? I should have the right to have as many dogs as I want and whatever breed I like!" In her mind, individual rights and preferences rule.

We were telling some Singaporean friends about this little interchange a bit later, and they said, "We *love* that law! Can you imagine if the people living in the flats above, below, and beside us had a bunch of big dogs? It's a small right to give up for the sake of everyone." Singapore is a very collectivist culture rather than an individualist one. So identity and decision making are based on what is best for the group rather than what is best for the individual.

But we Americans believe strongly in the words of Thomas Jefferson, *"that all men are created equal . . . with certain inalienable Rights . . ."* We celebrate our children's first steps into independence by preserving their shoes. This becomes an icon of their move toward exercising their inalienable rights as individuals.

Linda and I are forever giving our girls choices. I'm more aware of this because of having my South African friend, Mark, talk to me about it during times he has stayed in our home. One day he said, "It's remarkable. You guys let Emily and Grace make choices about everything. It starts at the breakfast table with asking them what they want to eat, then you let them decide what they're going to wear, how they're going to spend their time, and on and on it goes throughout the day. It's really quite amazing." That was his gracious way of saying, "Are you sure this is healthy?" I've viewed it as gradually empowering them to make decisions on their own. Mark wasn't so sure. Now I have questions about it too.

How has the "right" to pursue the American dream affected choices you've made? To what degree do you think as an individual? Begin thinking about this, and we'll take our understanding about this cultural value in ourselves and others further when we explore individualism in chapter 8.

Just Call Me Dave

I've been introduced to lots of "Rev. Dr. So and Sos" in my travels abroad. Even though I know some of the cultural reasons for these kinds of formal titles and introductions, it still unnerves me. It feels formal, hierarchical, and inauthentic. If the tables are turned and someone refers to me as Rev. Dr. David Livermore, I'm quick to say, "Just call me Dave!"

I'd love to tell you that my reason for eliminating titles in front of my name comes from my humility and from my sheer desire to be identified as a disciple of Jesus. But quite honestly, it's the American way to feign equality in all our relationships with a cloak of informality that applies to almost every interaction. As Linda and I train our girls how to politely greet people, we tell them, "Look them in the eye, shake their hand, and call them by name." We tell them to use the titles of "Mr." or "Ms.," but more often than not, the American adults they greet say something like, "Mrs. Evans is my mother. Just call me Susan."

Part of this is a shift in generational culture. My mom never told kids, "Just call me Marjorie." But across the generations, American individualism results in a priority of seeing all people as equal. Our practices and lifestyle might suggest otherwise, but we espouse the belief in the irreducible value of each person simply because of his or her humanness. So we love to feign the image of equality in everything.

Everyone knows American culture has a hierarchy of power relationships whether it is pastor to youth pastor, teacher to student, or rich person to middle-class person. But it is countercultural to be explicit about those kinds of things. Even when a superior needs to confront a subordinate, it is culturally appropriate to begin the conversation with small talk and to offer a cup of coffee. First names are preferred. And one of the greatest compliments to give someone in authority is "She's just a regular person. She doesn't lord her authority over you." Listen to how often political candidates seek to demonstrate their common roots. "He comes from a blue-collar family and is a self-made success. Even though he's brilliant and a world-renowned leader, he makes you feel like he's one of you!"

As a result, most Americans resist formality. Pomp and circumstance are reserved for unusual occasions such as commencement exercises and funerals, and even then, most of us prefer to not get too uptight. That seems inauthentic.

Many people from outside the United States dislike the ways we attempt to level all hierarchy with no formality. And many visitors to the United States are puzzled by the informality that permeates all kinds of relationships. One visiting pastor, John, said to me, "The hierarchies are so invisible here. I'm always guessing how I should be relating to people. I can't tell who are the pastors and who are the laity."

"John," I said, "just be yourself. We don't make a big distinction between the two. We're all ministers of the gospel—right? So why does it matter?" John continued, "That's really confusing to someone like me. You might see distinctions like that as pompous and arrogant, but among my people, these categories provide the context for how to behave and relate. It's just being honest about where the power lies!"

From the days of breaking free from the Old World monarchy, our culture has been shaped by a desire to look as if we treat everyone equally. This comes back to our obsession with individual rights. Just as Christ found aspects in his culture to protest and embrace, we too will find the need for both responses to these American values. The understanding gained by developing our knowledge CQ in regard to our own culture is pivotal to moving toward a place where we effectively love across the chasm of cultural difference.

All History Is Bunk

Yet another expression of our individualism and a characteristic of our American culture is our limited historical context. Most Americans who travel abroad, particularly on their first trips to Europe, are reminded of the youthfulness of our nation. I've joined countless other Americans in traveling to Europe and saying, "Wow! My town just had its 150th anniversary, and the village we just visited in France has bakeries that have been around since 1500!" As tourists, we enjoy the mystique of buildings and communities that have been around for centuries or even millennia. But when it comes down to it, the predominant American view of history is captured by that quintessential American, Henry Ford: "History is more or less bunk. It's tradition. We don't want tradition. We want to live in the present and the only history that is worth a tinker's damn is the history we make today."[6] Keep in mind, in some ways, there is no such thing as an "average American." So you might be a history fanatic who is offended by my stereotype of Americans as ahistorical. But stick with me. Even if you are an American who loves history, American culture as a whole is less interested in the past and more interested in the present. Seek to understand the subtle ways that might shape you.

Here's one of the ways I observed this tendency in myself. Last year I was teaching a group of pastors in Liberia. We were talking about some of the cultural issues that contributed to the recent civil war there. They helped me understand that the war partly stemmed from the exploitive, paternalistic rule exercised by the Americo Liberians—former American and Caribbean slaves who were repatriated to Liberia in the early nineteenth century. They explained that the Americos mistreated the indigenous people who had never left. Thinking I'd suggest some historical context for this conversation, I interjected the comment, "It's important we think about how the Americo people were treated as slaves. While that doesn't excuse their behavior, we often see that abused people abuse people." Some of the pastors in the room from Americo descent erupted to give me a more informed historical perspective. They said, "Oh, it's more than that. Some of the indigenous people were the ones who sold our forefathers and mothers as slaves to the slave traders. So it wasn't just a result of the abusive relationship on the other side of the Atlantic. It stemmed back to what happened to them before they left here in the first place." To which some of the pastors from a more indigenous background shot back, "Yes. But why did our forefathers and mothers sell your forebears to the slave traders? It was because your people exploited our people for so long."

The fascinating "rabbit trail" took over the rest of the class time that day. And as often happens in the classroom, I think the so-called teacher was the one learning the most. What a lesson in how little I understand about the deep, historical roots that shape the cultural patterns of so many places around the world.

As Americans, most of us know very little about the past, and we don't care. In our minds, we don't need the past. What we are interested in is the now, the moment, and the existential experience. All we need is pragmatic problem solving. That is the vision, or lack of vision, we've taken on as a country. We seldom look at the long-haul patterns of life and death. We are short-run people. Many of our American churches have this same mentality and view ancient rituals and church history as irrelevant for today.

In contrast, many European cultures stress abstract theory and historical dimensions, and the Japanese focus on concrete descriptions of what they observe. Meanwhile, Americans tend to focus on functional, pragmatic applications of thinking. We want action and measurable change. We want results.

Why should I be making apologies for what my great-great-grandparents did to African Americans? And what is the point of all the staid traditions in the church? These are the kinds of questions that reveal our ahistorical bent. They lead us to a now-oriented, problem-solving mind-set as we grab life by the reins.

Again, as with all these areas, I'm generalizing. Not all Americans disregard history as irrelevant. Former US president Harry Truman said, "There is nothing new in the world except the history you do not know."[7] There are American philosophers who aren't very interested in pragmatic implications, and there are emerging generations in the American church that see church history as the road to the future. There is a growing movement of many Americans who are searching for their generational roots. But as a whole, we're a nation that thrives on the present and on getting to the bottom line.

Our ahistorical, results-oriented nature affects our communication style. We value direct, bottom-line, straight-to-the-issue interaction.

We say things like, "Shoot straight with me," "Let's put the cards on the table," "Let's address the elephant in the room." This stems from our problem-solving orientation that wants to get straight to the source of the issue. It often leads to a very confusing dilemma for others who are trying to learn how to cope with us, because we have this equitable, cordial style of interaction that seeks to treat everyone fairly but that coexists with an explicit directness. Our American problem-solving exposes what appears to be the backbone of our American culture: whatever the problem, it can be fixed.

Our ahistorical orientation and subsequent problem-solving mode brings us full circle to individualism and our concern for equality and individual rights. Fairness is a big deal for us. I've had passionate debates with friends about special rights given to ethnic minority groups in light of our history. But an ahistorical, individualistic approach to life inevitably leads us to view any kind of systemic, structural response as unfair. By and large, we're antistructuralist. Mainstream American voters typically resist systems and structures that are meant to help entire cultures of people. And American evangelicals are especially resistant toward systemic responses to issues of inequality. For example, conservative Protestants are six times more likely than average Americans to cite lack of motivation among blacks to be the leading cause for the income differences between blacks and whites rather than seeing unequal access to education as a viable explanation.[8] Evangelicals tend to believe that giving attention to social structures and systems of inequality shifts guilt away from the root source, individual sin. On the whole, American evangelicals oppose programs such as affirmative action because they tend to go against an evangelical understanding of accountable, freewill individualism.[9]

Soon Ang is one of the leading researchers on cultural intelligence based in Singapore. As well as being a world-renowned researcher who consults with governments and Fortune 500 companies, Soon is a passionate follower of Jesus. She has become not only a mentor but a friend with whom I can freely interact. One day Soon asked me why I thought the United States doesn't regulate that neighborhoods and schools reflect the socioethnic diversity that exists within a community. I can't even imagine the revolt that would occur if a politician or an advocacy group tried to promote such legislation throughout the land of the brave and the free. Nor am I trying to take a position on whether that would be healthy, despite the near impossibility of doing so. But the point is, our dominant American values of individual rights combined with an ahistorical bias leads us to an emphasis on fairness and equality, and we use the cooperative nature of those emphases to get things done. The predominant American mind-set is that most problems could be solved if only people would put aside their prejudices and work together. History is irrelevant, and systems exist to provide equal rights to all individuals to enable them to become self-made people. What is good for you is what is good for me, and we can use each other to get closer to the American dream. This leads to one more thread of American life—our friendships.

No Strings Attached

Americans are known for being friendly and for having lots of relationships marked by friendliness and informality. Our friendships tend to be based on spontaneity, mutual attraction, and warm personal feelings. I had an Indian man stop me one day while I was walking around Connaught Place in New Delhi. "You're an American, aren't you?" he said. I was surprised because people often guess I'm European or Australian in this part of the world. I responded, "Yeah, I'm from the States. How did you know?"

"Oh, it's obvious," he said. "You're walking briskly like you're going somewhere really important, and you're looking at everyone and smiling. *Americans always think everyone is their friend. But they don't trust anyone.*" That led us into a fascinating walk together talking about the "no-strings approach" we as Americans take to friendship and family.

Google "no strings attached" or "NSA," and in a millisecond you'll pull up millions of listings—the top of the list being all kinds of options for NSA sex. Surfing for "hook-ups" through the Internet has become the epitome of "relationship" without any obligation. Although one-night stands are an extreme example, they exemplify a strong assumption that underlies American friendship. Friendship is an outgrowth of our individualistic orientation as Americans. We presume relationships shouldn't be obligatory. Relationships should be something that exist for the sheer enjoyment of them—not something to which you're obliged.

Of course, we don't *really* believe this. If I always ask you to coffee and you never reciprocate, I begin to see that this relationship is a one-way street. If you give me a birthday gift every year and I never even acknowledge yours, even the most hardcore red, white, and blue flag waver will get a little miffed. But on the whole, we avoid obligatory commitments to one another. Our friendships are based on freedom to come and go as we please. Children shouldn't be obliged to care for aging parents. There are professionals you can pay to take care of them. And unhappy married couples shouldn't be expected to hang in there just because their teenage romance led to wedding vows. If you aren't happy and fulfilled, you're free to leave. And friends can give input *when* it's solicited, but everyone should be free to make his or her own choices.

In contrast, my Chinese friends have taught me about *guanxi*, the personal relationship between people that obligates them to one another's needs and desires. In their minds, a relationship without any strings attached is no relationship. Friendship and familial relationships are built on commitment and the expectation that there will be reciprocal commitment. I have an American friend, Rob, who has worked as a physician in China for several years. Rob talks about how ill prepared he was for *guanxi*. He describes a dinner invitation he received soon after he moved to China. It was an "over-the-top evening" with all sorts of exotic foods, ceremonies, and gifts. Rob was overwhelmed by the hospitality of his new acquaintance. At the end of the evening, Rob thanked his Chinese host for his generosity. The Chinese man then asked Rob how he could arrange for this man's children to attend a university in the United States. Rob apologetically shrugged his shoulders and claimed there wasn't much he could do to get them into college. He might be able to recommend some places, but they would have to apply like anyone else. The Chinese host was appalled. How could Dr. Rob not see his ethical obligation to help?

As Americans, we find it hard to listen to an episode like that and not feel that it is exploitive and manipulative. But before we're too quick to get on our high horse of judgment, we need to realize that in most of the world, a relationship without any obligation is no relationship at all.

In the United States, social networks that go beyond our immediate group of significant friends and family are used primarily for information exchange. We want to gain information from others that we would not otherwise possess. In many Asian cultures, social ties are much stronger and involve more of a favor exchange. The favors need not necessarily be tit for tat. They represent obligations each party has to the other. Obligations tend not to diminish, unlike information exchange. Hence, the networks one develops at a conference in the United States are very different from what an individual might develop in many Asian venues.[10]

I assume not saying "thank you" to someone who holds the door for me or does something kind for me is rude. My Indian friend Joel tells me that if he were to say "thank you" every time a Punjabi doorman opens the door for him, the Punjabi would be insulted for the rudeness of that kind of formality. The action is a "given," therefore why would you be so formal as to say "thank you"?

While we prefer relationships that aren't obligatory, we do thrive on agreement and acceptance from friends and colleagues. We want to believe that people throughout the world will like us. This has been one of the most perplexing sentiments for Americans in a post-9/11 era. "After all we've done for the world, why do they hate us so much?" United States Agency for International Development projects have often been canceled in countries where the recipients appear ungrateful. Intercultural experts Edward Stewart and Milton Bennett write, "The glad handshake, the ready smile, the slap on the back, and other superficial signs of friendship are part of the American life. Whenever Americans are denied these expressions of friendship or popularity, they are confused, reacting as if one of the requirements for personal assurance has been denied. Social success is often a necessary part of achievement, and Americans tend to judge their personal and social success by popularity—almost literally by the number of people who like them."[11]

We consider our friends to be those with whom we get along and agree. One Italian ministry leader put it this way: "You Americans think, 'We're friends. Therefore we shouldn't argue.' As Italians, we think, 'We're friends, so now it's okay to argue!'"

Part of my daily rhythm is to take a morning run. As I run through the tree-lined streets of my neighborhood, more often than not, I nod and greet my fellow runners and walkers each morning. I tried the same thing the first time we lived in Singapore. The first challenge was that many of the people walking by were looking down at the ground. So it was difficult to even make eye contact, much less greet them verbally. But I decided these people needed to learn how to be friendly. So I made it a point of saying, "Good morning," which typically was received a bit awkwardly.

I prided myself on bucking the norm. A long time later, I was back in the States having lunch at a restaurant with Amos, a friend from West Africa. When the server came to take our order, I asked her, "How is your day going?" After she left, my friend Amos asked, "Do you know her?" I told him I had never met her before. He continued, "Then why would you ask her how her day was going?"

I replied, "I'm just being friendly. I don't necessarily expect she'll even tell me much in response, but it's just a way of being friendly with one another." He started laughing and said, "That's the crazy thing about you Americans. You talk so much about relationships, but you ask the same kind of question to a complete stranger serving us lunch as you would ask a close friend."

Smiling at passersby on a busy street in India and chatting with a restaurant server may at first appear to be personal ways of treating the Other, but it can potentially become depersonalizing because it treats everyone the same. This falls right in line with our desire for equality and fairness. When the same kinds of greetings and conversation are used with most everyone such that "even enemies are likely to be treated with a controlled friendliness"[12] it might look like we value our enemies, acquaintances, and intimate friends all equally. Of course, authentically loving the Other—friend or foe—is the revolutionary destination we're moving toward in this journey. But we're wise to consider the inauthenticity that might be communicated when we express our love to everyone in uniform ways.

Conclusion

For those of us who are Americans, it's helpful to consider how the thread of the American way is woven into the fabric of our being. How does it affect the way we see the world? How does it shape the way we relate? How does it shape our reading of Scripture?

Regardless of how you fared on the "average American" quiz at the beginning of the chapter, the very fact that we may vary widely in how we answer those questions speaks to our individualism as Americans. To be independent, distinctive, and have your own voice is to be American. At the same time, amid our individualism, we're shaped by the American way more than we might think.

The inward, transformative journey of cultural intelligence involves a heightened understanding of our own cultural background. In what ways are we shaped by the cultures of which we're a part? How does our cultural background shape the way we think, see, and love? Beware of too quickly defending or deprecating all that is part of your cultural background. And resist being hasty to differentiate yourself as not being like most other Americans, or whatever your cultural background. Instead, linger over the terrain at home for a bit and discuss with others how the way you see the world is shaped by your cultural background. As we do so, we'll probably see many things in our cultural orientation that reflect the "already" realities of God's kingdom and many that don't.

This kind of understanding about our own cultural background, especially when also applied to the other kinds of cultures of which we're a part, plays a significant role in helping us move forward in the journey of cultural intelligence. Having spent some time on the road that takes us toward seeing what knowledge CQ looks like in American culture, we want to look more specifically at knowledge CQ as it relates to all sorts of cultural contexts. Bring along a peanut butter sandwich for the ride.

> Think through the last week. What choices have you made? How have you spent your time? What have you done for fun? What does this say about what you value?

Consider this in contrast with the values of American culture (or whatever your primary national culture). How does your national culture shape the way you view the world?

Recommended Resources

O'Keefe, Kevin. *The Average American: The Extraordinary Search for the Nation's Most Ordinary Citizen.* New York: Public Affairs, 2005.

Rapaille, Clotaire. *The Culture Code: An Ingenious Way to Understand Why People around the World Live and Buy as They Do.* New York: Broadway Books, 2007.

Stewart, Edward, and Milton Bennett. *American Cultural Patterns: A Cross-Cultural Perspective.* Boston: Intercultural Press, 1991.

5

getting below the surface

What Is Culture Anyway?

I'm not sure culture has a whole lot to do with it," Scott said. Scott had been serving as a missionary in Eastern Europe for the last fifteen years. He was part of a focus group of American missionaries I was interviewing. "I just think the culture card is overplayed," he continued. "People are people. Sin is sin. Jesus is Jesus. That's not cultural intelligence. That's just a matter of knowing how to be humble and loving."

He began talking about how often he watched American visitors come through Romania who are invited to preach in some of the churches there. He said: "The Romanian pastors graciously invite the visiting Americans to preach, and the Americans all too willingly accept the invitation. One summer, our pastor didn't preach for three months straight because every week we had another American pastor who was too arrogant to turn down the invitation to preach. It doesn't take cultural intelligence to figure out you need to just humbly decline. That's just a matter of humility! It doesn't really have anything to do with culture."

A Korean pastor who had been sitting in on this focus group discussion pulled me aside later in the day and said, "What that missionary said about Romania isn't true in my country. It might be arrogant to accept the invitation to preach in Romania. But it would be an insult to refuse the invitation to preach in my Korean church."

I'm leery of generalizing either assumption to Romanian or Korean culture. But the point is this: can you see how vitally powerful yet invisible culture is? Cultural intelligence is needed to know what humility looks like in a specific context. What appears as arrogance in one place is humility in another.

Defining culture is much like defining air. We know what it is. We live in it. It lives in us. We can't see it, but it's there just the same. And like air, technical definitions of culture abound, but they don't necessarily move us any closer toward understanding what it really is and how it affects us. We want to tackle that challenge in this chapter. We want to better *understand* how culture shapes the ways all of us think and behave. You probably already have a great deal of understanding about culture. Culture is something we live in every day. So as much as anything, I want to provide language and pictures to build upon the understanding you already have. This will allow us to become more intentional in how we approach cross-cultural interactions.

A core part of knowledge CQ is to understand the notion of culture itself and how it interacts with what we all share as human beings versus what is unique to each of us as individuals. Increasing our knowledge of the very idea of culture and how it affects us is the goal of this chapter. I purposely didn't start the knowledge CQ portion of our journey with this chapter because I wanted to talk about something more tangible first—the American culture in which many of us live. If we can't first see our own culture with its own set of interests, emotions, and biases, how can we expect to understand what culture really is? But having looked at some of the interests and underlying values of American culture, we're now going to explore the abstraction of culture and observe its ubiquitous presence in our lives. We'll begin by looking at some definitions of culture. Then we'll distinguish culture from what we all share in common as human beings and from what differentiates all of us as unique individuals.

Culture Defined

Anthropologists and sociologists have heated debates about who originated the idea of culture, and they argue about how to define it. Most agree with James Clifford's statement that culture "is a deeply compromised idea I cannot yet do without."[1] Some of the more helpful definitions of culture include:

- Culture is the artificial, secondary environment superimposed on the natural.[2]
- Culture is "a pattern of thinking, feeling, and reacting to various situations and actions."[3]

- Culture is the *shared understandings* people use within a society to align their actions. "While culture is defined, created, and transmitted through interaction, it is not interaction itself, but the content, meanings, and topics of interaction."[4]
- Culture is the *collective programming of the mind* that distinguishes the members of one group from another. It is the software behind how we operate.[5]
- Culture is the way a group of people solve problems and reconcile dilemmas.[6]
- Cultures are comprised of "webs of significance" that people spin and in which they themselves are suspended.[7]

Several different metaphors are used to try to make the notion of culture more accessible. Earlier I compared culture to air to demonstrate culture's invisible but constant presence and influence on everything we do. Another way of describing culture is to see it as the software that runs the programs of our thoughts, speech, and actions. And others compare culture to a sport that runs by a certain set of rules. If you don't know the rules behind soccer, you can feel clueless watching a bunch of players kicking a ball around. But when you understand the rules of offside, unfair tackling, and ball handling, the game makes sense.

Visual metaphors such as those involving sight and references to lenses and eyeglasses are also frequently used to explain culture. Glasses are something through which we see the world. We see *with* a pair of eyeglasses, even though when rightly fitted, we don't see the glass itself. We're rarely conscious of the lens between our eye and what we're viewing, nor do we typically think about the way our glasses alter what we see. But we see differently because of them. That's what culture does. It is the pair of glasses through which we view the world.

Another important metaphor to help explain culture is the comparison of culture to an iceberg (see fig. 5a).[8] Iceberg metaphors are typically used to describe something that is only barely visible, with as much as 90 percent of it being submerged below the waterline. On the surface, we can observe a culture in light of its artifacts. Artifacts include things such as foods, eating habits, gestures, music, economic practices, dress, use of physical space (e.g., office setup), order of worship, art, and so on. When many people encounter a new culture, these are the things they are most inclined to talk about because they can see them. They're the part of the iceberg that is visible above water. This is a metaphor we'll continue to use throughout the book.

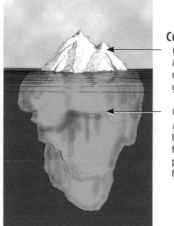

Culture
Cultural Artifacts
Art, clothing, food,
money, customs,
gestures, etc.

Cultural Values and
Assumptions
Unconscious, taken
for granted beliefs,
perceptions, and
feelings

Figure 5a. Cultural Artifacts and Values

Throughout my years of researching the experiences of American short-term missionaries, they have continually referenced the artifacts of culture when asked to describe the cultural differences observed. In response to the question, "What did you notice about the culture where you visited?" most North American participants, whether they are fifteen or fifty-five, make comments like these:

I remember them driving on the wrong side of the road, speaking a different language, and using strange-looking money.

Everything was different. The buildings were different. Their cars were different. Everything was so crowded, and people walked in the middle of the street and crossed whenever and wherever they wanted to. They don't have standards like we have.

The poverty is what I noticed the most. I mean, Mexico isn't that far away. It's just mind-boggling to think people who live so close to you live in such poor conditions.

I noticed it's not as modern as the United States. Walking down the stairs of a plane instead of walking through a jetway. That's the kind of stuff I observed. And it's not very clean.

I remember realizing how good I have it. You see these people around you with so little, but they're so happy.

Getting people to look below the surface of cultural artifacts has been one of the greatest challenges I've faced over the last several years. It is incredibly challenging to explore culture beneath the tip of the iceberg.

One of the most important roles for us as ministry leaders is to help people see what lies beneath the language, dress, food customs, and poverty of a culture.

The most significant aspects of culture are below the surface (cultural values and assumptions in fig. 5a). This part of the iceberg represents the values and assumptions of the culture. These invisible yet powerful elements include things such as the group's shared work ethic, identity, social etiquette, and view of authority. At its core, culture is not so much our habits, diets, and economic practices as it is the ideas and assumptions that are behind our habits, diets, and commerce. Culture represents the way a group of people organize their ideas and hence their lives. It's what lies beneath what we think and how we live.

One of our goals in this CQ pathway is to become more aware of the part of the iceberg submerged below the surface of the water. Or to switch back to the eyeglasses metaphor, we want to become more aware of the pair of glasses we're wearing to understand how they shape what we see and how they distort our vision. And we need to grow in our understanding of the glasses worn by people in other cultural contexts. The goal isn't as much to change our glasses as it is to become aware of them and respect the different lenses through which people view the world. This is a seminal aspect of knowledge CQ: understanding what culture is and how it shapes what we see.

One of the most important cross-cultural anthropologists of the twentieth century, Edward Hall, expressed it this way: "Most of culture lies hidden and is outside voluntary control, making up the warp and weft of human existence. It penetrates to the roots of [an individual's] nervous system and determines how he perceives the world. Even when small fragments of culture are elevated to awareness, they are difficult to change."[9] When wrestling with our cultural assumptions in tension with the values of the kingdom of God, we'll begin to see the aspects of our cultural perspective that should change as well as ways we need to be agents of change among others.

Finally, culture is not something that just happens to us. Though it becomes part of us subconsciously, that doesn't mean we're merely passive recipients of culture who have no choice but to become programmed robots of a culture. We're affected by culture, and we in turn are active creators of culture. It doesn't simply exercise determinative power over us. *Rather, culture is both an outcome and a product of our social interaction.*[10]

One step toward increasing our knowledge CQ is to become more aware of culture's influence on the behaviors of ourselves and others. This relates closely with the skills we're exploring as part of interpretive CQ. But before we can begin interpreting cultural behavior, we must have some rudimentary understanding of how culture shapes attitudes and behavior.

As you engage in the activities ahead of you this week, look for ways that culture is shaping what occurs. What can you learn about the corporate culture of the businesses you visit? As you interact with people who have lived in your town for their entire lives compared with people who are transplants there, what do you observe? Which of these observations can be attributed to culture, which are unique to the individual you encounter, and which are common to people everywhere?

How do we distinguish between what is cultural, what is universal to every human's experience, and what is unique to an individual? The interactive nature of culture with human nature and with individual personality is what we need to explore next.

We're So Much the Same. We're So Different.

Scott's statement, "People are people. Sin is sin," carries a kernel of truth while also being a dangerous standard by which to think about cross-cultural interaction. Delford, an African American pastor in Cincinnati, articulated a sentiment I heard from many ministry leaders of color: "I'm consistently invited to speak on behalf of African American pastors and churches. Somehow I'm supposed to be an expert on what black pastors think just because I'm black. Hello! I have areas where I have some expertise, and I'd love to be invited to speak about those topics. But the invitations are usually to come be the black guy speaking about issues of black churches." I don't think I've ever been asked to speak on behalf of all American ministry leaders or all white pastors. I'm never asked to speak for all white people nor for what men think about something.

One of the most important aspects of knowledge CQ is discerning when to look at something in light of culture, when to see something as common to all people, and when to see something as unique to one person, distinguishing her or him from the other 6.5 billion people on the planet. Applying the idiosyncrasies of one individual to an entire culture is one of the recurring errors made by ministry leaders when they interact cross-culturally. On the other hand, failure to appreciate the difference culture makes in how people view their faith is equally damaging to effective ministry leadership.

Geert Hofstede, one of the most important contributors to the study of the role of culture in international business, introduced the software metaphor to the descriptions of what culture means. Just as computer software affects the way a computer operates, culture shapes the way an individual thinks and acts. According to Hofstede, culture is the "collective programming of the mind."[11] He suggests three different levels of software that exist in each of us—human nature, culture, and personality. I've adapted Hofstede's three levels of software by adding them to the iceberg diagram we looked at earlier (see fig. 5b). These three levels of mental conditioning work iteratively with one another in shaping the ways we see the world and relate to one another.

As we reach across the chasm of cultural difference to express love to the Other, we'll encounter universal realities we share with all humans, cultural norms shared by large groups of people, and individual personality traits that are unique to each person. Human nature is represented by the very tip of the iceberg. These universal realities are fairly visible to all of us as we breathe, eat, and live. The middle level is culture, including both cultural artifacts above sea level and cultural values and assumptions below sea level, as we examined earlier. Finally, at the deepest level of the iceberg are the individual traits and experiences unique to each person. There is value in recognizing the distinctions and interconnection between these three levels of mental conditioning.

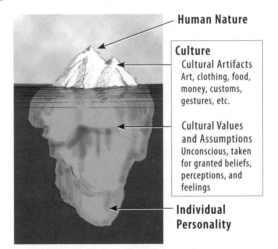

Figure 5b. Three Levels of Mental Conditioning

Human Nature

Confucius said, "All people are the same. It is only their habits that are different." Like the statement made by Scott, to a significant degree this is true. Many of our actions—whether caring for our young or communicating through language—are shared with people everywhere.

There's something redemptive about starting with what we have in common with all humanity. People are people, wherever you go. Thus we can be watching a news clip about people living fourteen time zones away and suddenly feel a connection with what they're experiencing. We all need to eat, and we all need to sleep. We're wired to survive, and regardless of personality or cultural background, in the midst of tragedy and disaster, people seem to overcome the insurmountable through an innate desire to sustain life. Hunger, sex drive, caring for our children, protecting what's ours—these are common human traits. Surely there are exceptional humans who don't share these traits, and the ways we live out these commonalities vary widely. But there are some underlying behaviors and understandings we share with the rest of humanity everywhere, past, present, and future.

Most importantly, we're all created in the image of God. A theological understanding of *imago Dei*, the Latin phrase for our having been created in the image of God, is essential for moving across the chasm from the desire to love the Other to actually expressing that love. To understand and see the Other as being created in the image of God is to recognize that he or she possesses special qualities that reflect God himself. No matter how different the Other is, he or she is in part a reflection of God. The Other was created as much in the image of God as you and I were. Our self-consciousness, our ability to make ethical choices and engage in moral reflection, and our volition are all universal traits we share as image bearers. The person with eating habits you find repulsive, the loud talker dining in the booth behind you, and the person who doesn't share your value for using deodorant are all image bearers of God. Even the villain who appears to be against all that we might deem good is at his core created in God's image. Few things are as sacred and worthy of our connection with other human beings than our shared identity as image bearers of the Holy Other.

Another important aspect to consider here is the cyclical phenomenon that exists among humanity. We as humans have some enduring ways of dealing with aging, sickness, conflict, and advancement. You can see this on a macro level by observing recurring cycles from one civilization to the next. History is a sequence of recurring patterns and cycles. This same cyclical phenomenon can be seen on the micro level by observing organizational cultures that shift from a focus on an organic, grassroots emphasis toward a more outcome-based, measurable approach to work. And sooner or later, many of these organizations cycle back to a more organic emphasis again. Or look at some of the recurring cycles involving the relationship between adults and adolescents. It has been said, "Young people nowadays love luxury; they have bad manners and contempt for authority. They show disrespect for old people and love silly talk in place of exercise. They no longer stand up when older people enter the room; they contradict their parents, talk constantly in front of company, gobble their food, and tyrannize their teachers."

It almost sounds like something you might overhear in the hallways of your church. But it was said by Socrates in 400 BC.[12] There's a cyclical nature built into how we as humans deal with some universal realities. We need to keep that in mind as we journey toward better loving the Other. But being an adolescent today is very different from being an adolescent fifteen years ago, not to mention two thousand years back.

The danger comes from too quickly lumping everything we observe about one another into this category of human nature. Deep down, we're inclined to assume that everyone thinks about and perceives the world as we do.[13] I love to sit in a busy train station or mall and watch all the people. Even in a faraway place where I don't know anyone, I can feel a level of connection simply by watching a father with his kids, a fellow traveler with her bags, or a couple laughing together. But when I move beyond feeling a connection with the father interacting with his child to making assumptions about their relationship based on my observations alone, I move into questionable territory. We assume others are like us because we learned how to behave by watching and imitating other people. "Thus while we may not choose to assume that others are like us, while we may even *know* better than to assume others are like us, and while we may very much wish we could stop expecting everyone to be like us, the force of our conditioning leaves us no other alternative."[14]

Beginning with what we have in common as human beings is a beautiful thing. But as we interact with various groups of people, we need to move toward understanding those individuals by seeing what they share with the cultural groups of which they're a part.

Culture

We can begin to distinguish one group of people from another by using the middle layer of mental conditioning, culture (refer to fig. 5b). Culture is learned, not inherited. It is formed in us both through explicit teaching and through our observation and interaction with others. We're socialized into our respective cultures first and foremost through the family setting. This socialization is further reinforced through school, the media, church, and eventually through our professional networks and environments.

Culture is the middle layer of mental conditioning because it is based on the uppermost layer of human nature wherein a group of people develop specific solutions for living out their humanity together in a particular environment. People from rural communities or even smaller cities throughout the United States are often caught off guard when they encounter rude salespeople in large urban areas. Research has demonstrated that the behavior of these salespeople is more a function of working in a busy environment than it is a reflection of their personal disposition. Of course, a continual pattern of relating this way reinforces this kind of behavior and furthers the socialization process.[15]

Culture also works interactively with the most submerged level of mental conditioning—personality—as each individual seeks to develop his or her personal identity. Therefore, cultural meanings are both psychological and social constructions. They relate to the symbolic dimension of life, where there is a continual process of making meaning and enacting one's identity. Cultural messages, which come from the groups to which we belong, give us information about what is meaningful or important. They tell us who we are in the world and in our relationships to others.

The cultural meanings that lie beneath the surface of cultural artifacts are developed through common experiences shared with a particular group of human beings. The group might be a very large grouping of individuals, such as all the people living in Brazil, or it might be a very small grouping of individuals, such as the people in your local church. Knowledge CQ gives leaders an aptitude and understanding for seeing the role of cultural values and norms in these endless varieties of cultural and subcultural groupings that we face in twenty-first-century ministry.

Despite the powerful role of culture in conditioning our minds, we're usually unconscious of its influence on our behavior. Yet culture, like the software running the beautiful Mac on which I'm currently typing, gives the brain messages to tell it how to process cues and what to do with them. The cultural layer of mental conditioning shapes our perceptions, attributions, judgments, and ideas of self and others. Neutral and positive stereotypes can actually be helpful as we begin to think about how to most effectively relate to certain groups of people amid the masses of humanity with whom we come into contact. Cultural norms are generalizations that are usually true among certain groups of people. But we must always beware of too quickly assuming a norm or stereotype applies to everyone who belongs to a cultural group. That leads us to the most specific part of mental conditioning: our individual personalities.

Individual Personality

Our personalities are central to who we are. They are what make us unique from all the other people who have ever lived. And our personalities distinguish us from the other individuals with whom we share a cultural context. Our personalities are rooted in our unique life experiences. They come from our genetic makeup and the things we've learned from our upbringing. The personality level of mental conditioning (see fig. 5b) comes from within and is both a product of our upbringing and of how we've learned to cope given the circumstances of our lives. In other words, personality is derived from both nature and nurture.

It is important to see the interactive, dynamic relationship between culture and personality. Our personalities are shaped by the cultures in which we're socialized. And through our personalities, we further shape the cultures of which we're a part. The nexus of self with the various cultures of which an individual is a part is often the cause for great dissonance and conflict within. As we look deep within ourselves, we need to be aware of some of these points of conflict and contradiction. For example, being a thirty-year-old American Presbyterian is very different from being a twenty-year-old American Pentecostal. We want to increase our appreciation for and understanding of the iterative relationship between the cultures of which we are a part and our individualized sense of self.

As we saw in our discussion about the "average American," assigning the idiosyncrasies of one individual to an entire cultural group is one of the most consistent errors made cross-culturally. There are quirks about me that many Americans wouldn't care to have generalized to them. And there are things that tend to be true about most Americans that might not necessarily be characteristic of me. We need to keep that understanding in view when we encounter people from other cultural contexts. What about that individual's behavior reflects her or his cultural context and what is more a reflection of the individual's personality?

In recent years, we've seen an explosion of books and assessments to help us understand our unique personality type, strengths, skills, and passions. An understanding of one's emotional intelligence and personal temperament is an important aspect of cultural intelligence. Unlike many of the other approaches to cross-cultural competency, cultural intelligence factors in the varying ways different personalities respond to cross-cultural interactions. Two American high school students can go through the same cross-cultural training to prepare them for working among the seasonal farm workers in a nearby community. But these two students will engage differently in that same cross-cultural encounter, relative to their unique personalities.

The relationship between human universals, cultural norms, and individual personalities can be identified by considering the greatest fears of adolescents. From what we know about human nature—which is certainly only the tip of the iceberg—it is clear that every human being experiences fear. It is a universal state that elicits cognitive and emotional responses. The middle layer of culture plays a large role in what we fear and how we express that fear. For example, one study compared the greatest fears of adolescents from Japanese, Singaporean, and American cultures. The study reported that Japanese teenagers' greatest fear is losing one of their parents. The greatest fear among Singaporean youth is academic failure. And the greatest fear of American youth is not fitting in with their peers.[16] All adolescents will feel varying degrees of these different fears, and they will express their anxiety in ways unique to their individual personalities—the deepest level of mental conditioning.

The dynamic relationship between these three levels of mental conditioning must be kept in view as we seek to understand ourselves and others. As we move ahead in increasing our knowledge CQ, we'll look at some key strategies for distinguishing between these varying levels of mental conditioning when observing the behavior of ourselves and others. For now, we simply want to understand the existence of the three levels of mental conditioning reflected in the iceberg. As we move toward interpretive CQ, we'll want to go deeper in actually understanding what exists in those various levels for us and in those with whom we interact and serve.

Conclusion

Culture is an elusive, dynamic concept that shapes everything we do. Things as basic as how we eat, sleep, and bathe ourselves and as abstract as how we read the Scriptures, relate to God, and communicate truth are all rooted in our cultural context. We live in a sociocultural world of our own creation. As a result, the cultures of which we are a part are always in flux. They are forever reinventing and interpreting themselves, and the final word on them can never be said.[17]

There is no such thing as a cultureless human. To be human is to live in culture. And as we visualize what culture is and represents and as we begin to explore the values and assumptions of our own cultural contexts, we're on the path toward increasing our knowledge CQ. Can you see what lies beneath? How does culture shape what you see? While knowledge CQ is cognitive and highly informational, it is deeply personal too. It is understanding what conditions our thoughts and actions. This kind of journey within is not merely self-serving. It is directly connected to lovingly serving the Other.

We have our magnifying glass on the knowledge CQ portion of the CQ pathway toward more effectively loving the Other. Knowledge CQ is understanding our own culture. It is understanding what culture is and how it shapes the way we relate to ourselves and others. By taking the time to read this book, combined with the everyday understandings and experiences you already have from serving and relating to people in your community, you're well on the journey toward better loving the Other.

Recommended Resources

Hofstede, Geert. *Cultures and Organizations: Software of the Mind.* New York: McGraw Hill, 1997.

Storti, Craig. *The Art of Crossing Cultures.* Yarmouth, ME: Intercultural Press, 1990.

6

hutus, presbyterians, and boomers

Cultural Domains

Kate was thirty years old when I met her. Six months earlier, she had moved to a small town in Alabama to become the youth direc-tor at a Presbyterian church. In her words, it was time to "grow up, get a real job, and put down roots." She hadn't exactly been sitting around during the eight years since college though. Between college graduation and moving to Alabama, she did two eighteen-month stints with a relief organization in Rwanda, she was a nanny for two years in New York City, and in between times she was a substitute teacher back home in Boston. We first met because Kate was interested in develop-ing a partnership between her youth group in Alabama and a Rwandan church. She was well aware of the huge gap between life for kids in her youth group and life for her friends in Rwanda. Quite frankly, she felt that her Rwandan friends had as much to offer her youth group as vice versa. I was encouraged by the respectful, loving way Kate talked about her friends in Rwanda.

We had talked for quite a while about some of the things she wanted to do through this partnership when suddenly she started crying. Through tears she said, "I don't know if I'm going to survive here. I thrived on life in Kigali. Sure, there were times it was hard, but I never experienced the culture shock I feel in Alabama. Maybe God is telling me I shouldn't be here. Everything is different here. I feel like way more of a foreigner here than I did in East Africa."

She went on to rant about "Presbyterians who are all caught up with their high-brow theology but can't live it out." She said her fifty-five-year-old senior pastor was obviously intimidated by a thirty-year-old female youth director and treated her more like a daughter than a colleague. I knew Kate was just venting so I simply listened for a while.

Later on, Kate described her high commitment to make sure anyone she took to Rwanda spent time reading and completing some training before going to East Africa. For example, she wanted to be sure her students understood what was behind the strife between the Hutus and the Tutsis. I affirmed her commitment to that kind of orientation, and then I asked her how much time she had spent preparing for life and ministry in Alabama. She laughed and said, "Yeah. Beyond looking for the best place to live and checking out the weather, I didn't give that much thought. I guess I should have though. This is definitely a cross-cultural experience!" We began talking about how Kate might be able to apply the same grace and understanding to her current context as she seemed to do in Rwanda. I could see myself in Kate's rant. I'm much quicker to suspend judgment and seek to understand first when I'm far away from home. But some of my worst examples of cultural intelligence are in cultural contexts right around the corner.

I'm not trying to suggest it's easier to go to Rwanda than to a new part of the United States. But going below the tip of the iceberg applies in cultures much closer to home as well. Knowledge CQ needs to be used to understand a variety of the cultural domains we encounter. I'm using the term "cultural domain" to refer to the various kinds of cultures and subcultures in which we find ourselves. We've already noted the ways we continually move in and out of various cultural domains weekly. Most of us are members of multiple cultural domains, and we interact with people from a wide array of domains. The nature of these cultural domains can be as broad as national cultures such as American or Chinese culture or even as broad as the emerging global culture that is being proliferated by organizations such as McDonald's and Starbucks. On the other hand, these domains can be as unique as the social grouping of your neighborhood or your local church. The possibilities for different kinds of cultural groupings in the world are nearly endless, including some of the contexts we've mentioned before such as those organized according to profession, gender, denomination, politics, tribe, and so on.

In my work and research among ministry leaders throughout the United States, three kinds of cultural domains surface most consistently for the majority of ministry leaders: socioethnic culture, organizational culture, and generational culture. I originally planned to write this book with separate parts for each of these domains. There would certainly be some advantages to the clarity and simplicity that could come from that kind of approach, but it is incongruent with the way we actually experience these varied cultural domains and apply cultural intelligence. We're bombarded with experiences from all three domains all the time, often more than one at a time. So it seemed more authentic to write the book in a way that walks through the cultural intelligence framework with continual application to all three domains. Socioethnic culture, organizational culture, and generational culture are the primary domains to which we're applying cultural intelligence in this journey together, so this chapter is meant to increase our understanding of how the notion of culture plays out in these three domains. And the concepts discussed throughout the rest of the book will be applied primarily to these domains.

Socioethnic Culture

Socioethnic culture is the domain with which we're most familiar. It is a broad and elusive domain because it includes national cultures such as the one shared by everyone who lives in the United States. Yet numerous ethnic cultures exist within the land of Uncle Sam, especially various African American, Asian American, Hispanic American, and Euro-American cultures. In the spirit of this tension, P. Christopher Earley, Soon Ang, and Joo-Seng Tan write, "Culture and country are slippery concepts at times. . . . Although every country has an overarching culture, many subcultures exist within a single country."[1]

Then there are many places around the world where national boundaries are artificial geopolitical lines created by colonizers. These national boundaries often separate more natural groupings of ethnic cultures. For example, tribes of Hutus and Tutsis are spread across Burundi, Rwanda, and Uganda. There are Akha tribes living in Thailand, China, Myanmar, and Laos. In some cases, ethnic cultures like these are dispersed across various nations due to displacement from war or natural disaster. Other times, they're living on the same land inherited by several generations of ancestors, but colonialist-imposed borders have separated them from others in their tribe. As a result, describing socioethnic culture is complex. Many people living in northern Thailand may be more "Akha" than "Thai." In fact, 90 percent of the Akha people living in Thailand aren't even Thai citizens. And large numbers of people in Minneapolis and Merced, California, are more "Hmong" than they are "American," even though they have American passports.

Despite these complexities, socioethnic culture is most often studied through the lens of national culture because it provides some definition to the slippery, elusive nature of socioethnic culture. National cultures have school systems, legal systems, and other social institutions by which to study culture, and these institutions further reinforce the dominant cultural values of the nation. As we think about applying cultural intelligence to socioethnic culture in this book, there are two basic kinds of cross-cultural encounters we want to explore: intercultural ministry within national culture and intercultural ministry across national cultures.

Within National Culture

Applying cultural intelligence *within* national culture means interacting with people in our own geographic context who come from different socio-ethnic backgrounds. In other words, this is when I as a Canadian American male of European descent interact with a Hispanic American friend who also lives in Grand Rapids. There are both similarities and differences at work when I interact with my Hispanic American friend living in Grand Rapids and with my Mexican friend living in Torreón, Mexico.

When I go to Mexico, I'm the minority. When I'm in Grand Rapids, I'm among the majority, dominant culture. Here are a few of the things that this means for me as compared to my Hispanic American friend:

If I wish, I can arrange to be in the company of people of my race most of the time.

If I need to move, I can be pretty sure of renting or purchasing housing in an affordable area where I want to live. I can be reasonably sure my new neighbors will be neutral or pleasant to me.

I can be sure my daughters will receive materials at school that reflect our heritage and race.

Whether I use a check, credit card, or cash, I can be confident my skin color won't work against the appearance that I'm financially reliable.

I can forego deodorant today and not have people attribute my body odor to my race.

If this book receives decent reviews, I can be confident it won't be called a credit to my race.

If a traffic cop pulls me over or if the IRS audits me, I can be sure I haven't been singled out by my race.[2]

There are many people living in my town who can't make those statements with confidence. Few books have helped me think as much about applying cultural intelligence within the subculture of church life in the United States as has Michael Emerson and Christian Smith's book, *Divided by Faith*.[3] Based on an extensive study using both qualitative and quantitative methods, Emerson and Smith explore the vastly different ways socioethnic culture affects the way American Christians view their faith and the issue of race. Any American ministry leader who is serious about applying cultural intelligence within his or her own community needs to read their book and the sequel written by Curtiss DeYoung, Michael Emerson, George Yancey, and Karen Chai Kim, *United by Faith*.

Debbie, one of the women interviewed by Emerson and Smith, expresses the commonly held white evangelical perspective about race in her response to the question, "Does our country have a race problem?" She replied, "I think we make it a problem."[4] When asked to expand on that statement, she said, "Well to me, people have problems. I mean, two white guys working together are gonna have arguments once in a while. Women are going to have arguments. It happens between men and women, between two white guys and two white women. It's just people. People are going to have arguments with people. I feel like once in a while, when an argument happens, say between a black guy and a white guy, instead of saying, 'Hey, there's two guys having an argument,' we say it's a race issue."[5]

Another woman responding to the same question said, "We have tried for thirty years to become a unified nation and now it is a big black push to be separate again. You know, like the Million Man March was for separation. It is very frustrating. I am not racist and I don't notice my friend's color. But it is frustrating when 'Oh, this is black heritage month, and this is Asian awareness and this is . . . Well then is there a basic white month?'"[6]

Both of these women, like most of the white evangelicals in Emerson and Smith's large sample, compartmentalized race as a marginal issue because it was not a focal part of their day-to-day lives. Emerson and Smith conclude, "White evangelicalism likely does more to perpetuate racialized society than to reduce it."[7] Conservative white Protestants are more than twice as likely as other whites to blame lack of equality (e.g., differences in income) between blacks and whites on a lack of motivation and work ethic than upon discrimination.

We'll continue to explore the issues of ministering within our own national culture while factoring in the growing number of socioethnic cultures that exist within most parts of the United States today. A starting point to more lovingly, respectfully, and effectively ministering among multicultural communities begins with enhancing our understanding of the varying ways we apply cultural intelligence within our own national culture.

Across National Cultures

We also want to explore how to apply cultural intelligence *across* national cultures. Moving across national cultures refers to when we leave the United States and become the minority in an entirely different place. This occurs when we travel to another part of the world on a short-term trip, take an overseas vacation, or accept an extended assignment serving in another part of the world.

Although there are similarities to what happens when we interact cross-culturally within our own country, some additional dynamics are at work when we apply cultural intelligence to people living in another nation. And those dynamics vary further based on the particular cultures involved. For example, the dynamics for me as a white male going to India aren't the same as a dark-skinned Indian coming to the United States. This is another example of the importance of a metaframework such as cultural intelligence that factors in a multiplicity of variables.

The upshot is, when we travel across national cultures, we're more likely to be alert to cultural difference. Cultural differences are often much more obvious when we move across national boundaries than they are when we interact cross-culturally within our own national culture. But it's usually far more challenging to be effective across national boundaries than it is to do so closer to home.

One of the big challenges in moving across national cultures is that we may well see artifacts that resemble what we see at home but might mean something different. For example, you can travel many places in the world and see people lining up to eat at McDonald's. An American stopping by McDonald's in Louisville is probably looking for a fast, inexpensive meal. However, a Russian stopping by McDonald's near Moscow may well be trying to show his status. This is one of the reasons interpretive CQ is so important. It helps us get beyond slowing down to observe what is happening and moves us toward trying to accurately interpret the meaning behind what we observe. It gets us below the artifacts of culture to understand the values and assumptions of a culture.

The domain of socioethnic culture is probably the most familiar one to us though it is perhaps the most challenging one for effective ministry. We'll continue to explore how one applies cultural intelligence to socioethnic culture. We're all conditioned by socioethnic culture, and we all minister in various socioethnic cultures. And most of us are called upon to effectively minister in a growing number of different socioethnic cultures wherever we serve.

Organizational Culture

Another important cultural domain experienced by ministry leaders wherever they serve is organizational culture. Organizations, like countries and socioethnic groups, have a "shared personality." Just like socioethnic culture, organizations have artifacts that provide us with cues about what is valued and assumed. For example, the arrangement of furniture in an office, the heroes of the organization—internally and externally—what members wear, and what they brag about all say something about the "software" that runs the organization. Effective ministry requires a growing understanding of the powerful values and assumptions that drive the organizations of which we're a part.

Different kinds of industries and professions are characterized by overarching cultural norms. For example, the health-care sector, the manufacturing industry, and the academic arena each have distinct cultural characteristics. The same is true for nonprofit organizations and churches. But far stronger cultures exist within specific organizations, guilds, and denominations. For example, while most American Christian churches share some broad cultural norms, Anglican churches or E-Free churches have much stronger cultures among themselves. And youth ministry has a strong professional culture with recurring jokes, fears, and gripes.

In the same way that socioethnic culture is an elusive, slippery domain, organizational culture can also be sliced up and applied in a variety of ways. The organizational culture with which you work is likely made up of numerous subcultures. One of your challenges is to grow in understanding which organizational culture most strongly affects how you serve. If you're in a local church, it is probably the church itself, though there may be a denominational culture and a youth ministry network culture that also require your understanding. If you're leading a Young Life group, it is important for you to understand the organizational culture of the school system in which you work as well as the specific culture of your Young Life chapter and of the Young Life organization as a whole.

Identify the most specific organizational context where you minister, such as your church, your missions agency, or the school where you teach. What are the values and assumptions that drive this organization? Who holds the power? What is deemed successful here? Write a few words in the margin or in your journal about the dynamics of this organizational culture.

Here's an activity you might want to try with some of your colleagues as a way to begin thinking and talking together about your organizational culture.

Have everyone get in a single-file line. Tell them you're going to list three words. They need to think about which of the three words best represents your ministry culture. If it's the first word in the list, they move one step to the right. If it's the second word in the list, they should stay where they are. If the third word in the list best describes the ministry culture, they should move one step to the left. They shouldn't overthink the question. After they've moved, ask a few people why they chose the word they did. Then have everyone move back into a single-file line and do the next three words.

Here's a sampling of words to try:

1 Step to Right	Stay Where You Are	1 Step to Left
Circle	Triangle	Square
Vision	Status Quo	Planning
Intuition	Reasoning	Emotion
Rock	Grass	Sand
Chocolate	Vanilla	Strawberry
Tight	Comfortable	Loose

This is a way to begin dialoguing about how your team views your ministry culture.

Jeffrey Sonnenfeld, of the Yale School of Management, has identified four types of organizational culture: the academy culture, the baseball-team culture, the club culture, and the fortress culture.[8] Churches and other ministry organizations seem to exist in all four of these types.

Academy Culture

In the academy culture, employees are highly skilled and tend to stay with the organization for an extended period of time while working their way up the ranks. The organization provides a stable environment in which employees can develop and exercise their skills and expertise. Universities, hospitals, and large corporations are the kinds of organizations that often embody this culture. As you might guess, ministry leaders in Christian schools often experience the academy culture, particularly those in higher education. Pastors are usually expected to be generalists who demonstrate an ability to teach, counsel, lead, balance budgets, and plan events. Professors, however, are expected to have a focused area of expertise and knowledge. Being a generalist in an academy culture may cause one to question whether he or she is valued and has anything of substance to offer.

Baseball-Team Culture

In the baseball-team culture, employees are "free agents" with highly prized skills for getting in, applying their expertise, and moving on. They are in high demand and can rather easily get jobs in other places. This culture is usually found in high-risk organizations such as investment banking and advertising companies. As a result, this kind of organizational culture isn't very common in churches. Churches aren't usually characterized as fast-paced, high-risk organizations. However, church-related subcultures, such as youth ministry, may be characterized by the baseball-team culture. Youth ministry used to be seen as a ministry culture that thrived on taking risks and bucking norms, but increasingly, it is becoming more of a stable, established professional culture. For example, despite the urban legend that says youth pastors only last eighteen months, the average youth pastor now stays five to six years in a church.[9] Ministry leaders with an affinity for the baseball-team culture more typically end up with parachurch organizations that thrive on innovation and pushing the envelope, or they pursue church planting, which brings a heightened degree of risk and room for innovation.

Club Culture

Many churches are characterized by Sonnenfeld's next culture type, the club culture. The most important requirement in the club culture is fitting into the group. Loyalty to the specific organization is highly valued. Usually employees start at the bottom and stay within the organization for a long time. The organization promotes from within and highly values seniority. Examples are the military and some law firms. A growing number of churches demonstrate characteristics of club cultures through their preference for internal rather than external hires. Many churches would rather hire an untrained but known entity than bring in an unknown seminary graduate who might stay only a year or two or, worse yet, might end up embezzling money or having an affair with a church member.

I used to work for an organization with a very strong club culture. Insider language and reference to people who "bled" the values of the ministry was a regular part of conversation in staff meetings and at organizational events. There was a deep bond shared by insiders. In that ministry, expressing a dissident perspective on the overall philosophy of something embraced by the organization needed to be done very cautiously. If it wasn't communicated carefully, it would be seen as disloyal. In contrast, when I came to the academy culture where I now serve, I experienced culture shock. Part of my learning curve included understanding that raising a dissident perspective within the organization often led to heightened respect rather than disapproval or suspicion. It isn't that disagreeing just for disagreement's sake brings respect from my colleagues at Grand Rapids Theological Seminary, but an ability to articulate a well-founded position that might run contrary to the widely accepted norms of the organization is embraced in our organizational culture as much as it was resisted in my last ministry context.

Coming back to the theological framework we laid out for cultural intelligence, the point is not to allow our organizational culture to dictate whether we should or shouldn't voice a dissident perspective. But knowledge CQ will help us understand the cultural challenges we face for expressing a viewpoint in light of the organizational culture. We must then filter that understanding through the kingdom-culture axis.

Fortress Culture

Finally, Sonnenfeld describes the fortress culture. "Fortress" doesn't refer to staid, unchanging organizations as much as it does to multifaceted behemoths that are continually called upon to undergo massive reorganization. Examples include savings and loan companies and large automotive corporations. Survival requires a culture of continually restructuring and shuffling staffing. As a result, employees are always uncertain about their jobs and fear they might be laid off. Many megachurches are characterized by this kind of culture. A simple choice to distribute a handout at Sunday services in a megachurch can mean a lot of money and personnel just because of the sheer volume. And like many fortress organizations, megachurches with multimillion-dollar budgets keep in mind the money spent annually on salary and benefits and continually look for ways to become more strategic and prudent financially. This inevitably leads to continual change. Many long-standing parachurch organizations exemplify fortress cultures. For example, missions agencies with personnel spread across countries often have a continual turnover of both support-based and salaried personnel. And many of the campus-based ministries started in the mid-twentieth century have been through countless cycles of reorganization and change throughout their existence.

Sonnenfeld's four organizational types don't fit the organizational cultures of ministry leaders perfectly, but they do provide helpful direction. Churches tend to mimic the organizational worlds around them, so it's not surprising we can find churches among all four of Sonnenfeld's types. More study is needed to explore the unique dynamics in the organizational cultures of Christian churches and organizations. In addition to understanding the dynamics raised by Sonnenfeld's work, ministry leaders need to grow in understanding how a ministry culture views tradition versus innovation, hierarchy versus collaboration, liturgy versus extemporaneous worship, emergent versus anti-emergent, and much more.

Just as with socioethnic culture, some aspects of organizational culture reflect God's kingdom, and other aspects work against the power of the kingdom. And many organizational dynamics are not overtly good or evil, but merely different. The challenge of the ministry leader is to know how to carefully live in light of the strong cultures where we serve and to discern when we need to work with God and others to try to change these cultures. There may be times when God will call us to be part of an organizational culture that elevates values very different from the ones we embrace. But for the most part, it is wise to join organizational cultures with which we have close alignment. "Persons who are culturally intelligent choose organizations that are culturally compatible with their own personality."[10] And when entering an unfamiliar organizational culture, we're wise to beware of our tendency to exercise the same kind of colonialist paternalism that some missionaries and businesses adopt when entering a new socioethnic culture. Listen and understand first.

Many ministry leaders give up on ministry because of the challenges of living within organizational culture and all its politics. We'll spend a great deal of our journey in this book thinking about how cultural intelligence applies to the organizational cultures where we find ourselves.

Generational Culture

The final cultural domain to which we want to apply cultural intelligence is the culture formed by generational difference. There are a couple of different ways we'll approach this cultural domain, including a consideration of subcultures formed around a particular age grouping (e.g., adolescence) and the subcultures created among those born during a similar era and time period. Generational subcultures exist to varying degrees in many places around the world. We'll look at some of the overriding ones in the United States. Also, we can't explore generational culture without at least acknowledging the cultural revolution of postmodernism, which creates an array of ministry challenges for most of us.

Youth Culture

Let's begin exploring the domain of generational culture with youth culture. Youth culture generally refers to the ways adolescents and teenagers differentiate themselves from the parent culture of their community. It includes the norms developed by youth between the stages of childhood and adulthood. In cautioning us against merely treating adolescents as "big kids" or "little adults," Chap Clark argues that the period of adolescence now expands well into an individual's twenties.

One can no longer simply refer to adolescence as a transition period. For young people growing up in the developed world, adolescence is a full-fledged stage of development. Clark tells adults we must beware of viewing the period of adolescence as being the same as when we were teenagers.[11] Cultural intelligence is needed to understand the evolving world of life in the adolescent subculture.

Increasingly, adolescence is a phenomenon in the developing world too. Youth in places such as India and Nigeria represent a far greater percentage of the population than do youth in places such as the United States and Canada. And as globalization continues to unify youth with a common taste in music, movies, and fashion, the need for culturally specific ministry to youth is growing all over the world. Ten years ago, I would talk with older church leaders in Indian churches who could not see the need for ministry specifically targeting young people. They viewed it as something that would merely segment the generations and breed disrespect among young people. To a certain degree, I echoed their concern and was resistant to importing youth ministry there. Now I, like many others, receive far more invitations than I can possibly accept to help develop church-based youth ministry in places such as India. India, not unlike Brazil, China, and Croatia, is a place where youth culture is burgeoning. This is especially true in urban settings where there are many university and polytechnic schools, the promise of better-paying jobs in call centers, and abundant accessibility to MTV.

Just as socioethnic and organizational cultures consist of slippery categories, youth culture also takes many different forms among various subcultures of youth. There is a blurring mosaic of cultural connections across the youth culture domain. Consequently, the job of youth workers goes beyond simply figuring out how to relate to "youth culture"; it also involves learning how to relate to a plethora of youth cultures. Several years ago, Mark Senter's work *The Coming Revolution in Youth Ministry* was a seminal piece for challenging the tired approach that said, "If you reach the jocks and student leaders, you'll reach the rest of the school." Senter pointed out that while jocks might have influence among jocks, they may have little or even negative influence among techies.[12] Youth culture itself is as diverse as the ethnic cultures popping up in our cities. Jocks, hip-hop kids, goths, techies, and thespian and artsy students are but a few of the subcultural groups that exist in most high schools throughout the developed world. Missionaries, church planters, pastors, youth leaders, and many other ministry leaders need to have some understanding of youth culture to be effective in most ministry contexts.

Generational Eras

A related but different categorization within the domain of generational culture encompasses the generational eras that exist within broader ethnic cultures. In light of the dynamic relationship between identity formation and the social context in which we're born and reared, our cultural perspective is shaped to a certain degree by the historical period in which we experience childhood and adolescence. During childhood, each generation subconsciously lives in response to the economic, political, and educational issues of civilization. The subculture of each generational era usually differs in significant ways from that of the generation preceding it.

There are many different ways of categorizing the generational cultures that exist in North America today. Some of the familiar ways of categorizing generations in the United States are as the builders or traditionals, the boomers or moderns, Generation X, and Generation Y. A brief explanation of each follows.

Builders: The oldest generation living in the United States is referred to as the builders or traditionals. They're usually classified as individuals born before 1946. They experienced the Great Depression and both World Wars. Most builders believe the Bible provides guidance for life, and they have a high level of trust in the government for having gotten them through the ordeals of the early twentieth century. Builders expect men and women to adhere to traditional gender roles, and rural and small-town life are viewed as more virtuous than big city or suburban life. Traditionalism "is shorthand for a complex cultural conservatism and refers to a real subculture of shared values and familiar customs, rich with the details of life. . . . This subculture is not primarily about politics. It's about beliefs, ways of life, and personal identity."[13]

Boomers: The next generation, baby boomers or moderns, were born after World War II and before the mid-1960s. They value making or having a lot of money and climbing the ladder of success. Most boomers are obsessed with pragmatism and efficiency. Their "do what works" approach to everything in life drives the other generations crazy. Most boomers value self-fulfillment, individualism, and progress. *USA Today*, with its simple, bottom-line, to-the-point style, is "their" newspaper. The boomers' perspective is the taken-for-granted viewpoint "of those who belong to the dominant culture. It's a whole system of belief that says, 'This is obviously how it is.' In the practical workaday world, it is, 'This is simply what works, the only way to do it.' Or 'It's the latest and greatest development.'"[14]

Gen Xers: Those of us born between the mid-1960s and the 1970s are considered the angst-ridden generation called Gen Xers. Many of my peers grew up in difficult circumstances both financially and socially.

A growth in the number of single-parent boomer households efficiently climbing the ladder of success left many of us abandoned and jaded. We're skeptical of big organizations, and we distrust presentations that are fully reliant on bullet points and manipulatively march us to the bottom line. Authenticity and vulnerability are key. We're more powerfully attuned to whole systems, and so we reject categorical thinking. Issues such as AIDS, poverty, and social injustice are a big deal to us.

Millennials: The newest arrivals to the adult world are the millennials or Generation Y. Growing up with the Internet, they have an unusual aptitude for assessing and applying information.[15] Their parents were more intentional about spending time with them, and in particular, their fathers were more likely to play a significant role in their lives than fathers had done historically in the United States. As a result, despite embarking on adulthood right around 9/11, this youngest generation of American adults tends to be much more optimistic than Gen Xers do.

Robert Webber's book *The Younger Evangelicals* is especially helpful to church leaders in describing three predominant generations of adults coexisting in North American evangelical churches: traditionalists (builders), pragmatics (boomers), and younger evangelicals (Gen X and Gen Y). He provides several helpful charts comparing things such as the theology, worship style, leadership, and apologetics of these three generational subcultures. See table 1 below for a sampling of Webber's comparison of these three generational eras in the American evangelical church.

Table 1
Comparison of Traditional, Pragmatic, and Younger Evangelicals

	Traditional Evangelicals 1950–1975	Pragmatic Evangelicals 1975–2000	Younger Evangelicals 2000–
Cultural Situation	Modern worldview Industrial society Post–WW II	Transitional paradigm Technological society Vietnam War	Postmodern worldview Internet society War on terrorism
Communication Styles	Print Verbal	Broadcast Presentational	Internet Interactive
Generation	Booster Traditional	Boomer Innovative	"Twenty-Something" Deconstruction/ Reconstruction
Attitude toward History	Maintain distinctives of twentieth-century fundamentals	Get a fresh start Ahistorical	Draw from the wisdom of the past The road to the future runs through the past

Continued on next page

	Traditional Evangelicals 1950–1975	Pragmatic Evangelicals 1975–2000	Younger Evangelicals 2000–
Theological Commitment	Christianity as a rational worldview	Christianity as therapy Answers needs	Christianity as a community of faith Ancient/Reformation
Apologetics Style	Evidential Foundational	Christianity as meaning-giver Experiential Personal faith	Embrace the metanarrative Embodied apologetic Communal faith
Ecclesial Paradigm	Constantinian church Civil religion	Culturally sensitive church Market driven	Missional church Countercultural
Church Style	Neighborhood churches Rural	Megachurch Suburban Market targeted	Small church Back to cities Intercultural
Leadership Style	Pastor centered	Managerial model CEO	Team ministry Priesthood of all
Youth Ministry	Church-centered programs	Outreach programs Weekend fun retreats	Prayer, Bible study, worship, social service
Education	Sunday school Information centered	Target generational groups and needs	Intergenerational formation in community
Spirituality	Keep the rules	Prosperity and success	Authentic embodiment
Worship	Traditional	Contemporary	Convergence
Art	Restrained	Art as illustration	Incarnational embodiment
Evangelism	Mass evangelism	Seeker service	Process evangelism
Activists	Beginnings of evangelical social action	Need-driven social action (i.e., divorce groups, drug rehab, etc.)	Rebuild cities and neighborhoods

Source: Robert E. Webber, *The Younger Evangelicals: Facing the Challenges of the New World* (Grand Rapids: Baker Academic, 2002), 18.

Much of Webber's discussion of what is emerging among younger evangelicals is a description of how they are responding to the realities of living and serving in a postmodern world. I'm not suggesting that postmodernism is simply an outgrowth of generational culture. It is a cultural revolution spanning all generations in numerous places around the world. But the younger generations have been socialized in the postmodern context far more than the older generations have.

The cultural implications of postmodernism are so broad and complex that I'm a bit reluctant even to raise the issue here. There are "probably a thousand different self-appointed commentators on the postmodern phenomenon and bewildering discrepancies between the ways many of these authors understand the term *postmodern* and its cognates."[16] It goes beyond the purposes of this book to thoroughly engage this issue; however, it would be negligent to talk about the cultural challenges facing most ministry leaders without some acknowledgment of the social revolution under way in the West and the somewhat parallel revolution occurring in many postcolonial contexts.

A concise, coherent definition of postmodernism is nearly impossible; however, John Franke suggests a basic, minimalist definition: "Postmodernism refers primarily to the rejection of the central features of modernity, such as its quest for certain, objective, and universal knowledge, along with its dualism and its assumption of the inherent goodness of knowledge. It is this critical agenda, rather than a proposed constructive paradigm to replace the modern vision, that unites postmodern thinkers."[17]

Some have carelessly written off postmodernity wholesale by equating it with relativism and subjectivism and calling it the enemy of morality and truth. Others are fearful of anything that sniffs of postmodernism because of the atheist assumptions of many of its most quoted thinkers, such as Nietzsche, Derrida, Foucault, and Lyotard. And others have been equally careless in uncritically embracing everything about postmodernism. Franke writes, "The postmodern condition is not something we simply choose to affirm or deny. It is rather a descriptor of the social and intellectual context in which we function. . . . Since this new postmodern paradigm is emerging but neither mature nor regnant, it continues to be hotly contested by both those who desire to embrace it for particular purposes and those who find reason to oppose it."[18]

I'm extremely interested in the realities of postmodernism and its implications for effective ministry leadership. Cultural intelligence must interact with these visceral cultural dynamics, and the postmodern condition is the ideal context for living between the tension of kingdom values and cultural values. There are new sensitivities and passions emerging in the postmodern era that reflect the presence of the kingdom. The spiritual craving, the interest in the mysterious, transcendent wonder of the supernatural, and the renewed interest in community are a few of the redemptive qualities we should embrace in our American context. Meanwhile, there are many things in our postmodern context where the kingdom has not yet come to bear. We have to protest consumerism, violence, sexual perversion, and nihilistic abandonment that leaves generations hopeless.

We'll continue to keep the challenges and opportunities of postmodernism in view as we journey toward cultural intelligence. Several books in addition to those cited can more thoroughly help us effectively serve and lead in light of postmodern realities.[19]

As with all the cultural contexts we've explored, we must take care not to automatically stereotype individuals because of their age. For example, Webber was in his seventies when he wrote his empathetic analysis of the "younger evangelicals," yet there are twenty-somethings who identify more closely with a D. A. Carson– or John MacArthur–like view of postmodernism than most millennials would. But as with all cultural descriptions, these are generalizations. Understanding, love, and respect are essential as we navigate the challenges of generational difference, and ultimately, the Other must be encountered up close as an individual rather than just as a generalized group.

If you're like me, you might find yourself far more forgiving of cultural differences among people from different socioethnic backgrounds than you are of people from different age brackets. But we must beware of rolling our eyes at the immaturity of the young or viewing older people as clueless and out of touch. Richard Rohr's words challenge me:

> Our grandparents were not stupid. The truth [was] already there. The patterns of the soul are not new, and our century hasn't discovered anything new in terms of how death is transformed into life. The price is still the same: "To create one new person from us who had been two . . . reconciling both of us to God in one body through the cross which puts all enmity to death" (Eph. 2.15–16). It's the only truly transformative pattern in human history.[20]

None of the cultural domains we're exploring happens independently from the others. The organizational contexts where we find ourselves operate in dynamic relationship with the socioethnic cultures in which they are rooted. And our church members usually come from a variety of generational eras, though the power is often held primarily by one generational culture. Developing our understanding of the subversive yet powerful role of culture in all three of these domains is a critical element of increasing our knowledge CQ. Throughout our pursuit of cultural intelligence in this book, we'll continue to move in and out of these three cultural domains just as we do in our day-to-day lives.

Conclusion

A couple of months ago Kate, the youth director in Alabama, e-mailed me. The subject line read, "Sweet home Alabama!" She wrote, "I'm in a lot better state than when we talked last year. I love it here now and I get along great with these Southern Presbyterians. And I even like my sr. pastor! . . . When I stopped feeling like I had to conform to being just like everybody born and raised here, I felt freed up to love and respect my kids and their families and they're even learning to appreciate this Yankee girl. . . . Okay. I'm off to eat my grits."

Kate brings me hope. As she sought to understand life in Alabama, Presbyterians, and her boomer pastor, she was free to be herself and free to let them be themselves. It took time, and the challenges and differences surely continue. This isn't just a "happily ever after" ending. But Kate exemplifies a leader who is willing to discover who she is and how she can best show her love for the Other she encounters.

We serve and lead in a variety of cultural domains, including socioethnic cultures, organizational cultures, and generational cultures. Note table 2 below for a summary of what we have reviewed in these three domains. Our identity is shaped by the nexus of these and other cultural contexts of which we're a part. And we live alongside others who move in and out of various cultures in these three domains. As we develop our knowledge CQ, we better understand the way these various cultures shape what is going on in and around us.

Understand your culture. Understand how culture shapes the way we live. Understand the varying domains where we and others live. There are two more areas of understanding for us to discover in the knowledge CQ category: language and cultural values.

Table 2

Cultural Domains Most Frequently Experienced by Ministry Leaders

Socioethnic Culture	Organizational Culture	Generational Culture
Within National Cultures	Academy Culture	Youth Culture
Across National Cultures	Baseball-Team Culture	Generational Eras
	Club Culture	Builders
	Fortress Culture	Boomers
		Gen Xers
		Millennials

Recommended Resources

Socioethnic Culture

Emerson, Michael, and Christian Smith. *Divided by Faith: Evangelical Religion and the Problem of Race in America.* New York: Oxford University Press, 2000.

Lingenfelter, Judith, and Sherwood Lingenfelter. *Teaching Cross-Culturally: An Incarnational Model for Learning and Teaching*. Grand Rapids: Baker Academic, 2003.

Lingenfelter, Sherwood, and Marvin Mayers. *Ministering Cross-Culturally: An Incarnational Model for Personal Relationships*. Grand Rapids: Baker Academic, 2003.

Organizational Culture

Bolman, Lee, and Terrence Deal. *Reframing Organizations: Artistry, Choice, and Leadership*. San Francisco: Jossey-Bass, 2003.

Schein, Edgar. *Organizational Culture and Leadership*. San Francisco: Jossey-Bass, 2004.

Generational Culture

Carroll, Jackson, and Wade Roof. *Bridging Divided Worlds: Generational Cultures in Congregations*. San Francisco: Jossey-Bass, 2002.

Clark, Chap. *Hurt: Inside the World of Today's Teenagers*. Grand Rapids: Baker Academic, 2004.

Howe, Neil, and William Strauss. *Millennials Rising: The Next Great Generation*. New York: Vintage, 2000.

Webber, Robert E. *The Younger Evangelicals: Facing the Challenges of the New World*. Grand Rapids: Baker Academic, 2002.

when yes means no and no means yes

Language

anguages are so much more than words. Words are merely the symbols used to represent ideas that lie far beneath the surface of what we can see in a culture. If we simply translate words from one language to another and presume that equals understanding, we might just end up being fluently foolish. I've had my own share of times when I've been a fluent fool in my own language. Notice my less than culturally intelligent rant in my journal during an extended time of living in Singapore:

> Every time I walk into a shop here, the first thing I hear is, "Yes?!" I've been hearing that for years during my many brief visits here, but now that we're staying much longer, it's really getting on my nerves. Yes what? I try to be polite, but can't I just look around freely without a Chinese shopkeeper invading my space asking, "Yes, Yes, Yes"? It just happened again a few minutes ago and under my breath I started muttering, "I didn't ask you anything!" Many of the business owners here could learn a thing or two about customer service. It almost makes me long for the annoyingly canned greeting, "Hi, how's it goin'?" from a college kid working at Blockbuster.

I confessed my rant to a few Singaporean friends who are very culturally aware. They started by laughing at me, and then they reminded me that English is a second language for many of these shopkeepers.

Their language limitations in English (and mine in Mandarin!) combined with the Singaporean value of efficiency makes their truncated greeting a welcome approach for many locals in Singapore. "Yes" covers everything from "Hello. Can I help you?" to "What would you like?" Similarly, Singaporeans use the word "can" to mean everything from, "Is the price right?" to "Are you comfortable with what I suggest?" to "Do you want this?"

Furthermore, in the same way that my West African friend Amos found it humorous that I asked our restaurant server, "How's it going?" the Singaporean shopkeepers I was ranting about would not likely think I wanted anything from them other than being given what I came into their store to get. So while my assumptions made me hear "yes" as poor customer service, their assumptions might make it seem the ideal way to let me get in, get what I want, and get out.

This exemplifies the last two areas we need to explore in our journey toward greater knowledge CQ: understanding language and cultural values. It would be hard to decide which of these is more important. To speak the language of a culture without grasping the values behind it could be a dangerous combination. But to have a strong understanding of what drives the culture without the ability to communicate verbally is equally problematic. Understanding these two core aspects of knowledge CQ really takes us below the tip of the iceberg to see what we might otherwise miss above the surface. We'll tackle language in this chapter and cultural values in the next, but as with everything in the cultural intelligence framework, one without the other is incomplete.

Language Is Culture

We've probably all heard the joke that says people who speak two languages are called bilingual and people who speak one language are called American. We're one of the most monolingual cultures in the world. That reality combined with our cultural dominance in many contexts often results in our expecting others to speak our language rather than vice versa. Many American travelers say things like what I wrote in my journal during my first missions trip: "They don't speak English, so I had to use an interpreter." It is subtle, but why is it we choose to emphasize a whole culture not speaking *our* language rather than saying that we, the guests, don't speak *their* language, therefore *we* need an interpreter?

It's hard to overestimate the importance of language to cultural intelligence. Some say language *is* culture. The very words used and how they're used are symbiotically wrapped together with culture. Of course, this poses a challenge. Given the abundance of cultural contexts in which we find ourselves in the course of a week, how can we possibly become literate in the languages of all the cultures we encounter? And for those of us who do itinerant work across national cultures, what kind of effectiveness can occur through interpreters?

We can't learn the language of every subculture we encounter. But before we let ourselves off the hook too easily, we need to understand the ubiquitous role of language in cross-cultural work and explore those instances where learning the language will become necessary. And perhaps we need to significantly rethink the number of short-term teams we send into places where they can't speak the language of the locals.

As we become fluent in a language, it becomes a semiautomatic, subconscious action. It has a huge effect on how we see the world. Not only is it a tool for communication, but more than that, it is an entire system of representation for perception and thinking. A great deal of study has been devoted to the connection between our first language and the way we view the world. A long history of academic controversy surrounds this topic, but it is widely agreed that language shapes how we think and live, and how we think and live shapes our language. To learn a culture's language is to learn the way it organizes its thinking and view of the world.

I've experienced this linguistic challenge when I've read some of my favorite Russian authors, such as Dostoevsky or Tolstoy. As I read their novels, I have a hard time keeping track of all the relationships among the various characters and understanding their motives. Part of the difficulty lies in the intricate web of extended kinship relations that existed in nineteenth-century Russia for which there were more than three hundred kinship terms. In Russian families, all the members of the household were considered relatives, even though they might not have been related by blood or marriage. They ate together, worked together, and defined their relationships to one another by use of very precise kinship terms. But without some knowledge CQ about that background, the translations of these Russian novels into English lose something when I read them.[1]

Language and Cognition

One of the most important theories regarding the connection between language and culture is the Sapir-Whorf hypothesis.[2] This theory posits that the nature of a particular language influences the habitual thought of its speakers. Different patterns of language yield different patterns of thought. And language itself is usually derived from the environment of the people who speak it.

Whorf writes, "We cut nature up, organize it into concepts, and ascribe significances as we do, largely because we are parties to an agreement to organize it in this way."[3] Cultures share an unspoken agreement that is codified in the patterns of its language. In Sapir and Whorf's view, these different language patterns result in cultures arriving at different pictures of the universe. They support their hypothesis by pointing to the multiple words Eskimos have for snow or the many Norwegian words that exist for our one generic term "fish." Culture and environment play a role in the development of language.

Opponents of the Sapir-Whorf hypothesis argue that language has absolutely no influence on thought. In this view, cognitive development occurs independently from language.[4] The most commonly held view falls somewhere in between; it assumes that language does in some way affect thinking, but the question is how and to what degree. My understanding of snow and fish might pale in contrast to how Eskimos and Norwegians understand them, but it doesn't mean I have no concept whatsoever of fish or snow. To follow the Sapir-Whorf hypothesis exclusively would leave little hope that cross-cultural communication about snow could ever occur between an Eskimo and me, much less between an Eskimo and someone from a tropical context.

For the purposes of cultural intelligence, it's important to realize that language is far more than simply learning new vocabulary and grammar. Words are symbols that represent tangible things and intangible ideas. Foreign-language instructors have increasingly incorporated this view into their methods of teaching a new language. The shift has been from simply teaching sentence grammar and informational retrieval to a more thoughtful mode of learning that invokes reflection on language and interaction with text and the cultures from which it originates.

Different Language

When ministering exclusively in a culture whose primary language is different from yours, there's no substitute for pursuing some fluency in the language. Not only will it endear you to people and enhance communication, it will also help you understand the way they view the world. Even for those of us who don't spend extensive time among cultures whose language is unfamiliar to us, learning a second language is a valuable contribution toward developing our cultural intelligence. P. Christopher Earley, Soon Ang, and Joo-Seng Tan argue, "People lacking an aptitude for learning languages, *at least at some reasonable level of proficiency*, will have a low CQ. That doesn't mean that learning a language causes CQ to increase or vice versa, but the two are related.

Learning a language is a complex behavior, since linguists tell us that language use and acquisition may be tied both to genetics and to early learning experiences."[5]

There's no substitute for studying a language while being surrounded by people who speak it as their first language. For those of us whose lives don't allow for that, other options include attending a language-immersion school for a couple of weeks and living with a native family in the country (e.g., the Christian Spanish Academy in Antigua, Guatemala, www.learncsa.com), hiring local immigrants at home to tutor us in their first language, or using a resource such as those available through Rosetta Stone.

Learning a language is more than just learning words. It might also include learning some general strategies for how to communicate in ways that are respectful and effective. What are some key ways to ask questions or get information? What are some key phrases that are needed, even if you can't achieve fluency in the language of the Other? Knowing the answers to these questions for any particular culture comes from both linguistic and cultural understanding. In particular, the cultural values we'll examine in the next chapter will aid in this process.

What does this look like practically? If you continue to do short-term missions trips to the same location, what are a few key cues, words, and phrases with which you need to familiarize yourself? If you're continually interacting with a specific cultural group in your community, look for the key words to which you need to pay attention. Noel Bechetti, executive director of the Center for Student Missions, shares the story of an American friend living in France who was trying to overcome her fear of how French people view Americans. Noel's American friend found that whenever she asked for something specific from a shopkeeper, for example, "Where can I find the lipstick?" she felt she was being treated curtly. One day, a French friend suggested, "Try starting with something like this when you walk into the store: 'Could you help me with this problem?' And if they say, 'Yes,' which they more than likely will, then ask for help finding the lipstick." The American woman tried it and couldn't believe how it seemed to consistently change the disposition of the French people waiting on her. The shopkeepers felt like they were helping someone in need rather than being treated as someone who was just there to respond to people's demands. What a contrast to my shopping experiences in Singapore. Complete fluency in French and in all the cultural values of the French is a great ideal. But to begin with, finding a couple of key filters like this one is a great way to start honing our literacy among different cultural groups.

There are both obvious and subtle ways that learning a foreign language contributes to cross-cultural understanding. Speaking the language of the Other plays an integral role in service that demonstrates love and respect mirroring the character of Christ.

Same Language, Different Country

Language challenges aren't limited to communicating in cultures where we can't speak the language. I travel many places where locals speak English fluently and often as their first language. But that doesn't automatically result in effective communication. One time my Indian friend Warris brought me to the train station. He dropped me off by the platform and said, "Wait here awhile." In my mind, I thought that meant I was going to be there for quite a long time. But in a minute or so he was there. I assumed things just went quicker than he had anticipated. But then I heard that phrase coming up again and again with other hosts. "Just wait here awhile." And it didn't seem to indicate a long amount of time at all. I began to wonder if "awhile" was no different than when I might say, "Wait here a second," even though I rarely mean "one second" when I say that.

And many of the people in English-speaking places I visit ask me, "Where do you stay?" At first I responded to that question by talking about where I was staying during my brief visit there, for example, in a nearby hotel, with friends, and so on. But people would almost always follow up by asking again where I live with my family. So I eventually learned that "Where do you stay?" meant "Where do you live?" And it took me awhile to learn not to respond to that question with an answer like "Grand Rapids" or even "Michigan." In fact many people I've interviewed who are from outside the United States have commented on how Americans are the only people they know who when asked by a foreigner where they live, respond by giving the city rather than just the country. Most people around the world have about as much an idea of where "Grand Rapids" is as most Americans have an idea of where Chittagong is, a Bangladeshi city of nearly four million people.

Interpretive CQ will teach us how to determine whether these kinds of language issues are one-time exceptions to the way we would say something or whether they're something that can be generalized to most people from a culture. We must be careful to test the kinds of assumptions we begin to make as a result of these interactions. But when we actually discover something that is accurate, it can be a helpful way of enhancing our knowledge CQ and, better yet, our ability to communicate with the Other. Don't think knowledge CQ is more complicated than it is. A lot of it is simply putting together what we already know with what we learn as we listen hard to what is and isn't being said.

Same Language, Same Country

We don't have to cross national boundaries or speak a different language to experience the communication challenges that exist when communicating with the Other. Language is an important issue when we encounter people from various subcultures where we speak the same national language but where our words don't correspond because of the cultural meaning, values, and assumptions beneath the words. I often encounter people, such as medical professionals, biochemists, or automotive manufacturers, who work in professional cultures that are unfamiliar to me. I immediately observe the difference between the cultural intelligence of those individuals who can talk to me about their work at the factory using language I can understand versus others who use all kinds of trade jargon that means nothing to me. A doctor or a nurse with knowledge CQ must adjust her or his verbal and nonverbal language when talking about a diagnosis with family members versus doing so with medical peers.

A youth pastor might be merely contextualizing the story of Esther to students when describing her as "one hot woman." But when preaching from the same text to a different generational subculture, knowledge CQ will help that pastor consider whether that word choice is still the most effective strategy for communicating the story. Someone might argue that I'm asking leaders to become chameleons to whatever their context. While that can be a temptation, it isn't the objective. *The point is to remain authentic and to draw on cultural understanding to best communicate to a cultural group who we are authentically.*

Communication frustrations across different age groups in the church was a regular theme I heard when exploring cultural intelligence among generational groups. One seventy-five-year-old church member, Thelma, said to me, "It really gets me when the pastor greets me every week by saying, 'Good morning, young lady. How are you today?' Who is he kidding? Does he really think I'm not well aware that he and I both know I'm an old woman? I'm not ashamed of it, so why is he?"

What is going on here? I cringed when I heard Thelma's commentary on her pastor's greeting. I've used similar greetings with older people, thinking it was a term of endearment. If I knew this woman better, I'd challenge her toward having some measure of cultural intelligence (though I'd apply cultural intelligence by not actually using the term with her) by trying to think about why the pastor is calling her that. Is her pastor purposely trying to mock her, as if to say, "Hah! You're anything but a young lady and we both know it!" I doubt it. He's probably trying to be warm and perhaps a bit humorous with her. But it's not working. And when we get to interpretive CQ, we'll find some cues that he may pick up on, making him aware that this regular greeting is hindering his interaction with Thelma.

Perhaps many of us can think of parallel encounters in our own families and marriages. Sometimes missing one another with language comes down to an inability to understand one another at the deepest level of mental conditioning, individual to individual. But culture provides a space for us to more confidently explore our communication with one another. So much of the communication on which we rely in our day-to-day work, whether it's talking over coffee with a colleague, an invitation to a wedding, a memorandum announcing a staff meeting, or calling in a complaint about a defective purchase, embodies social and cultural norms. These norms are actualized with reference, albeit subconscious in most cases, to previous encounters and language.[6]

We talked about the need to learn some basic filters and cues to be more effective in places like France, where asking, "Could you help me with a problem?" might get us further than "Where's the lipstick?" We need to understand similar strategies and filters when jumping into subcultural groups where the language differences are less stark. For example, my friend Andrew, a communications professor at Malone College, describes the relatively recent freedom he has felt in using profanity every once in a while. He writes:

> I've felt much more free to spew the occasional blue streak. *Not* of course gratuitously or prolifically, just as a helpful tool for reshaping our assumptions about the world.
>
> There are those who live close to me, though, who still do not appreciate this particular freedom I've discovered. Certain words just grate them like sandpaper. I realized this week, during endless hours of faculty in-service that there are, for me, similarly grating words. These particular symbols, when used in particular ways, feel *far* more painful to me than anybody dropping the F bomb. They are, in no particular order: *Loyalty* (when referring to the way that people with power cover one another . . .) *Professionalism* (when cited as a virtue) and *Leadership* (pretty much any context will make this one explode for me).[7]

You might be thinking Andrew just needs to have a good cup of coffee if words as simple as "loyalty" and "leadership" unnerve him. But what's behind those words for him? And how can we become more aware of how the people with whom we interact might have similar words that grate them. What are some of the buzzwords that might lend you credibility in one context and erode it in another? Words such as "liberal," "evangelical," "third world," "inerrancy," "metanarrative," and "democrat" may have very different meanings depending on the cultural context in which they're spoken.

Cultural intelligence helps leaders monitor their choice of words when communicating with people from subcultures who speak the same language but for whom the very same words might mean very different things. This is more an issue of knowledge and interpretive CQ than of behavioral CQ because it's less about saying the right words and more about understanding the meaning behind the words. The words themselves are also important, but what is even more important is understanding what they represent and how and what they communicate to the Other. We'll come back to this when we explore behavioral CQ.

Conclusion

"I'm illiterate!" Those were the words my American friend Chris declared after her first one hundred days living in China. She was eight weeks into language study, yet as she looked at the signs and listened to the conversations taking place around her, her PhD did little to keep her from feeling like a child all over again. Actually, to be a child there would have been easier. Language, like the rest of culture, is transmitted primarily through family. It just happens quite naturally among children. So when we attempt to become socialized into a new culture as an adult, the process is much more forced and laborious. But intercultural expert Craig Storti writes, "Those who cannot speak the language of the country where they reside and whose inhabitants can't speak theirs can never feel altogether at ease."[8]

There are several good books to help us specifically with growing in the area of intercultural communication. Knowledge CQ requires assessing, seeing, and reaching the embedded layers of emotions, judgments, and implicit connotations lurking behind a foreign reality and a foreign text, whether a literary piece, a news article, a story, or even an administrative document. We need to learn how to "compose in the act of writing, comprehend in the act of reading, to learn techniques of reading by writing, and techniques of writing by reading."[9]

Linguistic awareness and fluency play a key role in moving beyond the tip of the iceberg toward greater understanding of culture. Language is central to knowledge CQ and cross-cultural interaction. An understanding of the symbolic power of words and what they mean to the Other is an important part of the journey toward better expressing our love for the Other. Listen to the words used and not used. Watch the reactions of the Other as certain words are used. And seek to understand.

Recommended Resources

Center for Advanced Research on Language Acquisition (CARLA) at the University of Minnesota, http://www.carla.umn.edu/.

Intercultural Communication Institute, www.intercultural.org/.

International Association for Intercultural Communication Studies, http://www.iaics.org/.

Smith, David, and Barbara Carvill. *Gift of the Stranger: Faith, Hospitality, and Foreign Language Learning.* Grand Rapids: Eerdmans, 2000.

8

why we do what we do

Cultural Values

Look around you. What do you observe? What do you see people doing? Why are they doing these things? To empirically observe what is happening around us is one thing. But to move toward interpreting why they do what they do, and to ask the same thing of ourselves, is a much more challenging process. Looking below the surface of what we observe is the primary emphasis of part 3 of this book, "Go Deep: Interpretive CQ." This final chapter of the knowledge CQ part is about cultural values. Cultural values are the linchpin connecting knowledge CQ with interpretive CQ. As we begin to explore the cultural values that shape why people do what they do, we can begin to move from a surface-level understanding to a deeper one.

Last night I ran into an Indian woman who lives around the corner from us. Then I went to my kids' talent show at school and sat next to a teenager sporting some pretty alternative-looking clothes. This morning I received an e-mail from Ecuador and another one from Hong Kong. Next week I'm going to Uganda for five days. En route, I'll be stopping in the United Arab Emirates for a day of meetings. I'm doing a bit of reading to prepare me for my brief sojourns in Uganda and the UAE next week, but there simply isn't the capacity in my life to become an expert on all the cultures I encounter in a week or two. I would guess the same is true for you. Even if you don't plan to use a passport any time soon, you still encounter numerous cultures every week.

Cross-cultural training programs often distinguish between cultural-specific training and cultural-general training. There's a place for both. If you're going to work primarily with a group of Mexican immigrants in Orlando, you'd be wise to gain some depth of understanding about Mexican culture and in particular of Mexican American culture.

Increasing our understanding of some general cultural values such as the ones in this chapter won't make us experts; but it can improve our ability to interact with the barrage of cultural differences we face from week to week. There are many different ways to organize cultural values. Some categorizations are better suited to comparing broad national cultures; other methods are more appropriate for comparing organizational cultures and still others for understanding generational cultures. Given our desire to develop knowledge CQ in a more generalist way, I've chosen six cultural values that cut across all three kinds of cultural domains we're examining: socioethnic culture, organizational culture, and generational culture. There are entire books devoted to explaining cultural values, so the objective here isn't to cover them comprehensively, but instead to move us forward in gaining an appreciation for the kinds of things we need to understand as we seek to move seamlessly across the chasm of cultural difference.

Some of the material in this chapter will recall themes we explored in chapter 4 when we examined the American way. But in contrast to our focus in chapter 4, our interest now is to look more broadly at cultural values and see the variance in these values across several different cultures. And we'll consider what each of us as individuals values compared to the cultures of which we're a part. These cultural values are found in organizational and generational cultures as well as in socioethnic cultures. Actually, this kind of repetitive analysis is one of the most helpful ways to expand our cultural-general understanding. Knowledge CQ means we often encounter some of the same information multiple times and each time incorporate it a bit differently in light of a new set of experiences and insights.

In chapter 5, we discovered the three levels of mental conditioning represented by the iceberg: human nature, culture, and individual personality. Each one of these levels shapes how we think and live. An understanding of the cultural values that follow will help us more carefully distinguish between universal human behaviors, cultural norms, and individual differences. Cultural values are the key form of understanding that help us separate what we observe from how we interpret what we observe.

The six cultural values we're going to explore stem from long-standing literature on how human beings deal with their environments.[1] Throughout history, societies have been faced with the recurring issues of how people deal with one another, with environmental circumstances, and with time. The six values we're going to explore are identity, hierarchy, risk, time, communication, and achievement. We'll look at how different cultures and subcultures respond to the issues embedded in these values. Every cultural grouping interfaces with these values somewhat differently, and each of us as individuals falls somewhere along the continuum described for each value. Depending on the varied cultures in which we've been socialized, we may or may not closely identify with the way the dominant socioethnic culture in our context relates to this value. Once again culture and personal identity always work dialectically. These values are described primarily as cultural norms, but they can also be measured in individuals. Comparing your personal values with the values of the cultures of which you're a part and others you encounter is one of the most important ways to enhance your knowledge CQ.[2]

We want to incorporate an understanding of these cultural values into our overall repertoire of knowledge CQ. These are generalizations, and the measurements are always relative. But these six values help us to look beyond the immediate things observed on the tip of the iceberg and to explore the more important values and assumptions that lie beneath.

Identity: I versus We

The opposite ends of the identity spectrum are usually described in cross-cultural research as individualism versus collectivism. This cultural value considers the extent to which personal identity is defined in terms of individual or group characteristics. Earlier, we described individualism as one of the most pervasive currents in American life. We saw numerous ways that American culture is based on the individualist perspective of pursuing one's own interests and rights. At its core, this involves how we as Americans tend to view ourselves. It was the value at work when my daughter Emily was miffed with the Singaporean government's infringement on "the individual's rights" regarding dog ownership.

Of all the cultures studied, the United States has the highest individualism score, 91 on a scale of 1–100. Close behind the United States are Australia—90, the United Kingdom—89, and Canada and the Netherlands, which score 80.[3] People from individualistic cultures are more inclined toward self-reliance and retaining functional, relatively loose bonds with others. Individualists tend to look out mostly for themselves and their closest family members. This helps explain our American "no strings attached" approach to relationships.

China is on the far end of the collectivism side of the continuum, scoring 20 on a scale of 1–100 with 100 being the most individualistic, which helps explain *guanxi*—the personal relationship between people that obligates them to one another's needs and desires. Most Latin countries also have very collectivist cultures as do many of the African nations. Loyalty trumps everything else in a collectivist culture, and it overrides societal rules and personal gain. As a result, people from collectivist cultures usually have strong relationships in which everyone takes responsibility for fellow members of his or her group—whether that be one's extended family, one's church, or one's own village. It doesn't necessarily refer to one's loyalty to the state.

The identity value is played out in many different ways culturally. The organizational cultures of churches are shaped by the values of the socioethnic cultures in which they are based. For example, churches in individualistic cultures struggle with consumer-driven congregations whose members are quick to pull their membership and leave as soon as they become dissatisfied. For that matter, churches increasingly struggle to get people even to join as members because of the individualistic resistance to being tied to a group. In these churches, attendees usually see calling as something to be discovered alone on a personal retreat, and spiritual formation is a private matter.

A few years ago, my friend and ministry partner, Steve Argue, and I were in Phoenix for the National Youth Workers Convention, and we stopped at Starbucks for our morning fix. The twenty-something barista, TJ, started talking with us. TJ said: "Six months ago I was flying through Phoenix en route from Portland. I got off the plane, and I just knew God was telling me to stay here and start a church over at UA in Tempe. I called home to talk to a few friends, and they thought I was crazy. But I knew God called me to do this so I didn't get on the flight back home, and I've been here ever since." Steve asked him, "So how's it going six months later?" and TJ said, "It sucks. I hate it. It's nothing like Portland here, but I'm not going to give up."

The ironic thing is, TJ comes from a generational subculture (and a regional subculture in Portland) that espouses communal values over and above individualism. The communal atmosphere of coffeehouses, dialogue, and thinking in neighborly ways are core themes for the emerging generation in the church. Yet not unlike TJ, many of us like the warm buzz and rewards of hanging with a group of friends in community, but we resist giving them any authoritative voice in our lives.

This is one of my great fears as an American ministry leader. I identify with many of the ideals of a shift from so much attention on individual rights to more attention on community. I have far more hope for the redemptive impact of a group of people living out a communal apologetic of the gospel than I do of an individual rock-star pastor drawing crowds with his or her personality, charisma, and polished multimedia presentations. But the odds are stacked against me. *The more we travel, the more education, and the more money we have, the more likely we are to be individualists!*[4] By worldwide standards, I'm off the chart on all three of those. Furthermore, "voluntary organizations, research institutes, and academia are usually quite individualistic. Organizations such as the military, mass production facilities, and jobs requiring behavior according to exact standards are often collectivist."[5] To be an American is to be an individualist. This is not to say we can't be more collectivist in our orientation, but doing so is swimming upstream.

Lest we paint too rosy a picture of churches in collectivist cultures, many ministry leaders in these contexts express frustration with finding people who will rise to the cause of leadership and with members who appear to lack personal accountability and initiative. Bernard Tan, a pastor in Taiwan, expressed what many Asian leaders have said: "I can't get my congregation to become serious about evangelistic conversations. We're so loyal to our family and friends. And most of them are loyal to Buddhism or Taoism. So it's hard to even talk to family and friends about Jesus because it seems disrespectful or disloyal. And another thing: there isn't enough attention by my church members to personal responsibility for their own spiritual growth."

> Where is your church on this continuum of individualism versus collectivism? Do people in your ministry view their faith maturity primarily in light of their own journey with Jesus or in light of where your faith community as a whole is in relationship to Jesus? How about you? Are you willing to follow your community's guidance and decisions for you even if you disagree with them?

I've watched far too many ministry leaders live individualistically to the point that they're accountable to no one. Sure, boards and reporting structures usually exist. But no one really has authority over their lives. Knowing my own propensity for this, Linda and I are committed to living in community with a few other individuals and couples. We haven't gone the route of living on the same property and sharing a communal purse, but we do make decisions about where to live and where to go to church and about jobs together. This is more than just getting one another's input. It is actually trusting the community with a decision that affects our lives.

Here's a really simple example. Long ago, Linda and I were told about the value of giving each other veto power over our respective schedules. Surely I support the value of that kind of thing, but one day, while in the midst of way too much travel, I ran by her the opportunity I had been given to go to Sierra Leone for the first time to do some work with churches that were trying to pull themselves back together after the war. When I asked Linda how she felt about my going, she said, "I don't really like being put in this position. Of course, I don't want you to go. I want you here. But how do I know whether that's me just being selfish or a legitimate perspective?" When you add in that I'm a strong personality and know how to easily tap into Linda's gifts of compassion and mercy, I can get her to give the nod to nearly anything I want to put in my schedule. So a few years ago, we decided our community needed to have authority over the big items in our schedules. They aren't nearly as resistant as Linda to saying, "Dave, no! You aren't going to Sierra Leone. You've been gone too much. And by the way, what do you know about helping churches put themselves back together after war?" Okay, they aren't quite that brutal. And there are times when I've truly thought the community wasn't making the right decision for something that affected me. In one case, it was as simple as declining a speaking invitation. In another, it was as major as turning down a job offer I was really excited about. But even in those times when I don't agree with the community's decision, I find great protection and discipline coming from surrendering my choices to the community of which I'm a part.

Some of my friends in collectivist cultures describe how they've had to create similar structures for the opposite reason. They want to create accountability systems that keep them from merely conforming to what everyone expects of them. In order to be true to their personal calling, alongside the calling they share with their community, they have created ways to be sure they're living out their unique identities.

Individualism versus collectivism is found in all three of the cultural domains we're exploring. Churches that reflect a club culture expect pastors to make loyalty to particular congregations the highest ideal. Someone with a lot of personal goals for his or her own achievement will likely struggle in the club culture. Pastors with an interest in doing external ministry such as speaking for other churches or helping another church in town may not feel welcomed in the club culture church. Understanding the way a culture values identity enlightens our view of the artifacts that exist above the sea level.

The greatest amount of research on cultural values comes from the socioethnic domain. Ministry leaders working among collectivist socioethnic cultures have to think carefully about how to motivate people, how to approach learning, and how to recruit leaders. There are several resources available to help ministry leaders consider these cultural values when working with different ethnic backgrounds. A summary of this value and how it is exemplified in socioethnic culture is found in table 3 below. You can also note your personal orientation and those of another national culture.

Table 3
Individualism and Collectivism

Value	Individualism	Collectivism
Description	Emphasizes "I" and individual identity Prefers individual decisions and working alone	Emphasizes "we" and group identity (family, work, group, organization, tribe) Prefers group decisions and working with others
Examples	United States Australia United Kingdom	China Colombia West Africa

Comparing Scores: Scale of 1–100, with 100 being extremely individualistic and 1 being extremely collectivist

US Score[a]	Personal Score[b]	_____ Score[c]
91 Individualism		

a. Score of the United States culture as a whole.
b. Find your score through a CQ test from the Cultural Intelligence Center (http://www.culturalq.com) or make an informed estimate.
c. Fill in the name of another culture. Visit http://www.geert-hofstede.com for the scores of several nations.

Hierarchy: Top-Down versus Flat

The next cultural value we want to explore is hierarchy. Let me explain this one by talking about one of my encounters with this value when I was in India. One morning when I was preparing to start a three-day training module at a church in Delhi, I asked my host, Sagar, if the training materials were all printed and ready. "Oh, yes," he said. "They're at the print shop next door. They just need to be brought here." "Oh, great!" I replied. "I'll run next door and get them." "No, no," Sagar said. "I'll send someone to get them." I responded, "That's kind of you, Sagar. But I don't mind at all. I can use the exercise after the long flight. It's no problem. I'll just run next door and come right back." "Please wait here awhile," Sagar replied. "We will drink tea, and I'll have someone bring them to us."

What's going on here? Is Sagar just insisting on being a gracious host? Am I supposed to turn down his gracious offer to have someone bring them, or am I being too task oriented and missing the point that Sagar just wants to have tea together? Or is he just trying to save face and keep me from knowing that they haven't even been printed yet? It may have been any of the above. Interpreting the many possibilities of this type of exchange is the kind of dilemma we'll explore further as we look at interpretive CQ. But as I debriefed this encounter with a couple of

Indian friends afterward, combined with some reading I did elsewhere, I began to see this conflict was primarily related to the differing views Sagar and I had about hierarchy and status.

It seems I wasn't sufficiently status conscious to suit Sagar. A top-down, status-conscious culture views it as the lot in life of some individuals to courier materials and carry books while others are given the role of doing things such as teaching or being a pastor. For me to have gotten my own materials would not only have been a slight to Sagar, demonstrating that he doesn't know how to take care of a guest teacher, but it may also have been a slur on the importance of education itself. And by the way, the materials did show up right on time.[6]

Hierarchy as a cultural value is the degree of inequality that is assumed to be appropriate and normal. This value, often measured as power distance, reveals where the power lies and how it's structured. Power distance is the extent to which differences in power and status are expected and accepted.

There are a variety of above-the-waterline artifacts that can serve as cues to the degree of hierarchy existing within a cultural context. When visiting a new organization, notice how people address those to whom they report, what kinds of titles are used, and how they're displayed. How are you introduced to the senior pastor, and what does the office setup suggest about power dynamics? Don't miss these important observations when you're in the interviewing process with a new organization. As always, beware of too quickly assuming you know what the office layout means. And don't be too quick to assume one person's level of formality should be generalized to the entire organizational culture. But do take note of the cues and draw on them as you continue to observe the culture.

We've looked at how we as Americans prefer to see everyone as equal. We avoid formal titles as much as possible. We have to beware of too quickly making judgments about how this relates to the way we value hierarchy and power. For example, though we emphasize an informal, "he's just a regular guy" kind of communication, that doesn't mean there are no power structures in place. In fact, US culture is by no means the lowest in power distance. Places such as Israel, Austria, and the United Kingdom are at the lowest end of power-distance measurements.

To what degree does the organization where you serve value hierarchy? How does that compare with your own leadership preferences?

The hierarchy value is an instance where even those of us with a high level of sensitivity to cultural differences can be guilty of imposing our cultural value on another culture. I'm most comfortable in fairly flat, egalitarian types of cultures. I see my students as colearners, I'm grateful that our seminary president treats me more like a colleague than an underling, and I don't view the paid pastors at my church as any more "legitimate" pastors than many laypeople who function in pastoral roles in our congregation. As a result, I tend to see hierarchical structures of leadership as wrong and egalitarian structures of leadership as right.

I've listened sympathetically to many presentations on the biblical patterns supporting models of collaborative leadership over and above top-down, hierarchical models of leadership. The problem is, there are far more biblical descriptions of hierarchical leadership than of collaborative leadership. I question whether the Bible prescribes either model as right or wrong.

Without doubt there are hierarchical structures that allow leaders to exploit with power just as there are flat structures that allow people to hide behind consensus rather than taking responsibility for their actions. And that is a right-versus-wrong issue as prescribed by God's Word. But we're wise to beware of too quickly ascribing morality to one hierarchical structure versus another. We're also wise to know what kind of leadership structure best fits who we are. We'll further explore the tension that comes with this in part 3 in the discussion about interpretive CQ.

Table 4 provides an overview of this value and a place for you to compare your score with that of American culture and another culture of your choice.

Table 4
Low Power Distance and High Power Distance

Value	Low Power Distance	High Power Distance
Description	Expects that all should have equal rights Willing to question and challenge the views of superiors	Expects power holders to be entitled to privileges Willing to support and accept the view of superiors
Examples	Israel Austria United Kingdom	Malaysia Middle Eastern countries France

Comparing Scores: Scale of 1–100 with 100 being extremely high in power distance (hierarchy emphasized) and 1 being extremely low (egalitarianism emphasized)

US Score[a]	Personal Score[b]	_____ Score[c]
40 Low Power Distance		

a. Score of the United States culture as a whole.
b. Find your score through a CQ test from the Cultural Intelligence Center (http://www.culturalq.com) or make an informed estimate.
c. Fill in the name of another culture. Visit http://www.geert-hofstede.com for the scores of several nations.

Risk: Tight versus Loose

This next value, risk, deals with the degree to which a culture tolerates uncertainty and ambiguity. On one end of the spectrum are cultures that are tight, a value sometimes measured as high in risk or uncertainty avoidance.[7] As much as possible, people in these cultures try to control the unexpected through safety and security measures and through strict laws. People in tight cultures tend to prize order and self-discipline. Life is ordered by clear rules and is characterized by limited ambiguity. The majority of people in these cultures are uncomfortable in novel situations where the unknown and the surprising are apt to occur, so they attempt to minimize uncertainty in whatever ways possible.

There's no place outside the United States where I've spent as much time teaching as Singapore. Some studies have erroneously labeled Singapore as a low-risk-avoidance culture. While Singapore is cosmopolitan and allows for many expressions of culture and faith, on the whole, Singapore is a tight, high-risk-avoidance culture.[8] It's not uncommon for me to be asked twelve to fifteen times in advance of teaching there to provide another level of clarity about what I'll be covering. Even after I provide as explicit an explanation as I can, I'm often asked for more clarification. Similarly, when living there, Linda and I were often cautioned by Singaporean parents against allowing our kids to freely climb up and down the playground equipment in the park. It seemed the cultural aversion to risk caused them to be extremely cautious with the ways they would allow their children to play.

On the other end of the risk value are loose cultures. In these cultures ambiguity and unpredictability are welcomed. Strict laws and rules are resisted, and people are more accepting of opinions different from theirs. Loose cultures are often more individualistic because loose rules and room for ambiguity allow individuals to pursue their own objectives while not infringing on the rights of others. Undoubtedly you're seeing your own tendency in each of these values too. We continue to see each of these values manifested in individual personalities and as cultural norms.

Ultimately, this value is expressed by how people in a culture view truth. Tight cultures, such as those in countries where Islamic law and state law are one and the same, are sometimes called "one-truth" cultures. Tight cultures perpetuate the presupposition that there can only be one truth and "we have it!" Loose cultures are said to have a many-truths orientation that allows for the existence of many faiths coexisting together. These cultures are more relativist in their orientation to truth and are content to conceive of multiple understandings of truth and religion existing side by side. These kinds of cultures are often found in more cosmopolitan areas where the demographics have forced a looser, lower-risk-avoidance approach to life together.

What tendencies might a loose culture have that most reflect the kingdom of God? How can those be embraced? Ask the same questions of a tight culture.

We can probably easily think of ministry contexts characterized by one end of this continuum as compared to the other. And while there is a wide degree of variety in this value according to an individual's personality, generational culture also shapes the way one is programmed in regard to risk. Notice how Jeff, a pastor who had been serving for one year in a three-hundred-member Baptist church, describes a church with a tight culture, highly adverse to risk: "I've never seen the church as a place ready to take risks and try new things. But this church takes the cake! Forget talking about taking risks with shaking up the way we do worship or elect officers. They got all freaked out when I had us print the bulletin in-house instead of using the bulletin covers they had been using for fifty years. They were convinced this was the beginning of the end!" I asked Jeff, "Did you see any evidence of this when you were candidating?" He replied, "I told them I'm a risk taker. My final words to the congregation were, 'Don't call me here if you want status quo. But if you're ready to adapt to the needs of the twenty-first century, I'd be honored to serve here.'"

It's interesting that Jeff responded to my question by reflecting on what he had *told* them rather than by describing questions he had asked or observations he had made. A year later Jeff had left that church. Far be it from me to reduce the enormous challenges that faced Jeff to simply high-risk avoidance. But it's hard to imagine that a church so strongly shaped by a tight, high-risk-avoidance culture didn't demonstrate some "tightness" before Jeff arrived. I'm not surprised the congregation agreed to desiring relevance in the twenty-first century. And the language of the search committee may well have been about needing a pastor who would take risks and bring about change. But we have to understand language and cultural values to understand what's really going on below the surface.

Think about the cultures with which you interact and how they interact with this value of risk. Surely there's a place for high-risk-oriented leaders to serve in contexts that are risk averse. But they had best do so understanding how powerfully the cultural forces against risk will shape how they serve there.

Table 5 provides an overview of this value and a place for you to compare your scores with those of American culture and another culture of your choice.

Table 5
Low-Risk Avoidance and High-Risk Avoidance

Value	Loose: Low-Risk Avoidance	Tight: High-Risk Avoidance
Description	Prefers few rules, little structure, and few guidelines Tolerates unstructured and unpredictable situations	Prefers written rules, structure, and guidelines Uncomfortable with unstructured or unpredictable situations
Examples	Jamaica Sweden Malaysia	Greece Uruguay Japan

Comparing Scores: Scale of 1–100 with 100 being extremely high in risk avoidance and 1 being extremely low

US Score[a]	Personal Score[b]	_____ Score[c]
46 Low-Risk Avoidance		

a. Score of the United States culture as a whole.
b. Find your score through a CQ test from the Cultural Intelligence Center (http://www.cultur alq.com) or make an informed estimate.
c. Fill in the name of another culture. Visit http://www.geert-hofstede.com for the scores of several nations.

Time: Short-Term versus Long-Term Orientation

Time and the way a culture views it might be the cultural value with which we're most familiar. The most basic level is the distinction in socioethnic culture of clock time versus event time. Clock time is most typically found in industrialized cultures where punctuality and tight adherence to a schedule are the overriding values in order to efficiently manufacture products. Event time prevails in cultures where time is meant to serve the relationships and events that occur within a given day. As more and more cultures in the developing world become industrialized, work life is becoming more strongly shaped by a clock-time orientation.

Although this understanding about time is a helpful part of knowledge CQ, some issues go deeper into the water when we're thinking about how a culture views time. In the world of organizational culture, an organization's orientation toward time is said to be the most important cultural value to understand. The most critical understanding of time for the organizational domain is whether the organization is most oriented to the past, the present, the near future, or the distant future. Churches oriented to the past often had a period of perceived success known as the "glory days," and as a result, old-timers in the church continue to look back longingly, remembering what it was like back then. In these kinds of churches, homegrown staff members are likely to fare better than outsiders who come in. Many churches and ministries are caught up with the present. To be fair, the very real ministry demands of broken homes, unemployment, and funerals keep many pastors and their teams focused on tending to the immediate needs of today. Ministries that are most oriented toward the future can be divided into those primarily interested in the near future—What do we see happening here in the next three to six months?—and those interested in the distant future, which have regular conversations oriented toward big, audacious dreams for what they are going to be in their community and in the world.

Just as we would want to be sensitive to working with a Mexican group that might not be as concerned about starting promptly at 7:00 p.m. as the Anglo congregation in Manhattan would, so also a new leader entering an organization must be sensitive to its orientation toward time. Those in positions of senior leadership may have more ability to shift the culture than those in midlevel positions of leadership. But even senior leaders should bear in mind that organizational cultures don't change easily, and new leaders need to discern carefully when it is appropriate to change the organizational culture, when the leader needs to adjust to the culture, and when the two just aren't a good fit. Church cultures form quickly—and people bring church cultures with them from previous church experiences. I've talked with many church planters who were surprised by how quickly people in a newly formed church began using the phrase, "But we've always done it that way!"

An additional way time is measured as a cultural value is whether the people in the culture have a long-term or a short-term orientation toward the future. This cultural dimension was identified by a group of Chinese scholars who used a questionnaire in twenty-three different countries around the world to understand each culture's view of virtue. The Chinese scholars drew on their Confucian heritage, in which virtue is dealt with devoid of any religious content. Confucius left the question of truth open-ended. His interest was in an individual's humanity, loyalty, and goodness. Virtue and time orientation are categorized together because virtue is believed to be something that is developed over time, rather than something that can be quickly manufactured or mastered. In collectivist cultures, virtue is something shared as a community rather than something possessed as individuals. And it's something possessed by a community over many generations.

The cultural value of virtue is often held in contrast to the previous one we examined, truth. While some cultures hold truth and the quest for truth as the ultimate ideal, others are most concerned about virtue and goodness.

Cultures with a short-term orientation toward time and virtue are concerned with quick results. There is a concern for possessing the Truth with a capital *T*. Cultures with a long-term orientation toward time and virtue have a general sense of perseverance. They're comfortable with slow results, and their focus is on the long-term future.

These varying ways of approaching time are all important aspects of understanding the cultures we encounter. We're pretty aware of how age tends to shape the way generational cultures view the past, the present, and the future. In the developed world, youth tend to see themselves as invincible. The future seems inaccessible and the past irrelevant; therefore, a "live for today" mind-set dominates the lifestyle of the young. Older people are more likely to spend a great deal of time reminiscing about the past, while forty-somethings are known for wanting to make the next couple of decades of life count for something.

> Are you most concerned with the past, the present, or the future right now? How might that shape the way you interact in the various cultures you regularly encounter?

"They're on Latin time," Carol said. She said it half jokingly, but there was a pejorative bite to her tone as she talked about the chronic lateness of her Hispanic colleagues at the youth center. Most Americans "believe punctuality is a virtue and have never thought about other ways of being on time, other than noting the 'clock' time."[9] Understanding

Table 6
Short-Term Orientation and Long-Term Orientation

Value	Short-Term Orientation	Long-Term Orientation
Description	Emphasizes the present or the recent past Values quick results	Emphasizes perseverance for future opportunities Values long-range planning
Examples	Pakistan Nigeria United States	China Brazil India

Comparing Scores: Scale of 1–100, with 100 representing a very long-term orientation toward time and 1 representing a very short-term orientation

US Score[a]	Personal Score[b]	_____ Score[c]
29 Short-Term Orientation		

a. Score of the United States culture as a whole.
b. Find your score through a CQ test from the Cultural Intelligence Center (http://www.culturalq.com) or make an informed estimate.
c. Fill in the name of another culture. Visit http://www.geert-hofstede.com for the scores of several nations.

the varying ways time and virtue are valued is essential to serving with cultural intelligence.

Table 6 provides an overview of this value and a place for you to compare your scores with those of American culture and another culture of your choice.

Communication: Explicit versus Implicit

Given the highly behavioral nature of communication, it could be argued that communication is as much a reflection of the other cultural values as it is a value itself. But communication and its process have value-laden dimensions for many cultural contexts, so it is germane to our discussion of cultural values.

> Think about a cultural context of which you're a part—whether it's your socioethnic group, your ministry, or your peers. What kind of information is important to you as a group? Are people in the group most drawn to stories and experiences or to research and statistics?

Like the other values, the way communication is approached will vary from person to person according to our unique personalities. But there are some overriding values within cultures regarding the kind of information deemed valuable. Some cultures are very interested in what comes from experts, while others are suspicious of it. And this is where the multiple cultures of which each of us is a part can cause internal conflicts for us. This is one way to think about how a culture values communication.

Another way of thinking about communication is seeing the degree to which explicit versus implicit communication is valued, sometimes referred to as direct versus indirect or low-context versus high-context communication. Direct communication refers to instructions that specifically state and direct an action, whereas indirect communication relies on input and understanding from the listener and the surrounding environment.

Western nations such as the United States and the United Kingdom tend to be very low-context cultures, which use very direct communication. Very little of the context is assumed for knowing how to act. As a result, directions are visible and explicit.

Many Latin cultures are high-context cultures, where information about how to act and instructions are assumed and indirectly implied rather than explicitly stated. Most of us who are used to low-context, direct cultures have felt the challenge of being in a place that we label as "not well marked" because there aren't "good signs" to tell us where to go.

One would assume that a high power-distance culture, in which authority structures are clear, would utilize very direct, explicit communication. In some sense that's true. There's little ambiguity to the directives given to underlings. At the same time, some of these cultures are the places most often characterized by intercultural experts as being high-context cultures, where information about how to act is assumed rather than explicitly given. Sagar didn't need to give very explicit directions to the print shop that prepared my materials for teaching in India. There was a protocol for what would be expected of the courier in delivering the materials ordered.

Though US culture is very direct and low context, many ministry organizations are very indirect and high context. Churches in particular tend to assume a high level of understanding based on history with a church culture. It's assumed people know when to sit, stand, and close their eyes. Many churches following a liturgical tradition do little to explain the meaning behind the liturgies taking place.

I score very high on the value of direct, explicit communication. Clarity is important to me. That spills over into how I approach conflict, the area where communication differences are felt most profoundly. If there's a conflict between someone and me, I want it resolved, the sooner the better. I'm not one to play games by leaving the "elephant in the room" unnamed. That direct approach works pretty well for me in most of the cultures in which I interact in the US. But it has often gotten me into trouble elsewhere.

My direct, bottom-line approach got me into trouble one day when I was working with my Liberian friend Moses. We had been working with Moses to create a collaborative partnership to train Liberian pastors. Moses cautioned us against working with one particular organization in Monrovia, given his concerns about the integrity and ethics of the primary leader of that organization, Dr. Jones. One day, Moses and I were visiting another Liberian pastor, an individual who had a great deal of contact with Dr. Jones. Drawing on my value for direct communication, soon after we got through the perfunctory introductions, I went for it. "Tell me, pastor. I've heard some less than flattering things about Dr. Jones. I'm not looking for dirt, but we're considering a partnership with him and his ministry. What can you tell me?" The Liberian pastor talked about the organization, affirmed it, and didn't say a word about Dr. Jones. I wasn't going to play this game. I tried again. "That's great. But tell me about Dr. Jones himself. Would you feel good endorsing him to us as a potential partner?" Again the pastor affirmed the good things the organization had done. Beginning to pick up on the cues (at last!) I threw in, "And you feel good about Dr. Jones's part in the things the organization has done?" The pastor replied, "Dr. Jones has done many good things. He's a good brother."

As we walked away from the meeting, I tried to quickly reassure Moses by saying, "Moses, I don't want you to think I don't trust the validity of your concerns about Dr. Jones. It's just that it was important for me to get this other pastor's input. But even though he didn't offer any reservations, I'm not discounting yours!"

Fortunately, Moses had learned enough cultural intelligence to talk to a direct-communication American like me in a way that I would understand. He replied, "Don't you see, Dave? Don't you see? Of course he wasn't going to tell you his concerns about Dr. Jones. You should never have asked him that, especially with me there. He would never speak disparagingly about a Liberian brother in front of another Liberian brother to a complete stranger from the States." Later that day, I wrote in my journal: "Okay. I blew it. All this talk about cultural intelligence and I still have so far to go. But when do we need to blow to pieces the idea of cultural intelligence for the sake of truth? I need the truth about Dr. Jones, not a bunch of antics that worry about offending someone. But then how do we negotiate the ethics of truth-telling vis-à-vis collective virtue? Few things challenge my abilities to relate cross-culturally as much as interacting with the issue of indirect, high-context communication."

Either extreme of this cultural value has aspects that reflect kingdom values and that conflict with kingdom values. I must beware of too quickly seeing all the redemptive dimensions of my orientation and too quickly missing the redemptive lessons to be learned in seeing the way the Other approaches communication. The reverse is also true.

Table 7 provides an overview of this value and a place for you to compare your scores with those of American culture and another culture of your choice.

Achievement: Being versus Doing

Achievement is the cultural value that measures the importance given to action. The question examined through this value is, "How does this cultural group define and perceive activity?" This value was measured by Geert Hofstede on a continuum of masculine versus feminine cultures. The idea was to examine the degree to which gender shaped the kind of roles held by people in various cultures. Feminine cultures were said to emphasize nurturing behavior and cooperation, while masculine cultures were said to emphasize assertive behavior and competition.[10]

Given the growing range of views about what roles are appropriate for men versus women, it seems more helpful to measure this value on a continuum of being versus doing, rather than masculine versus feminine. Every culture will have some individuals who are more inclined toward

Table 7
Low Context and High Context

Value	Low Context	High Context
Description	Emphasizes explicit words Values direct communication	Emphasizes roles and implicit understanding Values indirect communication
Examples	United States Israel Australia	Brazil East African countries Thailand

Comparing Scores: Scale of 1–100 with 100 being extremely high context and 1 being extremely low context

US Score[a]	Personal Score[b]	_____ Score[c]
Very low (numerical score not available for United States)		

a. Score of the United States culture as a whole.
b. Find your score through a CQ test from the Cultural Intelligence Center (http://www.cultur alq.com) or make an informed estimate.
c. See Edward Hall, *Beyond Culture* (Garden City, NY: Anchor, 1976) for help in determining the scores of several nations.

spending time with people and engaging in nurturing, feeling-oriented activities and other individuals who are more inclined toward completing tasks and spending their time in thinking-oriented activities. Patty Lane, an intercultural expert with the Baptist General Convention of Texas, writes, "The US culture, which is a doing culture, has persons who function within a large spectrum of behaviors, some appearing extremely doing-driven and others quite being-driven. When compared to a being culture, however, even someone who seems very being-driven will come across as a 'doing-driven person' to people in a high 'being' culture."[11]

Doing cultures value results and materialism. Being cultures value relationships and quality of life. Boomers tend to be far more oriented toward results and action than younger generations. It isn't that boomers don't care about relationships or that Gen Xers don't care about results. But boomers will often be more motivated toward activity that is measurable and quantifiable, whereas Gen Xers are more interested in quality.

Think of an individual you know who seems to value "being" over "doing." How does that affect the way you relate to this person? How do you see it affecting his or her interactions in various cultural contexts?

The generational contrasts in this cultural value are something I observe in the differing approaches to mission by established leaders in missions organizations compared to many younger leaders who are interested in mission. For the most part, emerging ministry leaders are skeptical of ambitious programs and campaigns to complete the evangelization of the world. Slick marketing campaigns that overstrategize how the kingdom is going to be consummated, or overstated descriptions of what any one organization or leader is accomplishing, leave this generational culture unimpressed. Hierarchy, organizational power, and grand strategies are met with suspicion as are the endless military metaphors of mobilizing beachheads all over the world and waging war against other faiths.

Instead, there's a longing among the emerging generation in mission for more "being-oriented" values, including relationships, deep connections, and stories about God working through the underdog. There's a desire for us to be honest about the pitfalls of Western missions. As a result, there are countless stories of emerging leaders leaving large, stable evangelical organizations to work with friends in small, off-the-radar ministries.

Richard Tiplady, a young missions leader in the United Kingdom, says to Western missions organizations, "Don't try to bamboozle us with talk of the 'big picture.' Whatever 'big picture' you develop, it will be wrong. The world is too complex, life is too changeable, and God is too mysterious, for us to get fired up by that kind of language."[12] Instead, the interest is in the kinds of supernatural things God will do through people devoted to him. The emphasis is away from the doing end of the spectrum. This is yet another instance where we must discern in community the strengths and weaknesses of culture's varying ways of viewing achievement.

Table 8 provides an overview of this value and a place for you to compare your scores with those of American culture and another culture of your choice.

Conclusion

Understanding cultural values plays an integral role in our becoming more culturally intelligent. They allow us to begin to understand some of the dynamics shaping how people see the world. They're generalizations, so they're not the whole story. There is no substitute for building relationships and sharing experiences with individuals and coming to know one another more deeply over time. But cultural values provide a starting point. They're immeasurably valuable to knowledge CQ.

Table 8
Being and Doing

Value	Being	Doing
Description	Emphasizes contemplation and reflection Values quality of life	Emphasizes action and proactive behavior Values efficiency and results
Examples	Israel Brazil Sweden	United States (extremely high) Austria India

Comparing Scores: Scale of 1–100 with 100 being extremely focused on doing and 1 being extremely focused on being		
US Score[a]	Personal Score[b]	_____ Score[c]
Very high "doing" (numerical score not available for United States)		

a. Score of the United States culture as a whole.
b. Find your score through a CQ test from the Cultural Intelligence Center (http://www.cultur alq.com) or make an informed estimate.
c. See Patty Lane, *Beginner's Guide to Crossing Cultures* (Downers Grove, IL: InterVarsity, 2002), 98 for help in determining the scores of several nations.

What do we do with all these discoveries about ourselves, our cultures, and the cultures of others? This understanding is what is needed to go beyond the 10 percent of the iceberg that's visible—human nature and cultural artifacts. And as we begin to understand what lies beneath the waterline, we gain an appreciation for the need to think and listen first and to act and speak second. All this increased understanding *is* leading us somewhere. It's moving us toward more effective love and service.

> Observe the cultural values at work in how the Other behaves. Think about what your own behavior reveals about your values. If you journal, what phrases show up again and again? In your conversation, what are the phrases you often hear spoken by yourself and others? And how does your personality align with the cultural values we just explored?

Knowledge CQ is valuable for every believer as we seek to live out the presence of Jesus among the varied cultures in which we find ourselves. But it is essential for leaders. "If [leaders] do not become conscious of the cultures in which they are embedded, those cultures will manage them. Cultural understanding is desirable for all of us, but it is essential to leaders if they are to lead."[13]

The journey toward culturally intelligent love and service is impossible without ongoing growth in knowledge CQ. We have to understand culture's ubiquitous presence in how we see the world and the way others see it. But information and understanding are not enough. There is an abundance of training programs in workplaces across the United States that teach men how to appropriately relate to their female colleagues. But far too many inappropriate behaviors still exist in organizations that have invested lots of money in that kind of training. And parenting seminars about adolescent culture don't seem to reduce the number of counseling appointments most youth pastors have regarding parent-student conflict. Several volumes already offer good information about culture, and there's no shortage of training given to ministry leaders working in cross-cultural contexts. Training and information have their place, but something more is needed. The journey may lead us to the middle of nowhere if all we do is develop our cultural understanding. Knowledge CQ is essential but must be wed with the other factors of cultural intelligence.

Understand yourself. Understand the Other. Understanding *is* an essential part of this pathway toward more effectively loving the Other. Many of these discoveries are things we already know through life experience. We're going to use our enhanced knowledge and our life experience to further our understanding and to explore more deeply the iceberg of others and ourselves. And we're going to be free to admit when we're clueless about what something means. Because, as Confucius said, "When you do not know a thing, to allow that you do not know it—this is knowledge." Understand?

Recommended Resources

Hofstede Cultural Dimensions scores, http://www.geert-hofstede.com/.

The Intercultural Competency Scale, developed by Muriel Elmer, http://www.icsprofile.org/ics.

Lane, Patty. *A Beginner's Guide to Crossing Cultures: Making Friends in a Multicultural World*. Downers Grove, IL: InterVarsity, 2002.

Lanier, Sarah. *Foreign to Familiar: A Guide to Understanding Hot- and Cold-Climate Cultures*. Hagerstown, MD: McDougal, 2000.

Lingenfelter, Sherwood, and Marvin Mayers. *Ministering Cross-Culturally: An Incarnational Model for Personal Relationships*. Grand Rapids: Baker Academic, 2003.

part 3

go deep: interpretive CQ

CQ MAP

Figure 6

From my journal:

I feel so alive sitting here this morning at this little café. Looking at the endless motorcycles driving by with entire families. Smelling the unfamiliar scents. Seeing the street vendors move around with vigor. It's almost easy to forget the tragedies that so recently took place on these streets.

I spent more time than usual preparing for my time here. I rented the *Killing Fields*, I skimmed a couple of books, and I talked with the Cambodian man who works at the Asian food store in Lansing. But I just don't have the slightest clue as to whether my preaching last night really connected in any kind of way with these Cambodian believers. The interpreter was phenomenal—at least it seemed like he was. There wasn't even a hesitation between my pauses. And people seemed to be listening. But how do I begin to assess my effectiveness in a place like this? Was he really "interpreting" what's on my heart? And how could I expect him to?

—December 3, 1997. Phnom Penh, Cambodia

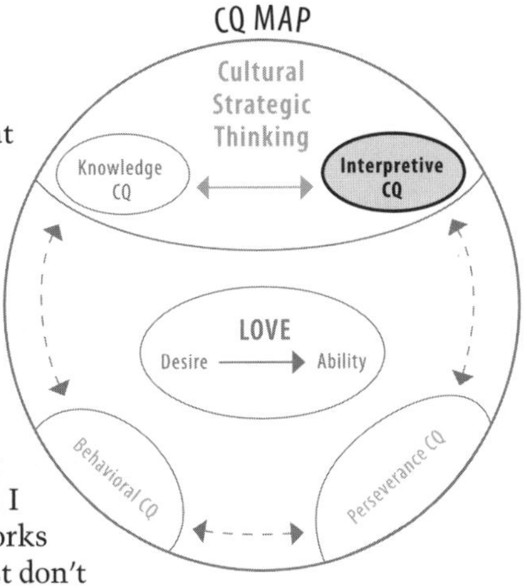

Go deep. We've already started that process by seeking to understand the varying layers of the iceberg. Learning about our own cultural context, the role of culture in shaping behavior, the various cultural domains we encounter, and the language and values that lie beneath the tip of the iceberg yields important discoveries about ourselves and others. And now we want to draw on these understandings to go much, much deeper. Be encouraged. You're well on the way. There's a world that lies beneath what we readily see that when more fully explored makes us far more effective as twenty-first-century ministry leaders.

One's level of interpretive CQ is the degree to which one is mindful and aware when interacting cross-culturally. It's almost impossible to separate interpretive CQ from knowledge CQ, which is why some authors and researchers have kept them together under the umbrella of "cultural strategic thinking." The way we become more aware and more accurately interpret what we observe is largely tied to our level of cross-cultural understanding. At the same time, given the critical linking process that interpretive CQ plays in translating knowledge CQ into culturally intelligent behavior, there is value in viewing knowledge CQ and interpretive CQ separately.

When measuring your interpretive CQ, a few questions to ask yourself include:

- Am I conscious of what I need to know about a culture that is unfamiliar to me?
- Am I conscious of how my cultural background shapes the way I read the Bible?
- Do I determine what I need to know about a culture before I interact with people from that culture?
- Do I compare my previous ideas about a culture with what I actually experience during cross-cultural interactions?
- Do I check for appropriate ways to talk about my faith in cross-cultural situations?[1]

This is the kind of depth measured when testing interpretive CQ.

"Individuals who are culturally intelligent are able to see past the stereotypes that a superficial understanding of cultural [values] provides. Those [values] are only a first step—knowledge CQ—of developing CQ."[2] The cultural values we explored in the last chapter are signposts that provide direction toward more culturally intelligent behavior, but we need the interpretive skills that come from metacognition, thinking about thinking, to actually serve in culturally intelligent ways.

Interpretive CQ doesn't occur in a neat, linear fashion, but if it did, the process might look something like this:

Step 1: Become mindful and aware
Step 2: Empathize with the Other
Step 3: Simultaneously monitor my internal and external world
Step 4: Seek out information to confirm or negate my interpretations

The chapters in this part walk through this process of going deeper. The first chapter considers the need to grow in awareness when we interact cross-culturally. Most of the cross-cultural mistakes I've observed in other ministry leaders and myself have not come from overt intentions to be inappropriate. They often happened unbeknownst to us. So interpretive CQ begins with heightened awareness and alertness. Then we'll consider how that aids us in empathetically identifying with the Other. We'll work toward seeing what is apparent to the Other by trying to put ourselves in their shoes. Throughout this journey, we must keep the end goal in mind: more effectively expressing love and the gospel to the Other.

The next two chapters, 10 and 11, deal with the fascinating field of attribution theory, research that explores how we name and label the world. This investigation will help us improve our ability to monitor our internal thinking process as compared to the thinking processes of people from other cultural contexts. We'll look at this skill in chapter 10 by thinking about how we name and categorize our world (e.g., what makes something a fruit and what makes someone a Christian). In chapter 11, we'll look at the notion of category width, a construct that measures our ability to deal with things that don't neatly fall into one category. In particular, we'll look at how we deal with things that fall into neither a right nor a wrong category but simply into a category of difference.

In the final chapter of this part, we'll synthesize the material explored in the preceding chapters on interpretive CQ by looking at the relevance of praxis and critical reflection to how we interact cross-culturally. We'll draw on some of the educational literature on transformational learning to enhance our ability to seek out information to confirm or negate the interpretations we make throughout our cross-cultural interactions. We'll explore a very practical model for engaging in interpretive CQ in our daily lives.

Each of these chapters takes us deeper into learning how to interpret what occurs in ourselves and the Other as we encounter one another. Let's go deep so we can express Christ up close.

cruise control off

Awareness and Empathy

D riving is a metaphor often used for thinking about the awareness needed to exercise interpretive CQ. When we drive around familiar places, we can drive on autopilot. Similarly, when we interact in familiar cultural contexts, to some degree we can comfortably behave with our cultural cruise control on. For example, when I gather with a group of evangelical leaders in the Midwest, I know the norms and rules. I understand what's typically viewed as humorous, I know what kinds of questions to ask, and I can jump into small talk pretty naturally.

When I drive into a city that's unfamiliar to me, I inevitably turn off the cruise control, slow down, and turn down the music. I'm wise to do the same when I interact with people from different cultural contexts. I may see some of the very same behaviors or hear some of the same terms from a more familiar cultural context. But I ought to question whether similar language and behaviors in a different context mean what they do in my context. If you put me with a group of evangelical leaders from a very distinct denominational group that's unfamiliar to me, or in the midst of a group of Korean American ministry leaders, I'm wise to turn off the cultural cruise control. When moving into such new cultural contexts, I need to question everything from how I should dress for the meeting to when I should and shouldn't speak up.

The journey into interpretive CQ begins with awareness of what lies beneath the external objects and behaviors in our environment and the environment of others. We have to intentionally become conscious of

what lies beneath material things, appearance, reputation, social acceptance, and belonging. Going deep means going beyond the norms of what
the dominant group tells us about ourselves and the Other to empathizing
with the Other while remaining fully whole in who we are personally.

One of our goals along the CQ pathway is to move to a point of being
able to engage in interpretive CQ *while* in the midst of cross-cultural
interactions. That is, we want to get to the point where we can monitor
and adjust our thoughts and behaviors right in the midst of action, not
merely after the fact. Some careful thinking about what it means to be
aware and how we use awareness to empathize with the Other is the
starting point for the seamless connection between interpretive CQ and
actually behaving in ways that are culturally intelligent.

In the beginning, we usually aren't aware of the expectations and assumptions behind behavior, neither our own nor others'. So we have to
settle for retrospective awareness through intentional reflection. This
might mean taking time at lunch or the end of the day to deliberately
recall moments when we were agitated or frustrated by something that
happened and to reflect on why we reacted the way we did. The key is
not further reacting but moving toward awareness. By disciplining ourselves to recall cultural incidents like these, we come face-to-face with
what lies behind the behavior of ourselves and others.

We're going to begin our journey into interpretive CQ by looking more
fully at this discipline of awareness. We'll work toward an understanding
of the concept of awareness as a whole, awareness of what's going on in
both us and others. Then we'll explore some ways to nurture awareness
and how to use awareness to empathize with the Other.

Seeing the Invisible

It might be easier to begin by defining what awareness is *not* rather
than what it *is*. Awareness is not just active, focused thinking, though
that is certainly part of it. Neither is it simply the ability to be intui-
tive and sense what is going on. Awareness is stepping back from what
we're doing and reflecting on it. It's disciplining ourselves to see what
we otherwise miss.

Awareness is one of the primary tools that enables us to discern between the three levels of mental conditioning we examined earlier—
human nature, culture, and individual personality. All three levels play
a part in the formation of consciousness, but as we saw earlier, without
awareness, we often assign individual personality traits to entire cultures;
or we fail to distinguish between what is common to all humanity and

what is unique to a particular culture. Awareness helps us deconstruct and make apparent the various levels of mental conditioning.[1]

Awareness of our own consciousness and mental conditioning begins with an inner journey that seeks to understand how we've come to think and act the way we do. That kind of inward dialogue with ourselves enhances our ability to explore this with others as well. As we engage in dialogue with ourselves and others, we can continue to explore an "experiential understanding of a deeper, more expanded self, whether as temporary levels and states, or developmentally, as structures of consciousness."[2]

Awareness is important because most of the influences that shape our patterns of interpersonal interaction are unknown to us, and the patterns themselves are largely outside our awareness.[3] Think about it this way. One of the ways we simplify our lives is to develop habits and patterns of behaving that we perform semiautomatically. We brush our teeth the same way day after day. Even those people who aren't multitaskers can easily watch the news or listen to a conversation while brushing their teeth. This same kind of semiautomatic behavior is at work on January 1 when we write last year's date. It's what occurs when we drive with the cruise control on.

To be aware is to shut down some of our semiautomatic behavior and to stop and think about what we're observing, thinking, and feeling. For example, we might catch ourselves feeling irritated, bored, or lonely in the midst of a cross-cultural encounter. With a heightened sense of awareness, we transcend merely being defined by our irritation or loneliness and seek to understand what's behind it.[4] In the same way, intentional awareness might mean shutting down our assumptions about what we presume is meant by a familiar behavior and considering what it means for the Other.

Tapping into anthropologists' use of the term "liminality" might enhance our understanding of the importance of awareness to interpretive CQ. Liminality describes a transitional state of openness and ambiguity.[5] It often involves some kind of inner crisis that occurs to bring about adjustment to a new set of circumstances. Liminal space is always an "experience of displacement in the hope of a new point of view."[6]

Arnold van Gennep originated the idea of liminality when studying the rites of passage that many cultures use for transforming a boy into a man. These rites stem from the idea that an individual needs to be led out of the world of "business as usual" and moved into a liminal space for a while in order to become *aware* of the world. The displacement that occurs through liminality is thought to shock the individual into seeing that one's own context is not the only "world." "There is another world, much bigger and more inclusive, that both relativizes and reenchants this world we take as normative."[7] Rites of passage are created based on the assumption that adults must see the world differently than they did as children. A period of liminality helps nurture that shift.

Actually, cross-cultural encounters, particularly travel to a new cultural environment, can be one of the most effective tools to elicit liminality. When cross-cultural travel is approached with a measure of intentional awareness, encountering the Other when we travel is an optimal way to experience liminality, which in turn creates the environment for personal transformation. Of course, we must beware of exploiting the Other merely for self-serving purposes.

One more way of thinking about awareness is to associate it with the idea of mindfulness, a concept that originated in Buddhism.[8] According to Buddhist scriptures, mindfulness is complete awareness of everything that happens within one's own body, mind, and consciousness. The same kind of awareness is also applied to one's environment. The discipline of mindfulness comes with practice and moves toward gaining control over one's thoughts and as a result one's behavior. Since all truth is God's truth, we're wise to learn from the discipline of mindfulness as a way to slow down the rpms and become conscious of our thinking and behavior. It requires commitment to seek out multiple perspectives and, when helpful, create new mental categories, something we'll explore further in the next couple of chapters.

The concept of mindfulness was applied to psychology literature by E. J. Langer[9] and has since been applied to cross-cultural communication and cultural intelligence.[10] In the cross-cultural context, mindfulness means moving out of our automated habits of thinking and behavior that come to us naturally in our familiar environments. In particular, mindfulness draws on the cultural understanding we derive from knowledge CQ to see its role in shaping motives, goals, and emotions in ourselves and others. It's stopping to think about how to approach a conflict-laden situation, such as my need to gain information on the Liberian leader Dr. Jones as compared to how I'd approach that issue with individuals from my own cultural context.

Adopting a state of mindfulness in the midst of cross-cultural interaction allows us to step back and observe the automatic behaviors of ourselves and others. "It is thus the critical link between knowledge and effective behavior."[11] Shutting down our semiautomatic impulses, choosing liminality for a period of time, and remaining mindful throughout cross-cultural experiences are all part of what it means to become more aware. Awareness is active, not passive, and it's thought to be the most novel aspect of cultural intelligence in comparison to other theories of cross-cultural interaction. It's the key linking process between knowledge and action.[12]

Of all the comments made by American short-term missionaries who travel to underresourced places in the world, the most common reflection goes something like this: "Even though those people have so little, *they're so happy!*" There is something endearing about hearing a group of wealthy Americans talk about their amazement that people with so little could be so happy. The question is, are the people they observed really happy? I've asked several hundred short-term missionaries, "What made you think they were happy?" To which they most often responded, "They were always smiling and laughing. You could just tell."

Part of being mindful is for us to take an observation like that and ask some deeper questions. In many contexts, a language barrier results in a nervous interaction of smiling and laughter. It goes something like this:

"Hola!" (giggle, giggle)

"Hi!" (giggle, giggle)

"How are you?" (nervous laughter)

"Bien, gracias." (more nervous laughter)

Have you been there? I sure have. The smiles might reflect genuine happiness, but they just as well might be a nervous cross-cultural response that indicates little about one's level of contentment.

Furthermore, there are cultures like one in a small community in New Zealand where extremely polite, smiling reactions are a way of expressing that the people feel deeply offended. And in Thailand, there are at least twenty different smiles to communicate at least that many different thoughts and feelings.[13]

Or consider what a fifteen-year-old means by wearing his baseball cap through the communion service as compared to what his grandparents think he means by doing so. So much of our behavior is culturally informed without our even being aware that it is.

Can you see how important it is to be mindful about what's going on in any cross-cultural interaction? We need to question our assumptions anytime we interact with someone else, even if that person is from cultural contexts very similar to our own. If I don't know you and I see you smile or laugh, it doesn't necessarily mean you're happy. You could be clinically depressed yet still feigning happiness as an expression of social etiquette. Mindfulness is a skill that will enhance all our interpersonal relationships. But in particular, when we interact with individuals from different cultural backgrounds, the rules for behavior change. Interpretive CQ starts with being mindful of what's going on beneath what's immediately visible.

Notice the way awareness occurs in Nate, who describes what it was like for him as an almost glow-in-the-dark white boy to move into an urban neighborhood. One day soon after Nate and his wife, Melissa, moved into the hood, they brought home Scooter, their solid-muscle American bulldog. Nate introduced Scooter to his neighbor Ed. As he did so, he noticed some resistance on Ed's part. Now here's where awareness kicks in. Nate could have thought, *Oh. That's exactly what my uncle does because he isn't a big fan of dogs. Ed must not be a dog lover either.* And that could have been the end of it. Instead, Nate stopped to consider what Ed's body language meant. This occurred both because of Nate's overall mindfulness *and* because Nate and Ed had been developing a relationship of trust. This led Nate and Ed into a weighty conversation about the civil rights movement. Ed explained to Nate that dogs like Scooter used to be used by police to prey on black people in the South. Nate says, "Ed is originally from the South, and he proceeded to show me the length of the scar on his leg from such police brutality. Ed later asked me to walk Scooter through his backyard in the hope that Scooter would get used to him and his family. He now frequently pets Scooter, and our friendship continues to grow. Did I mention that Ed hadn't told anyone in nearly thirty years about his civil rights dog attack?"[14]

I'm not surprised. Awareness is more than just a theoretical issue of liminality and mindfulness. It determines whether white boys from the burbs and black men haunted by the past can become neighbors and friends. One of the things we're interested in exploring all throughout this book is both a heightened awareness and mindfulness of what's going on inside the Other as we interact cross-culturally and a heightened awareness of what's going on within *us*. If we're honest about our cross-cultural encounters, we'll experience all kinds of emotions and thoughts. We need to turn off the cruise control on our internal drive as well as on our view of what's going on inside the Other. We have to pay careful attention to what we're feeling and thinking as we interact with different issues cross-culturally.

Nurturing Awareness

There are several ways to develop a better sense of awareness and mindfulness as we move toward more culturally intelligent behavior. Awareness begins as we find ways to become more conscious of the assumptions, ideas, and emotions going on within ourselves and within those we encounter. A few of the steps that are likely to enhance our awareness include making time to process alone, making time to process with others, following the spiritual disciplines, and traveling cross-culturally. I want to expand on these briefly.

Time Alone

Learning to become more aware of what lies beneath the tip of the iceberg in encountering the Other might mean actually scheduling time to journal after having lunch with a friend from another cultural context. What questions linger in your mind? What assumptions do you think you had in common? Notice what is apparent about the other person and work toward tuning into his or her assumptions, words, and behavior. Of course, it's important not to simply rely on listening to the words spoken but to tap into other senses for becoming aware of these realities.

Consistent with what we're doing all along this journey, the awareness is as much looking below the iceberg in ourselves as well as in the Other. When you're seated on the plane and wondering who will be seated next to you, stop and think about who it is you'd least want to sit there. Why? It might simply be due to physical comfort that you prefer one person as compared to another, but might there be other reasons that you're hoping for someone like you to sit by you? Pay attention to those thoughts and emotions and jot them down.

Another powerful opportunity for nurturing awareness on our own is in moments of great frustration or disgust. Cross-cultural expert Craig Storti suggests that awareness itself is a way of abating anger for a time. It's pretty difficult to remain angry while simultaneously stepping back to reflect on it. "So long as our attention is diverted from whatever is making us angry, for that period . . . the emotion, cut off from its object, is checked. It is likely to return, of course, as soon as our awareness lapses (or another object comes along), but so long as our awareness is sustained, the anger cannot intrude into our consciousness."[15] Of course, ridding ourselves of anger isn't necessarily the point as much as it is pulling away from the emotion for a time to better understand what is eliciting the anger we feel. There are several things we can do on our own to begin nurturing awareness. Many of the practical ideas listed in chapter 15 also play a part in nurturing awareness, such as reading novels, watching movies, and attending cultural events. But we can only get so far down this road on our own.

Time with Others

Becoming more aware of what's below the surface might mean finding a mentor or a peer with whom you can process the questions, thoughts, and intuitions surfacing for you in a cross-cultural encounter. This is one of the many reasons I love traveling with Linda. We process our cross-cultural encounters together. She's a wonderful "CQ peer" because she's quick to challenge my assumptions and she's never too ready to assume my interpretations of a situation are accurate.

Traveling with a thoughtful sojourner is a valuable asset to any cross-cultural experience. On some occasions, I've been fortunate enough to travel with one or more colleagues from different socioethnic cultures. This kind of multicultural perspective really enhances the potential for nurturing awareness. Of course, similar approaches can help enhance awareness when crossing organizational and generational cultures too. We almost always have the chance to tap into people around us who come from different cultural contexts organizationally and generationally. As we engage in awareness and reflection in community with others, it allows us to begin viewing situations from as many different perspectives as possible. Even in future situations when we don't have immediate access to fellow sojourners, we can begin to more accurately think about how we might reflect on a particular encounter if they were along. Or we can hypothetically ask ourselves questions such as, "How would I view this if I were twenty years older/younger?" "What if I were the opposite gender?" "What if I were a layperson or from a different denomination?" Consciously asking ourselves these kinds of questions begins to make us more aware of our own assumptions and those we intuit the Other to have.

When we're pulling together a team or group, we need to seek ways to diversify it with people from varying cultural perspectives and domains. It grieves me to see a church leadership team reflecting only one age group, ethnicity, or gender. Sometimes teams have uniformity in all these categories, such as a leadership team consisting of only white, fifty-something men. More discussion about forming a culturally intelligent ministry as a whole is found in appendix D. To become more aware of ourselves and others, we have to pursue time with people of difference.

Spiritual Disciplines

One of the most powerful ways to become aware is through the spiritual disciplines. They train us to see what is behind our emotions and to see what we do not naturally see. For many centuries, the church fathers and mothers have used the spiritual disciplines to banish illusions in order to be fully present with themselves and others. Cultural intelligence isn't something we should compartmentalize as a separate skill apart from the rest of our faith and formation. It ought to be an outgrowth of our inward spiritual journey as we live out devotion to God in relationship with the Other. The "disciplines exist so that we can see what is, see who we are, and see what is happening."[16] This is exactly what is needed in developing awareness for interpretive CQ. Prayer, for example, is more than just saying words and thinking thoughts. It's a stance and a posture. It's a way of living *in* the presence of God and living in *awareness* of his presence as we interact with people wherever we go.[17] Henri Nouwen asks us, "Are the leaders of the future truly men and women of God, people with an ardent desire to dwell in God's presence, to listen to God's voice, to look at God's beauty, to touch God's incarnate Word and to taste fully God's infinite goodness?"[18] The disciplines enable us to remove ourselves from the bombardment of stimuli in our environment to see what is within, what is in the Other, and what is in our surrounding environments. They're one of the most important tools for going deep.

International Travel

Earlier, I mentioned that cross-cultural travel itself can be a way to experience liminality, which in turn creates the space for awareness. We cannot come to know our cultural selves without the benefit of an equivalent vantage point. But when we leave home, there's greater potential that we'll become more aware. The average tourist "returns from a stay abroad knowing more about his or her own country than about the one just visited."[19]

In fact, international travel is consistently listed as being among the top three to five transformative experiences in the lives of adults. Experiencing the jarring nature of being removed from our familiar surroundings, when combined with these other practices, is one of the most powerful ways to look below the tip of the iceberg. Those of us with opportunities to travel abroad are entrusted with an amazing resource for deepening our interpretive CQ.

We're least likely to gain the awareness benefits from cross-cultural travel if we stay in American chain hotels and complain, "The Big Macs here aren't quite like they make them at home." And traveling with a large group of people from back home also limits the transformative impact. We don't really enter the disorienting, liminal space when we retain all the comforts of home as we travel. But when we really immerse ourselves in another culture and interact up close with the Other there, we have an ideal space in which to question our fundamental assumptions. We can begin to see that not everyone views things the way we do nor are our questions the only ones being asked. Cross-cultural encounters can be an ideal way of exploring whether our faith is the only sensible way of looking at the world. Many Christians fear even allowing themselves to question their faith, but a serious engagement with the Other should cause us to explore our faith with a heightened sense of curiosity.

Unfortunately, short-term missionaries rarely talk about their cross-cultural experiences as opportunities to question and rethink their faith. Notice the kinds of responses that came when I asked several short-term missionaries about their experiences before and after their trips. I said, "Talk to me about how this cross-cultural trip changed you as a person. How, if at all, will it influence the way you will go about your daily life as a follower of Jesus? How are you rethinking your faith as a result of what you encountered?" The following responses exemplify what most of the subjects in this study said:

> I notice how much we have in our country versus what they don't have and how much it can be a plus or a minus. It can be a plus in the fact that we are so blessed. I mean, we have all this running water and dependable electricity and cars. We have freeways, telephone systems, and e-mail. But these things can be a hindrance because they can keep us from really focusing on God.

> The big challenge I've faced is seeing the living conditions of these people and the way they respond. I've been encouraged actually, to see how they deal with so little and their strong faith.

> One of the biggest things I learned was the power of prayer. We really saw incredible answers to prayer.

> I never want to forget some of the things I've seen this last week. These people do so much with so little. I have it so good. Why can't I be content with what I have? Maybe God wants us to get along with less. Maybe we should sell our home, our second car? How can we live more simply? That's what's on my mind.

Remember my initial question: "Talk to me about how this cross-cultural trip *changed you* as a person. How, if at all, will it influence the way you will go about your daily life as a follower of Jesus? How are you rethinking your faith as a result of what you encountered?" Prayer, contentment, broadening one's horizons, and similar themes were the recurring responses given regarding how this trip changed them. These are the kinds of things I expect to hear from a group of high school students or middle-aged adults going on their first overseas trip. But these weren't teenagers or inexperienced laypeople. This study looked specifically at the short-term missions experiences of professional church leaders. The vast majority of the pastors interviewed as part of this particular study made comments similar to the ones above. I was shocked. I expected a group of Christian leaders such as those sampled in this study to be more inclined than the typical person to engage in deep, critical thinking about the role of culture in shaping the beliefs and ethics of ourselves and others.

Almost any discussion about the personal transformation these pastors experienced as a result of their cross-cultural experience was immediately relegated to commonplace spiritual themes in Christianity. These were rich, life-changing conclusions. A transformed prayer life and an increased measure of contentment are surely worth celebrating among any of us. But I expected more from pastors and church leaders. I anticipated more discussion about the uncertainty ministering abroad raised in their convictions and beliefs about life and ministry. *I expected to hear them describe an increased awareness of the role of culture in shaping how they were thinking about life, knowledge, church, teaching, ethics, ministry, and more.*

At one point in the study, I became more proactive to see if I could prod the pastors toward a heightened level of reflection. I said things like, "It's great to hear you were stretched to pray more and that you were challenged to think about materialism. What about your theology? What questions did this experience raise for you in that way? How did it affect your view of Christianity alongside other religions?"

With one exception, all the responses, even to these leading probes, mirrored Ken's. Ken said, "It certainly didn't raise doubts for me. Instead, it was kind of like a personal revival for me. It showed me how true Christianity is and what a blessing it is to be from a country founded on Judeo-Christian values as compared to these other religions. God just seemed more real to me while I was there."

Again, intimacy with God that yields increased contentment and prayer is not insignificant. But to move closer to the journey of effectively expressing love for the Other, we have to go deeper below the surface to become more aware of how culture shapes the way we live out our faith. International travel affords us an unusual opportunity to be transformed not only in our prayer lives but also in the way we respect, understand, and appreciate the Other. With just a little more awareness while traveling, we can gain far more from these experiences. "The world is a book, and those who do not travel read only a page."[20]

Examples of some healthy, below-the-surface questions about our faith might include questions like these when we encounter the Other at home and abroad:

- How does my cultural background enhance my understanding of the Scriptures? How does it hinder it?

- What am I observing here that causes me to question God's ways?

- What do the Christians in this culture seem to understand that I can learn from?

- What aspects of the faiths predominant in this culture reflect something I need to learn?

In chapter 11, we'll come back to the role of critical reflection in interpretive CQ, and we'll look at some additional ideas for how to become more aware and how to translate that awareness into more culturally intelligent love and service. But for now, we want to focus on the essential role of awareness in enhancing our interpretive CQ. As we become more aware, not only of the things above the surface of culture but also of the values and assumptions that lie beneath, we move one step closer to more culturally intelligent behavior, which in turn allows us to better love the Other.

Empathy

The fullest expression of awareness occurs when we move beyond simply understanding what lies beneath the behavior of the Other to actually entering in and empathizing with the Other. By empathy, I mean noticing what's apparent about another person and trying to tune into her or his thoughts, emotions, and feelings. This can be hard enough for two individuals coming from the same cultural context, so it's especially challenging when it involves empathizing with someone with a different set of values and assumptions, as is often the case when we relate cross-culturally.

One way that interpretive CQ relates to knowledge CQ involves using our understanding of culture to appreciate what we have in common with all humanity as compared to our differences. The greater the cultural distance, the harder it is to empathize. But there's value in starting with our most basic connection as human beings. We understand what it means to lose a loved one. At some level we know what it is to feel hopeless. We understand the joys that come in having meaning and purpose. So there are some basic aspects of being human with which we can all empathize, though we're in danger of some colossal cross-cultural mistakes if we think those commonalities mean that we fully understand what another individual is experiencing.

It's difficult to empathize from afar. The knowledge CQ gained by reading novels, watching movies, and visiting museums and restaurants are all part of how we learn to empathize. But there's nothing like being immersed in the world of the Other to truly grow toward empathizing. Beware. It's possible to teach in a middle school for thirty years or take twelve short-term missions trips to the same village without ever empathizing with the people living in those cultural landscapes. This is where mindfulness needs up-close relationships to build empathy.

Youth ministry researcher Terry Linhart observed firsthand a group of American high school students who, though they spent several days with a group of Ecuadorians, failed to empathize with them. He compares their interaction with the Ecuadorians to an interactive museum. The students gawked at the "living artifacts" from Ecuador without really encountering them. The Americans worshiped alongside the Ecuadorians, they performed for them, and they poured out affection on their children. However, with limited ability to cross the chasm of language, the students were unable to make accurate perceptions about the Latinos. Linhart writes, "Without spending significant time with the person, visiting his or her home, or even possessing rudimentary knowledge about the person's history, students made quick assessments of their hosts' lives and values."[21]

In part, it is to be hoped that empathy will be the natural outgrowth of becoming more mindful of the assumptions, ideas, and behaviors of ourselves and others. But even empathy is not the final objective. Accurately seeing and interpreting what's going on and allowing ourselves to empathize with the Other must eventually translate into behavior and culturally intelligent ministry that effectively and lovingly draws people to Jesus. And the way we express empathy is fraught with cultural assumptions. What might appear empathetic in one cultural context could be seen as interference and meddling in another. However, empathy is an essential part of the process for moving toward more culturally intelligent service and relationships.

Empathy is the ability to imagine ourselves in someone else's position and to intuit what that person is feeling. In many cross-cultural interactions, the degree to which we can empathize is seriously limited. My own experiences with congregational life in churches give me plenty of room to empathize with church leaders in many different contexts who are trying to bring about restoration among church family members who have had a falling out. But as I hear the stories of my brothers and sisters in Rwandan churches where Hutus and Tutsis are learning to be restored to one another, I realize the limitations of my ability to empathize. Watching the restoration of two Kansas City church members after a business deal has gone bad is a beautiful picture. Watching the restoration of two Kigali church members after one of them has killed the other's brother during civil war is miraculous.

So part of the process of empathizing relies on a realistic understanding of just how far we can put ourselves in another person's position and intuit what he or she is feeling. But as we grow in our ability to become mindful and aware, it enhances our ability to stand in the shoes of the Other, to see with that person's eyes, and to feel with his or her heart. "Empathy is a stunning act of imaginative derring-do, the ultimate reality—climbing into another's mind to experience the world from that person's perspective."[22]

It's important to note that empathy is not the same as feeling sorry for someone. Empathetically interacting with the Other may well elicit emotional responses such as sympathy and sorrow, but if we're not careful, those emotions can lead us to patronizing the Other and reinforcing tired power structures. True empathy leads to mutuality and investment rather than condescending sympathy. When we get to perseverance CQ in chapter 13, we'll further explore the delicate balance between compassion and power.

Some individuals have personalities that are more naturally oriented toward being empathetic than others. Left-brained, reason-dominated individuals sometimes have a harder time empathizing with the Other than more right-brained, emotive people do. But with increased awareness, everyone can grow in the ability to see the other side of an argument, to comfort someone in distress, and to bite one's tongue instead of muttering something snide. Empathy is a means of understanding a situation and the Other's feelings toward it and learning to view it from the cultural context of the Other rather than purely from our own.[23]

Empathy ought to be a part of how we go about cross-cultural evangelism. The point is not to respect different religions merely for political correctness, but instead, to truly become incarnational in seeking to empathetically identify with what following Jesus will mean for an individual. Think about how empathy shapes the way we read the conversation between this missionary mother and her daughter:

"Mom, wait a minute," Emma said to me. Something had been troubling her ever since she first came home from school. "What would you say if . . ." I set the plates back on the table and sat down. "What would you say if I told you I was going to become a Hindu?"

It was a good thing I sat down. "What did you say Emma?" I stalled.

"What would you say if I told you I was going to become a Hindu?" She didn't take her eyes off my face.

"You're not joking?" I knew she wasn't. Her deep brown eyes could not have been more serious.

"I am not joking," Emma replied.

What was there for me to say? The sweet, earnest, devout child before me, flesh of my flesh, a Hindu?! I had never thought of her in any way except as a child of Christ. I had failed her, and I had failed God. I had failed the other missionaries and the Indian Christians. How could I face anybody? All this came over me in a flash, and I was then more deeply shamed in the realization that my first reaction was one of loss of face.

She let me sit in silence until the whole impact of what she had said sank in. I saw her whole life before me including her marriage to. . . . Where was her father?! Perhaps he would be able to cope with this better than I could.

I must have looked very stricken, for she suddenly said, "I'm sorry, Mom. I just want you to know how Rani's mother will feel. Rani is going to tell her mother, this vacation, that she is going to become a Christian. It will affect her family as deeply as it would affect you if I became a Hindu."

When I think how close our family has been, it makes me hurt all over to think how hers will suffer.[24]

There are times when I "hurt all over" from empathetically thinking about the discipline I need to use with my daughters. That doesn't keep me from doing it, but empathizing with them causes me to go about doing it differently. In the same way, empathy for Rani and her mother doesn't run into conflict with calling them to follow Jesus. But it surely informs the way I would go about doing so.

> Practice empathizing today. When you stand in line at the store, look at the stranger in line ahead of you and imagine your life in her or his shoes. Beware of hasty assumptions. But think about what life might be like for this individual based on your brief observation. As you have coffee with a friend, sit in a meeting, or share dinner with an acquaintance, put yourself in the shoes of the Other. How might you be feeling right now if you were that person?

Conclusion

Awareness and empathy are the first steps toward going deeper with interpretive CQ. There's little hope that we can make accurate interpretations of what we observe cross-culturally without first growing in our ability to be aware and to identify with the Other. Social interactions are our best way to actually develop cultural intelligence. But the interactions by themselves aren't enough. Social interactions combined with awareness and mindfulness allow us to draw on the understanding that comes from studying cultural values (chapter 8) without too quickly stereotyping people merely because of their cultural context. Although understanding a culture's values gives us clues about a group of people, it indicates little about the particular individual. "The culturally intelligent person does not jump to conclusions from only one or two clues but collects much biographical information before making a judgment" about an individual.[25]

Interpretive, or metacognitive, CQ is thinking about thinking. It's stepping back from activity to examine how we think about, conceptualize, and interpret what we observe. And consistent with our journey thus far, it's something that begins internally by thinking about the ways we think and act and then observing that in others. The next two chapters are devoted to two secondary variables within the interpretive dimension of cultural intelligence: logic sets and category width. Both of these variables relate to how we categorize and classify information, and they shape the way we see the world and how we interpret the behavior of the Other. They submerge us into greater depths of thinking about how we see the world.

Recommended Resources

Merton, Thomas. *New Seeds of Contemplation.* New York: New Directions, 1972.

Pink, Daniel. *A Whole New Mind: Moving from the Information Age to the Conceptual Age.* New York: Riverhead, 2005. See chapter 7 on "Empathy."

Rohr, Richard. *Everything Belongs: The Gift of Contemplative Prayer.* New York: Crossroad, 2003.

10

what makes an apple an apple?

Labeling Our World

As we become more aware and observe the world around us, we're bombarded by stimuli and images. Looking out my window this morning, I see grass, trees, birds, toys my kids haven't put away, weeds we haven't pulled, a messy garage, and a chipmunk scurrying across our deck. I hear the sounds of construction on a nearby street, birds chirping, and runners talking together on their early morning jog. As I taste and smell my coffee, I feel a nice breeze blowing through the window behind me. Those are only a tiny fraction of the stimuli currently bombarding me. Why did I name the things I did? Why did I lump certain things together (e.g., toys, weeds, and birds) while separating others? Why did I order my description around the sensory nature of the observation (sights, sounds, smells, etc.)? And how did I choose what to list as compared to the thousands of things around me that went unmentioned and quite possibly unobserved? Social psychologists have devoted a great deal of study to examining how we name and categorize what we observe and experience. Exploring that dimension of our cognitive processing is an important element of going deeper into interpretive CQ. Interpretive CQ is all about drawing on the understanding we gain from knowledge CQ and using that to help us go below the surface to see what's behind what we observe. What's going on in ourselves? What's going on in the Other?

One of the ways we deal with the complexity of our environments is to classify the world into different categories. Deeper thinking about our own journey and the journey of others includes thinking about the continual subconscious decisions we make to eliminate confusion. It helps us distinguish between a garage and a chipmunk, coffee and wind, weather and food. And we further separate those categories into other lists, such as separating food into fruit, meat, and vegetables. The categories of distinction continue. We label certain fruits oranges when a fruit possesses features common to what we've decided make up an orange while ignoring many other features of the object that may be irrelevant. This is one of the most amazing features of being human. We name everything in our world. And the names become the categories by which we think. The nature of how we classify the world is known as attribution theory.[1] Our ability to classify and name things is part of what makes us image bearers of God. We can understand and explain what we see in the world. We can ask, "Why?" It allows us to look at something we've never seen before and appropriate it into a category. Understanding this phenomenon is what lies behind attribution theory.

Attribution theory is important to interpretive CQ because culture significantly shapes how we organize the world, and interpretive CQ is focused on looking at how we see the world. It takes us deep below the surface of activity to understand how we think. Most stimuli in our environments don't fit neat categories, so we create categories that fit the things we see in the world around us. Psychologist M. A. Wallach says, "The world more often than not provides a person with stimulation that does not clearly fit the definition of any one class or label, but rather stands at the boundary of a particular label's applicability: it can be labeled with equal or near equal appropriateness by more than one term."[2] Attribution theory examines the way one's cultural background, personality, and upbringing shape the way an individual explains what is observed and what happens. For example, some students receiving a low grade draw on external explanations for what happened (e.g., a poor teacher and a bad textbook) as compared to others who draw on internal explanations (e.g., inadequate study or rest). A variety of tenets within attribution theory help us examine why we categorize things the way we do.

We want to specifically examine the aspects of attribution theory that have the most relevance to culture and to interpretive CQ. First, attribution theory helps us see how culture shapes the way we form categories, referred to as logic sets. That's what we'll explore in this chapter. Second, attribution theory provides perspective on the degree to which we're comfortable with things that don't neatly fit into our culturally formed categories, referred to as category width. We'll explore that idea in the next chapter.

There are many ways to approach how culture influences the way we form categories. Paul Hiebert's work on centered sets and bounded sets is one of the most helpful approaches for applying interpretive CQ to ministry leadership. A great deal of what I've included in this chapter is informed by his work on this topic.[3]

For an example of how culture shapes the way we see, label, and describe the world, consider the juxtaposition of Hebrew and Greek cultures and their respective influences on Christianity. A Hebrew view of God is relational in nature. To the Hebrews, God is Creator, Judge, and Lord. He is called "the God of Abraham, Isaac, Jacob, and our forefathers." Hebrew culture sees and describes reality in relationship to other people and things, rather than describing objects in and of themselves. Paul Hiebert refers to this approach as a "centered-set" way of seeing the world.[4] Things and people are described in relationship to other things and people.

In contrast, the Greeks view the world using what Hiebert calls "bounded sets." People and things are classified in light of their intrinsic value, and there are clean boundaries that set them apart from other people and things. To the Greeks, God is supernatural, omnipotent, and omnipresent. This is who God is independent of his relationship to others.

Understanding these different ways of seeing and thinking about the world is a critical aspect of interpretive CQ. Ironically, these very sets themselves are an expression of our human tendency toward classifying and labeling. We need to further understand the basis by which we organize the world and how that understanding relates to culturally intelligent leadership in the ministries where we serve.

Basis and Boundaries

Vijay is an Indian American friend of mine who became a Christian during medical school at the University of Chicago. When Vijay came to the United States, he was a devout Hindu, but several friendships and experiences played a part in his becoming a Christian.

Stop right there for a second. What kinds of assumptions are you making about Vijay in light of my telling you about his conversion? In your mind, what must be true about Vijay for me to refer to him as a Christian compared to when I said he was a devout Hindu? Of course, the way you answer will in part be a reflection of your theological stance on salvation. But it will also say something about how you categorize people as Christians and non-Christians. What does it take for you to label one person a Christian and not another?

That's really what is at stake in thinking about this issue of how we classify and categorize things. In talking about the relevance of how we categorize things with how we do mission, Hiebert describes two kinds of variables that are essential to forming categories and how those in turn affect the way cultural intelligence shapes our view of conversion, the church, and the gospel.

The first variable refers to the *basis* on which the elements are assigned to a category. Hiebert offers two choices: an intrinsic basis (the Greek approach) versus an extrinsic basis (the Hebrew approach). "*Intrinsic sets* are formed on the basis of the *essential nature of the members themselves*—on what they are in and of themselves."[5] God is. God is omnipotent. God is omniscient. God is omnipresent. God is holy. God is immanent. God is transcendent. This way of describing God flows from an intrinsic way of categorizing God. He is who he is with or without relationship to anyone or anything else. Of course, those attributes are meaningless apart from relationship with his creation, but the emphasis is on God's internal nature.

The other option Hiebert offers is extrinsic sets. "*Extrinsic, or relational, sets* are formed, not on the basis of what things are, but on their relationship to other things or to a reference point. For example, a *son* and a *daughter* are *children* of a *father* and *mother*. If they are children of the same parents they are *brother* and *sister*, not because of what they are intrinsically, but because of their relationship to a common reference point."[6] It's more difficult to exemplify external sets in English because English is based on a Greek worldview, which defines reality in terms of the internal essence of things rather than the external relationship of things. As demonstrated by the Hebrews, an extrinsic view of God describes God as the Creator of the universe. He is God the Father, Ruler, and Savior. He is best understood in relationship to us and the rest of creation.

Whether cultures create categories intrinsically or extrinsically depends on the *basis* for how things are organized, independently or relationally. The second variable concerns the *boundaries* of how sets are formed, labeled as well-formed or fuzzy sets. "*Well-formed sets* have a sharp boundary. Things either belong to the set or they do not. The result is a clear boundary between things that are inside and things that are outside the category. *Fuzzy sets* have no sharp boundaries. Categories flow into one another. For example, day becomes night, and a mountain turns into a plain without a clear transition."[7]

Both the Hebrews' and the Greeks' view of God situates God in a well-formed set. The boundaries are clear, but the basis is different. Hebrews base their view of God extrinsically or relationally. Hiebert refers to this as an extrinsic well-formed set or as a "centered set." No one else can be God. His relationships are his alone, and they define him as God. The Greeks' view of God is described as an intrinsic well-formed set or what Hiebert calls a "bounded set." Again, God alone is God, though he is defined as such first and foremost because of his internal essence and attributes. Given that both cultures use well-formed sets, there is no question whether other beings are part God or whether God is partially something other than God. He is God, and no one else is. In contrast, a fuzzy set might see something as partially God and God as partially something else.

In summary, Hiebert's four possibilities for how cultures classify the world include:

1. Intrinsic Well-Formed Sets, or Bounded Sets
2. Extrinsic Well-Formed Sets, or Centered Sets
3. Intrinsic Fuzzy Sets
4. Extrinsic Fuzzy Sets[8]

These are summarized as follows:

	Boundaries	
	Well-Formed Sets	Fuzzy Sets
Intrinsic Sets Based on what something is in and of itself (e.g., apple)	**Bounded Set** • Category created by listing essential characteristics (an apple is fruit, round, etc.) • Defined by a clear boundary • Tied to ultimate, changeless reality	**Intrinsic Fuzzy Set** • Like bounded—based on its essential characteristics • Boundaries are fuzzy (things may be 30 percent or 70 percent but rarely 100 percent) • Because boundaries are fuzzy, thing may belong to two or more sets at a time • Tied to a reality that is a spectrum and continuum
Extrinsic Sets Based on what something is in relationship to a reference point (e.g., daughter)	**Centered Set** Created by defining a center or reference point • Things related to the center belong to the set, and those not related to the center do not (family; geographic reference points, e.g., center of equator) • Not created by drawing boundaries but they do have sharp boundaries • Definition comes from movement to or away from center	**Extrinsic Fuzzy Set** Relationship based not on the intrinsic nature of something but entirely on how things relate—everything is relative • Fuzzy boundaries • No definitive point of movement—can continually be moving toward and away from

(Basis)

There is tremendous value in a deeper understanding of all four of these ways of classifying the world. They're closely related to the metacognition process we're exploring with interpretive CQ. It is well worth reading Hiebert's and other analysts' work in this regard. But the most helpful contribution of this work for culturally intelligent ministry is the distinction between bounded sets (intrinsic well-formed sets such as the Greeks use) and centered sets (extrinsic well-formed sets such as the Hebrews use).

Bounded Sets

Ethnocentrism, the tendency to look at the world primarily from the perspective of one's own culture, has been a recurring theme throughout each of the studies I've done exploring the cultural intelligence of American ministry leaders. This was true across the cultural domains of socioethnic culture, organizational culture, and generational culture.

Joe is a thirty-five-year-old pastor who is passionate about calling his suburban church to reach out to some of the families and kids in the inner city nearby. In talking about the challenge of getting his congregation to join this cause, he said, "They're committed to the idea of reaching out to inner-city kids until they actually show up in our youth room. God forbid one of their precious Wonder Bread children brush up against a kid from the hood. You won't believe what one of my elders said last week. He said, 'I know this isn't a very politically correct statement, but you can't deny the facts. Most of the crime reports on the evening news involve black kids. Are we sure we're up for this?'"

Joe was appropriately frustrated by the ethnocentric, racist attitudes present in his congregation and even his board. He spent several minutes talking about his concern for teaching his congregation about cultural sensitivity before they could be effective in reaching some of the different ethnic groups in town. Ironically, during the same interview, Joe said this about his congregation: "I know they love their hymns and their suits, but watch them on a Sunday morning. They're lifeless. They just go through the motions, following the order of service, waiting for the service to get out so they can get on with their lives." His statement was not unlike the comments of many younger leaders regarding the older generation in the church. Joe seemed unaware that the very ethnocentric attitudes he was describing in his board seemed to be present in his own description of the older generation of people who don't approach worship the way he does. We might argue that the dangers of the board member's attitude toward kids from the inner city is more problematic than Joe's attitude toward the older generation, but both stem from the same kind of ethnocentric, "my way is best" mentality. Ethnocentric behavior is further exacerbated by bounded-set thinking, also evident in most of the ministry leaders sampled.

Bounded sets are the basis of life in the West. Most of our nouns are bounded sets—apples, oranges, pencils, and pens. We use adjectives to allow for some blur such as green apples or fully ripe apples, but they're all still apples because of their intrinsic nature. Something cannot be partially an apple. Either it is an apple, or it is not. The bud and blossom that precede the tangible fruit are not considered apples. Things are identified based on clear boundaries. The logical inference for cultures using bounded-set reasoning is that there can be no blurring of the boundary.

The focus in bounded-set thinking is on the boundary. Bounded-set cultures develop taxonomies and logical systems and categories for everything. As already noted, classifying the world into different sets is common to all cultures, but the bounded-set approach is much more concerned about clear categorical distinctions than are the forms of thinking used by other cultures. From personality types to taxonomies of plants and animals to the ten loci of systematic theology, bounded-set logic permeates our lives. We think in terms of opposites and simplistic categories: good versus bad, rich versus poor, and literate versus illiterate.[9] Historically, an American is either Republican or Democrat, blue collar or white collar, liberal or conservative, modern or postmodern, and environmentalist or industrialist. Postmodern thought has been eroding these categories for the last several years, but either/or categories continue to permeate a great deal of American logic. "Bounded sets are fundamental to our understanding of order. We want uniform categories."[10] Going deep to see this form of logic allows us to engage in the dynamic process of interpretive CQ.

I was brought up in the subculture of fundamentalism. Nowadays, that term applies as much to Islamic extremist groups such as al-Qaeda as it does to Baptist dispensationalists. But the term originated in the 1920s to refer to militant evangelicals. An American fundamentalist was said to be "an evangelical who is militant in opposition to liberal theology in the churches or to changes in cultural values or mores."[11] The fundamentalist movement in which I was reared was committed to an idea called secondary separation. This is the epitome of bounded-set reasoning. Secondary separation came from the conviction that to remain pure one must remove oneself from any hint of worldly influence. It was unacceptable to associate with people of other faiths in any kind of relationship beyond an evangelistic one. Baptist pastors shouldn't collaborate in community events with Jewish rabbis or Catholic priests, and, yes, Jews and Catholics were put in the same category. Anyone who wasn't in "our" category was in the "other" category. But secondary separation created harder boundary lines than just those. It maintained that you also shouldn't associate with anyone who associated with those in the other category. So if a like-minded church up the road associated with people following Billy Graham's ecumenical approach, we wouldn't associate with that church. The boundaries were clearly determined, though consistency was pretty difficult. What kind of library could a pastor have if the only options were books by authors who draw the lines in the same places and authors who only associate with people who draw the lines in those places? And the points of delineation grew even more extreme among some fundamentalist Christians who followed third- and fourth-degrees of separation.

These examples might feel extreme compared to the shape of American evangelicalism today. But notice the bounded-set thinking behind these comments that surfaced in the research: "I was really tracking with this guy who came to candidate for youth pastor until he said Brian McLaren's writings really shaped his thinking."

This senior pastor felt that acknowledging McLaren's writings must mean this candidate aligned himself with everything that Brian McLaren, a key voice in the Emergent Church movement, represents. The Emergent Church movement is a controversial twenty-first-century movement of Christians who are reconstructing the faith in light of postmodernity. I'm increasingly frustrated by the ways the Emergent Church issue is polarizing many churches and Christians. Bounded-set thinking leads many church leaders to immediately label people one way or another. I've heard countless stories that reflect this pastor's sentiment, that simply reading or being shaped by McLaren automatically puts someone in the category of aligning himself with all that McLaren thinks. And it works both ways. I've heard Emergent Church proponents discount many of the valuable works of D. A. Carson on the New Testament simply because they don't agree with his harsh critique of the Emergent Church.

We apply our bounded-set thinking to our politics as well. In one of the focus groups discussing interracial church relationships, one white pastor said, "I know African Americans more typically vote for Democratic candidates, but how can they vote for these guys who are pro-abortion?"

I remember the consternation in our home when born-again Jimmy Carter was running as the Democratic candidate for president against divorced Hollywood star Ronald Reagan as the Republican candidate. As Canadian citizens, my parents didn't have to make a decision, but many of their friends were forced to choose one sacred category over another. In more recent days, I've sat with some leaders from the Emergent Church movement who can't fathom how any kind of thoughtful Christian who cares for the poor could vote Republican. Bounded-set thinking can be found on both sides of the Emergent/Non-Emergent poles. And bounded-set thinking is often the reason that many American Christians make their voting decisions based on a single issue. The subculture of Christianity isn't alone in this, however. There are many in the homosexual subculture whose bounded-set nature also leads them to practice single-issue voting, such as, "What's the candidate's view on homosexual marriage?"

When talking with a new acquaintance, what might that person say or do that would prompt you to view him or her as someone with whom you don't connect or belong? Which authors or bands would the person need to reference? What political views would she or he need to espouse? How would tattoos, an effeminate voice, or extremely conservative clothes make you classify a new acquaintance? Honestly answering these kinds of questions nurtures the awareness we talked about at the beginning of our journey into the depths of interpretive CQ. And it moves us toward thinking about how we categorize people and issues.

Step away from these examples for a moment and consider the pervasive influence of bounded-set logic throughout American life as a whole. The cultural artifacts in our homes make this obvious. We want forks with forks and knives with knives. The walls of a room are usually uniform in color, and when a creative shift in color does occur, it usually happens at a corner or along a straight line midway down the wall. Pictures are framed with straight edges, molding covers up seams in the wall, and lawns are edged to form a clear line between the sidewalk and the lawn. Why? Because we're so strongly shaped by creating boundaries and keeping the boundaries clean. And cleanliness itself is largely defined by the degree of order that exists. It has little to do with sanitation and far more to do with whether things appear to be in their proper place. "Maintaining boundaries is essential in a bounded-set world, otherwise categories begin to disintegrate and chaos sets in."[12]

Make no mistake about it. I'm terminally American when it comes to my love for order. There's far too much dust and who knows what else around me in my office, but I can't write unless things are organized and in their "proper place."

Most Americans want dandelion-free lawns and roads with clear lanes prescribing where to drive and where not to drive. Men wear ties to cover the adjoining fabric on our shirts that we put on before going to the symphony, where we listen to classical music based on a scale with seven notes and five half steps. Each note "has a fixed pitch, defined in terms of the lengths of the sound waves it produces."[13] A good performance occurs when the musicians hit the notes precisely.

In contrast, many Eastern cultures have little concern in everyday life for sharp boundaries and uniform categories. Different colors of paint may be used at various places on the same wall. And the paint may well "spill" over onto the window glass and ceiling. Meals are a fascinating array of ingredients where food is best enjoyed when mixed together on your plate.

Let's go back to my friend Vijay. What do you assume occurred when I tell you Vijay became a Christian? A bounded-set definition of someone becoming a Christian would usually include a verbal affirmation of belief in a specific set of doctrines and a prescribed set of behavior. Given his Hindu background, most of us would probably be interested in knowing whether Vijay has fully renounced Hinduism—an interesting challenge when you consider "Hindu" means "Indian" and "Indian" means "Hindu." The bounded-set approach is concerned about when and how Vijay crossed the boundary from being outside the Christian circle to inside it. Conversion is seen as a "single dramatic crossing of the boundary between being a *non-Christian* and being a *Christian*. We would expect all believers to enter by the same door, share the same basic theological doctrines, and behave in the same basic way."[14]

The boundary of being a Christian is protected carefully in bounded-set thinking. Historically, Western churches have been careful not to baptize people until there's certainty that the individual knows and affirms the church's creed and follows its practices. The precise things that make up the boundary vary across denominational and theological contexts. In many church contexts, the sinner's prayer, followed by baptism, church attendance and eventually membership, witnessing, and not smoking would be among the central boundaries by which Vijay would be deemed legitimately "in."

In bounded-set organizational cultures, people accept the rules of the organization before being allowed into membership. The boundaries provide walls of demarcation and define identity. As a result, the primary role of leaders in these cultural contexts is to move people across the boundary into the set.[15]

Another expression of bounded-set thinking within American Christianity is the strong emphasis on the radical differences between Christianity and other faiths. Everything that comes from other religions is viewed as pagan and false, so the boundaries of Christianity need to be protected.[16] Many readers may struggle with my Buddhist reference to mindfulness in the last chapter because bounded-set logic would say we shouldn't be spending any time with something that comes from a pagan religion. A bounded-set approach to Christianity radically disowns anything from a different religion, even if it could have a place in our faith, for fear that it promotes syncretism. For that matter, Baptists in bounded-set cultures are often suspicious of practices used in the Catholic Church, such as Lent, and Catholics in bounded-set cultures are often resistant to extemporaneous worship services more akin to life in an evangelical megachurch.

Rob Bell, founding pastor of Mars Hill Bible Church in Grand Rapids, Michigan, describes a Christian lecturer who said, "If you deny God made the world in six twenty-four-hour days, you've denied Jesus died on the cross." Bell writes, "It's a bizarre leap of logic to make."[17] But it *is* "logical" from a bounded-set approach. For this creationist, six-day creation is part of the boundary that makes someone "in." Subcultures within American Christianity create different boundaries, but this creationist has lots of company in looking for boundaries such as six-day creation to determine whether someone is really a Christian.

Bell takes a lot of heat for his follow-up commentary to this illustration, in which he asks what happens if we were to discover that some of our other boundaries weren't true or relevant. Would our whole faith fall apart? For a bounded-set way of thinking, it *would* fall apart because the boundary is what holds it all together.

Bounded-set thinking has strongly permeated American life and hence American Christianity for centuries. I don't expect it to go away anytime soon. But the influences of postmodernism are causing many among the younger generational cultures to be less inclined toward a bounded-set approach to life and faith. And the hard-line boundaries are gradually eroding across North American churches for many generational groups. Many American believers resist being bound to any particular church or denomination based on a particular set of beliefs and rules. "This situation is illustrated by the widespread tendency to make the process of becoming a church member as simple and unchallenging as possible."[18]

Denominations are feeling the shift away from bounded-set thinking. Denominations used to provide parishioners with a clearly defined identity. People could travel from one church in the denomination to another, and the culture within those churches would have a uniform commonality. Members knew what it meant to belong, and constitutions described clear processes for getting in and what would cause someone to be voted out. But those boundaries are gradually weakening.

I'm not sure we're moving away from bounded-set thinking. Instead, it seems we're often just replacing the old boundaries with new ones. It used to be that good Christians didn't smoke, dance, or drink. Perhaps today the boundaries are that good Christians have read the *Purpose Driven Life*, stand against homosexuality, and support Christian-based movies. The boundaries themselves may be good or bad. But the Hebrew way of seeing the world, centered-set thinking, offers us an entirely different way that still allows for the redemptive values important to us as followers of Jesus.

Centered Sets

A centered-set way of thinking is not *determined* by its boundary, though it may have one. It is determined by its center. If the objects to be organized are moving toward the center, they are considered to be in the set. In this case, anything moving toward becoming an apple, such as an apple bud or blossom, can easily be considered an apple, even though it looks nothing like the "boundaries" used by Westerners to define an apple.

Objects that in some sense may be considered near the center but moving away from it are seen to be outside the set. Thus, the boundary is determined by the relation of the objects to the center and not by essential characteristics of the objects themselves. The emphasis is on the center and the relationship to the center rather than on the boundary.

Labeling me a "man" in light of my DNA, my appearance, and my anatomy is a bounded-set label of who I am. Many bounded-set cultures and subcultures further define manhood by several more boundaries, such as appropriate roles, dress, hobbies, and interests. But concluding I'm a "man" because I'm a father or a brother creates the classification in light of a centering reference point (my children, their mother, my siblings, our parents, etc.) rather than emphasizing the boundaries as making the classification. There *is* still a clear boundary. I'm a man or I'm not, but centered-set logic places the emphasis on who I am in relation to others rather than on the boundaries.

We've considered the ways that many Western ministry leaders draw on bounded-set thinking, albeit subconsciously, to define what classifies someone as a Christian. In contrast, many Eastern Christians are less concerned about identifying the boundaries that characterize someone as being a Christian. Instead, the focus is on the center; thus if someone is moving toward Jesus, the values he represents, and his followers, those factors more clearly define someone as a Christian than do boundaries established around a prescribed set of doctrines or behaviors.

How would someone with centered-set logic determine whether Vijay is a Christian? Christians are deemed to be followers of Jesus when they make him the center or Lord of their lives and join in covenant community with others who are following in the way of Jesus. A Christian using centered-set logic might claim Vijay must have some basic knowledge about Jesus, but the mental assent itself is not what classifies him as a Christian. Someone is a Christian when that person has made a covenant commitment to personally follow Jesus and join the community of Christians not because she or he independently and intrinsically has accepted the Christian creeds and said the right prayer.[19]

Christians from cultures using a centered-set approach still acknowledge that a clear separation exists between Christians and non-Christians, but they invest little energy in figuring out who is in and who is out. Instead, the emphasis is on calling everyone to follow Jesus, whether it be someone who has been walking toward him for fifty years or someone who is hearing about him for the first time. The call is always the same: "Follow Jesus." As a result, centered-set logic finds little reason to pit ourselves against those who aren't "in" as a way to preserve the purity of the set. "You rarely defend the things you love. You enjoy them and tell others about them and invite others to enjoy them with you."[20]

This kind of perspective recognizes that a great degree of variation exists among Christians. Hiebert writes, "By recognizing variance in the set and the need for growth, a centered-set approach avoids the dilemma between offering cheap grace that allows new believers to become Christians but leads to a shallow church or costly grace that preserves the purity of the church but keeps them out of the kingdom."[21]

As a result, when we move from a bounded-set approach to a centered-set approach to mission, we emphasize the lordship of Jesus and calling everyone to him as the best way to live rather than investing undue energy in proving other religions false. Ministry cultures shaped by centered-set reasoning constantly invite people to move into covenant relationship with a discipleship community. This kind of church is open to all who may want to be on this journey. "It has a permeability that is open to others since it seeks to draw others alongside and minister to people at every level on the way."[22] Hiebert reflects on the ways this more centered approach to mission plays out on the mission field. He writes, "A mission with a bounded view of Christianity baptized only a few 'converts' after twenty years of ministry in a West African city. Another mission, with a centered-set view of conversion, baptized two hundred in the first year of its ministry in the same city."[23]

Boundaries still exist in a centered-set way of thinking about the faith. But the boundaries emerge in relationship to the center and from those who gravitate toward the center. "The center has an identity and location among a people. Here the language of the 'city on a hill' is appropriate."[24] For the purposes of cultural intelligence, it seems there are greater strengths inherent to a centered-set approach to classifying the world than to a bounded-set approach. A weakness of the centered-set approach, taken to extremes, could be that someone might end up thinking that any kind of boundary is wrong. Boundaries are needed at some point; but when categories emerge in light of the center, the boundaries form in relationship to the center rather than being created for the safety and clarity of having boundaries in and of themselves.

The Israelites' identity was rooted in their covenant relationship with God, and therefore as people in community. They were to marry insiders, not outsiders. The boundaries were the result, not the deciding factor. "The primary values were relational in character: justice, shalom, love, and mercy."[25]

All cultures use both centered sets and bounded sets to classify the world. But cultures tend to focus on one reasoning approach more than the other as the basic building blocks for constructing their worlds. A metaphor sometimes used to help clarify bounded versus centered sets is fences versus wells. Most farmers in the United States build fences around the land where their animals roam as a way to keep their livestock in and the livestock of neighboring farms out. But in many rural communities around the world fencing is not an option, either because of the cost or because of the expansiveness of the region. In many of these places, such as several ranches across Australia, farmers use wells instead. They sink a bore and create a well in order to provide a precious water supply in the middle of the outback. "It is assumed that livestock, though they will stray, will never roam too far from the well, lest they die. . . . As long as there is a supply of clean water, the livestock will remain close by."[26] I'd rather see Jesus as a well of water to which we're drawn to slake our thirst than view him in light of boundaries that keep me in. Interpretive CQ is committed to exploring the discoveries that come from seeing how we organize our thinking.

Conclusion

Metacognitive, or interpretive, CQ is thinking about how we think. And it's also thinking about how others think. All this abstraction isn't a distraction from getting to the place where we better express love for the Other. Going deep to see the ways others and ourselves categorize the world is an integral part of reaching across the chasm of cultural difference.

A couple of years ago, my friend Vijay, who was teaching in the Chicago area, traveled to Delhi the same week I did. I was there en route to teach in Chandigarh, a city three hours away, and he was lecturing at a nearby university for a couple of days. We decided to grab dinner together in Delhi. He stopped by the YMCA with his driver to pick me up. As we began driving the Delhi streets at rush hour, I commented, "It just cracks me up how the lanes mean nothing here." Vijay replied, "Ah, but it's not that they mean nothing, Dave. It's that they're flexible." I laughed, "Yeah! That's one way of describing it." "No! Seriously!" he replied. "The lanes ebb and flow as needed depending on the volume of traffic. It's not static like the Eisenhower [a congested Chicago-area highway]. On the Eisenhower, you have traffic gridlock going one direction in the morning and an open highway on the other side. By 3:00 it's the opposite. Here the space is available for whichever vehicle needs it most, depending on the time of day."

Soon Vijay and I arrived at the restaurant. I listened to the atonal (to me) music serenading us in the background, quite a contrast to the classical music Linda teaches her piano students back home. After we ordered our meal, I said, "So, Vijay, I've never really heard how you became a Christian. I'd love to hear your story."

He started by saying, "Well, I'm *still* becoming a Christian, Dave." I had enough cultural intelligence not to start preaching to him just yet. But his was unlike most "salvation testimonies" I've heard. Three hours later, Vijay was still going strong in telling me about the many years he had been on a journey toward Jesus, from as far back as his years in primary school. He talked about the local Christian evangelist who stuck up for him as a seven-year-old when some older kids in the village were picking on him. He grew teary-eyed when he recalled the Swedish missionary who paid the bond to free him at age twelve from enslavement to the storeowner to which his parents were indebted. Then he told me about the day he put a picture of Jesus up on the wall in his parents' home to join the other gods hanging there. And there was the miraculous healing of the Christian neighbor's son, which was in part the reason that Vijay prayed a year straight that he would be able to study medicine in the States. He brought some other gods along with him to the States, but one night after spending a weekend with his "adopted family" in the Chicago area, a Christian family, he decided to put all his other gods away and make Jesus his only God.

I began to understand a centered-set way of thinking about conversion. Knowing when he "crossed the line" didn't seem very important to me. Even as we sat there in the dimly lit restaurant, Vijay was drawing me closer to Jesus through his story. This was yet another part of my own journey in moving toward Jesus and, in turn, becoming more culturally intelligent about how I view the world and the Other. Thanks, Vijay!

Recommended Resources

Frost, Michael, and Alan Hirsch. *The Shaping of Things to Come: Innovation and Mission for the 21st-Century Church.* Peabody, MA: Hendrickson, 2003.

Hiebert, Paul. *Anthropological Reflections on Missiological Issues.* Grand Rapids: Baker Academic, 1994.

11

being okay with gray

Category Width

The journey continues. Love. That's why we're trekking along this CQ pathway. Understand. That's the beginning of the journey. Go deep. That's the part of the journey we're currently exploring. We're looking deep within ourselves and into the Other to improve how we relate. The ways in which we label and categorize the world have something to teach us about what lies beneath the tip of the iceberg. The last chapter began with a brief description of attribution theory—learning how people classify the world. Interpretive, or metacognitive, CQ is thinking about thinking. Therefore, when we step back to think about how we categorize the world, we're making progress in becoming more culturally intelligent. The way we process information is culturally determined, so an understanding of how the thinking processes of people in various cultural contexts work is an important and necessary skill. Although all this critical reflection might seem irrelevant to the real demands of serving and leading in culturally intelligent ways, these very disciplines are what make interpretive CQ the key linking process between knowledge CQ and behavioral CQ. It's all part of the expedition toward loving people of difference in ways that more clearly reflect Jesus.

One more aspect of attribution theory is directly relevant to interpretive CQ: the notion of category width. We've noted that many things in the world don't neatly fit into our preexisting categories, regardless of whether we use bounded-set or centered-set logic. Our ability to deal with ambiguity, tension, and paradox is all part of what we want to explore through this chapter. We'll spend time familiarizing ourselves with the notion of category width, discuss its relevance to cultural intelligence, and talk about the particular tensions this creates for a Christian perspective on the world.

Category width refers to the number of events individuals place under one common label.[1] It has some similarities and overlap with bounded-set and centered-set logic but is distinct in that it specifically looks at how cultures socialize their members to tolerate things that don't neatly fall into one category or another. Category width exposes the reality that individuals, largely due to the cultures in which they are socialized, differ consistently in the extent to which they use broad or narrow categories for labeling the world. Some people are consistently wide categorizers, while others are consistently narrow. The hypothesis is that the breadth one uses in categorizing things extends across all types of judgments. Going deep to see how we think about things that don't neatly conform to our experience and understanding is an essential part of the interpretive CQ process.

Narrow categorizers focus on differences. Things must be very similar to be put into the same category, so they look for what is different. This tends to correlate with bounded-set thinking, where clear boundaries define what places something or someone into a category or classification and what keeps others out. Narrow categorizers watch the behavior of people from different cultures and categorize them based on what those actions would mean in one's own cultural context. A narrow categorizer has subconscious lists that include words that should be used by educated people, clothes that shouldn't appear on Christians, and norms for how married couples should relate. When there isn't a category in which to place the behavior of an individual, narrow categorizers judge it as an exception and don't entertain it as possibly being another whole category altogether.[2] Those with narrow category width are much quicker to characterize things as right versus wrong.

Broad categorizers focus more on similarities and demonstrate more tolerance for things that might not fit into preexisting categories. And a broad categorizer is more willing to place discrepant things in the same category. For example, this kind of individual may be much more content talking about Lutherans, Assemblies of God, Eastern Orthodox, and Catholics all in the same category of Christians, or just as likely, he or she might be more ready to believe that not everyone faithfully attending the local E-Free church is necessarily a follower of Jesus. Broad categorizers might be quicker to acknowledge that healthy parent-child relationships in one cultural context might include monthly, planned times together such as "date-nights," but that particular custom may be nonexistent among healthy families in another cultural context. Broad categorizers are much more apt to apply new behaviors observed cross-culturally into a category of "different" rather than right versus wrong or normal versus abnormal (see fig. 7).

Broad categorizers are more likely to have heightened cultural intelligence because they have a greater ability to accept a wider range of items in a particular category. Broad categorizers are more flexible in their thinking, and they're more open to understanding that different behaviors can have the same meanings and the same behavior can have different meanings. For example, two guys holding hands in American culture would likely be categorized as homosexual. The same behavior in Bangladesh would likely be categorized as an expression of friendship. Or a tribal woman walking around with exposed breasts might be put into an immoral category by many American Christians, but in many cultures no such categorization would occur. Such issues are addressed by the category-width concept.

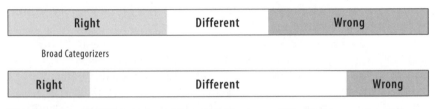

Figure 7. Category Width. (Adapted from T. F. Pettigrew, "The Measurement and Correlates of Category Width as a Cognitive Variable," *Journal of Personality* 26 [1958]: 532–44.)

Category Width and Culture

Category width is a variable of individual difference. Some people are narrow categorizers, and others are broad. But culture plays a significant role in socializing an individual more toward one end or the other. Richard Detweiler, a cross-cultural psychologist who has devoted a great deal of study to category width, writes, "Within any given culture, individuals should vary in their category width, but whether the variation is distributed toward the narrower or wider end would be expected to be a manifestation of cultural differences."[3]

Consequently, the number of different behaviors that are acceptable within a given culture is largely a reflection of where that culture lies on category-width differences. "A narrow categorizer might be less able than a broad categorizer to classify the different behavior of a person from another culture into the normal, acceptable category."[4] People in narrow-width church cultures are unnerved when the slightest change happens in the order of service or when there is a shift in how worship is led. People in broader-width church cultures are more likely to enjoy different genres and expressions of music and worship week after week. People coming from a generational subculture with narrow category width will have many right-versus-wrong views about how husbands and wives should relate, expecting those relationships to mirror their own. Broad categorizers will acknowledge that there are many different ways husbands and wives can relate. Some marriages might have dual incomes, and some might be solely dependent on one spouse's income. Some will schedule quarterly getaways, and others will never vacation apart from their kids. Both kinds of categorizers will have practices that fall into distinctions of right versus wrong, but the broad categorizers have much more room for practices that fall into the "different" category, rather than making almost everything a right-versus-wrong issue.

There's a high level of correlation between category width and where a culture falls on the scale of risk avoidance (described in chapter 8). Tight cultures where risk avoidance is high tend to be narrow categorizers, whereas loose cultures with a low risk avoidance embrace creativity and risk taking and, as a result, are more apt to apply that risk orientation in the ways they categorize people and things. Jeff, the pastor who had a short tenure at the church where they flipped out over the change in the bulletin template, was likely dealing with a very narrow-category-width church culture.

There is also correlation between logic sets and category width, but neither is a predictive variable of the other. The emphasis of bounded-set thinking on hard boundaries seems to correlate positively with narrow category width. Yet many Western cultures use bounded-set logic but have ever-widening category width. Much of the developed world functions using bounded-set logic. However, most cultures in the developed world socialize their members to be broad categorizers than many cultures in the developing world do. This is largely due to the increasingly cosmopolitan, diverse nature of many Western cultures; therefore, rules are limited, and the ones that do exist are imposed loosely. Younger generational cultures in the West are far more tolerant of difference than many among the older generational cultures. For example, 75 percent of eighteen- to thirty-four-year-old Americans think it's okay to be homosexual, whereas 50 percent of those over fifty-five do not.[5] Tolerance is lauded as a very important value in the West. So American culture as a whole is believed to nurture broad categorizers even though it leans toward bounded-set logic.

Category-width measurements have been used to predict overseas success by expatriates. Research has consistently found that broad categorizers have more success cross-culturally than narrow categorizers do.[6] Duane Elmer of Trinity International University writes, "A person with narrow categories has some tendencies that can hinder relationships. For example, narrow categorizers tend to be more ethnocentric, more reactionary and seek less information before forming judgments. Wider categorizers, on the other hand, tend to seek more information before making judgments and are more likely to put cultural differences in a neutral category rather than in the 'wrong' category."[7]

Elmer says that he begins his graduate courses on cross-cultural communication by telling students the course will serve their marriages or their relationships with their roommates more than anything else. At the most basic level, one can begin to see the notion of category width in the level of tolerance our roommates or spouses have for various ways of hanging the toilet paper, different ways to cook spaghetti, and ways to trim the Christmas tree, if there is a tree! Those same sensitivities are needed as we interact with groups of people coming from varying cultures.

Category Width and Christianity

The widening category width throughout American culture and the shift toward increased tolerance for many different moral choices run into conflict with some of the core tenets of Christianity. How does category width fit with the theological framework we established in chapter 2, which should direct our thinking about cultural intelligence? We considered the need to embrace the realities of the kingdom whenever we find them in a culture and to protest those realities conflicting with kingdom values. But some of the greatest challenges lie in those many expressions of culture that don't neatly fall into either category. What do we do with those cultural nuances that are not clearly right or wrong but are merely different? The degree to which we're even comfortable thinking about that notion is directly connected to our category width. And doing the hard work of going deep to think about this idea enhances our interpretive CQ.

Let me talk about my own journey toward becoming a broad categorizer. The fundamentalist subculture in which I was reared operated with extremely narrow category width. There were clear categories of right versus wrong. The length of your hair, the clothes worn, the beat of the music, attendance at movie theaters, and the times when church should meet were clear issues of right versus wrong. Very few things fell into the category of being neither right nor wrong but simply different. The category of "different" was reserved for inconsequential things such as your favorite flavor of ice cream, and even then, it had better not be something like rum raisin. That might veer too close to the "wrong" category of behavior. I'm serious! We were taught to find God's will for everything from our career and mate choices to how we should spend a Sunday afternoon. Gray areas should just be avoided.

The longer I've worked through my understanding of the faith and the more I've encountered people in various places around the world, the larger my category of "difference" has become. This has often been unnerving to some people who know me from my fundamentalist past. Don't get me wrong. I'm not suggesting everything is up for grabs or that nothing falls into the right-versus-wrong categories anymore. In fact, I have things in those categories that previously were not even part of my thinking. For example, today I have strong convictions about discrimination, the abuse of power, and how we treat the environment. Those issues weren't even part of my consciousness in my earlier years. But many things that used to seem like clear categories of right versus wrong have become more blurred to me.

The tension lies in the fact that Christianity, at its core, predisposes us to espouse universal morals that apply regardless of cultural variance. There is wide agreement among Christians around the world that there are some defined categories of right versus wrong. Many other faiths also affirm universal perspectives on morality. Local culture is not given complete liberty or authority to define and construct morality to be whatever it wants. There are some universal issues of morality that apply regardless of culture. For example, almost all Christians see the disregard for human life as wrong, not something simply to be left up to a culture's own interpretation and values. And Christianity is opposed to corruption and embezzlement by businesses, governments, and religions regardless of the cultural norms. It holds that it is not simply the option of a culture to socially construct a moral code that allows for these kinds of practices. Instead, Christians believe that the morals taught and lived by Jesus supersede cultural notions of ethics.

Category width is one of the areas I've been exploring in my research examining the cultural intelligence of ministry leaders as they function in various cultural domains. The ministry leaders examined across multiple studies displayed varying degrees of category width, but most of the subjects tended toward being narrow categorizers. This could be seen in everything from how they viewed denominational differences to leadership practices and biblical interpretation. Notice a few of the comments exemplifying the overarching presence of narrow category width among the subjects surveyed. In talking about the challenges he faced as a campus-based counselor working with international students, Dean said: "I think so much of this comes down to love marriages versus arranged marriages. Many of these couples don't even know each other when they get married. It's no wonder their relationships are so dysfunctional. One of the things we work on is trying to help them see that a marriage based upon a courtship of love and understanding will be a much better option for them and their children."

I asked Dean if he was saying arranged marriages are "wrong"? He was resistant to labeling them as "wrong," but he said, "I think it's fair to say they're inferior." Ironically, I've talked with young Christian men in India who have said to me, "We've heard some American Christians have *love* marriages. Is that really true?" They had no category for thinking a Bible-reading Christian would pursue anything other than accepting the spouse chosen by his or her extended families. Both views are demonstrations of narrow category width.

Sandy, a youth pastor near Charlotte, North Carolina, said, "Nothing causes more problems in our ministry than the homeschooled families. Their heads are in the sand and their kids are not learning to be salt and light. How can I teach them that being a biblically responsible parent and citizen would be sending their kids to a quality school where they get social interaction with others and can be incarnational instead of cloistered in a holy huddle?"

And Jake, a church planter in Michigan, said, "We're really trying to get back to the Early Church model—meeting in one another's homes and getting rid of so many of the trappings that exist in many churches today. The traditional churches are so stuck with all these rituals that have little to do with the New Testament church and the megachurches just put all their energy into their weekly show. I'm not trying to say we have it figured out, but we're trying to do church without all the trappings of tradition and culture."

A good researcher is not supposed to intervene with judgmental, leading questions, but I couldn't hold back on this one. I asked Jake, "Which early church model are you trying to replicate?" "What do you mean?" he asked. So grateful he took my bait, I jumped in, saying, "Most New Testament scholars would say there was no such thing as one normative church in the first century. Some met in homes, others in town halls, some in synagogues, and some met outside along the river. Isn't there a place for all different kinds of churches?"

I can join the rants about megachurches or traditional churches as much as anyone. But I can't write off the megachurch where I'm an elder as being nothing more than a show. Nor can I write off the very traditional, denominationally based churches—churches where many of my friends worship—as being trapped in stale practices. And during my youth ministry days, I saw strengths and weaknesses in all different kinds of educational approaches among various high school students. Narrow category width predisposes us to elevate our preferences to the "right" category and to see the rest as "wrong."

The issue of category width presents the greatest challenge when it relates to hermeneutics and teaching the Bible. The various studies examining cultural intelligence in American ministry leaders reveal their subjects' limited awareness of how significantly culture shapes the way one reads the Bible and hence views morality. Most of the ministry leaders missed out on the rich hermeneutical treasure that exists in encountering fellow Christians in another part of the world who hold to some similar presuppositions of Jesus's moral teaching but often interpret it differently.

In my dissertation research that examined the short-term training trips done by North American pastors, the subjects kept talking about the importance of teaching only biblical principles. In their minds, as long as they exclusively taught principles rather than describing specific programs in their churches, the teaching would be transcultural. Subjects frequently said things like, "We teach timeless, transferable principles; therefore, our biblical teaching applies worldwide, whatever the context." There was limited cultural intelligence evident in that the North American pastors failed to see the ways the principles they taught were embedded in cultural narratives.[8]

New Testament seminary professor Mark Powell describes how culture shapes the way Americans, Russians, and Tanzanians differently interpret the parable of the prodigal son. He compares their responses to questions like, "Why does the young man end up starving in the pigpen?"

- All the American readers responded to this question by saying the prodigal ended up starving in the pigpen because he squandered the money he "inherited."
- Nearly all the Russian readers (84 percent) said it was because of the famine.
- And nearly all the Tanzanian readers (80 percent) said it was because no one gave him anything to eat.[9]

Which is the *right* interpretation? Look at the text in Luke 15:13–16. "The younger son got together all he had, set off for a distant country and there *squandered his wealth in wild living*" (v. 13, my italics). So the Americans are right—yes? But hang on. The next verse says, "After he had spent everything, *there was a severe famine* in that whole country, and he began to be in need" (my italics). This fits with the Russian interpretation. And verse 16 supports the Tanzanian interpretation, "He longed to fill his stomach with the pods that the pigs were eating, *but no one gave him anything*" (my italics).

A narrow categorizer would have difficulty believing there can be more than one legitimate interpretation of this story. Allowing for a wider categorization—that is, acknowledging that there are different, viable interpretations—doesn't mean there are no wrong interpretations. Not all interpretations are equally valid. But Bible students with equal concern for authorial intent can arrive at different readings of the same passage, even if they all go back to the original language. Our cultural context shapes everything we see and think.

Given the ubiquitous role of culture in shaping how we read and teach Scripture, Eddie Gibbs of Fuller Seminary challenges us to rethink how we train pastors and church leaders. He writes,

> Whereas the training of church professionals provides a good grounding in biblical languages, exegesis, and church history, it is deficient in equipping students to critically engage their culture, and to exercise the risk-taking, entrepreneurial leadership that many will have to provide in leading their churches through a time of transition and revisioning. We have too quickly claimed that while methods may change, the message remains the same. Such an attitude indicates a lack of awareness of the extent to which our cultural biases and theological blinders cause us to overlook important truths in Scripture. We cannot simply assume we have got it right without re-examining the text in light of fresh questions and with the intellectual prodding of Christians from other traditions and cultures.[10]

Where do we draw the line between differing valid interpretations of Scripture and inappropriate syncretism that compromises the truth of the gospel? Richard Cunningham's words are a helpful encouragement and caution: "Our challenge is always to remain open to a new word from God or a new breeze of the Holy Spirit without being enticed by every siren's song that catches our ears. Throughout the universal church, we must learn how to say 'no' as well as how to say 'yes' to local theologies and how to achieve the wisdom to know when to do which."[11]

Dean Flemming suggests four criteria from the New Testament that can guide us as we seek to recognize both the possibilities and the parameters of a category of difference.[12] First, the biblical witness to what God has done in Jesus is core. All interpretations of Scripture must be tested against the revealed gospel in Scripture (1 Cor. 15:3–5, 11; Gal. 1:6–9; 2:1–21). "The gospel is not an empty form into which everyone is free to pour his or her own content."[13] Second, all interpretations must be guided by the Spirit, who leads the community into all truth (John 16:13). Third, all Christians in different local contexts must be willing to test their interpretations in light of the wider Christian community.

We've seen this exemplified from as far back as the Jerusalem Council. And finally, Flemming suggests authentic contextualization must bear "fruit in the furtherance of Christian mission and the transformation of individuals and the community."[14]

God is the source of all knowledge. I am confident there is an objective body of knowledge that constitutes universal truth, some of which is discernible as belonging to right and wrong categories. At the same time, the way we come to know universal truth is always shaped by our context. We come to know the Bible and its truth experientially and through the working of the Holy Spirit among those who are in covenant relationship with God through Christ. The acquisition of knowledge must happen in community with the people of God, past, present, and future. Although some universal truth is knowable empirically, a great deal of it is not and must be accepted purely on faith. It is with faith more than reason that I accept the Bible as the objective source of God's truth, although even the Bible has been written and rewritten through many revisionist lenses. I further interpret it through my own revisionist lens. This doesn't mean we can't know anything with certainty, nor does it mean that all interpretations are equally valid. But our interpretive CQ will be enhanced by living in the tension of universal morals that we come to know and experience in community with others.

It's easy to identify the narrow category width of those we might view as intolerant fundamentalist groups. We can point to the cultural blinding that comes from thinking one style of music is the only right way to worship or how continuing the Awana program suddenly gets leveraged as an issue of right versus wrong.

We must beware, however, because we're all susceptible to employing narrow category width in viewing different aspects of ministry according to our cultural bias. Earlier, I mentioned our tendency to do this in the way we think about leadership. The temptation can be to biblicize our preferred model of leadership, whether more hierarchical or more flat, and to proof text the other model as wrong. In our earlier discussion about this, we acknowledged the existence of evil within all models of leadership. But we have to be leery of too quickly throwing a whole cultural model of leadership into a right-versus-wrong category.

Or take an issue such as vegetarianism. What group might be stereotyped as more tolerant, open-minded, and progressive than a group of Christian vegetarians? Yet many vegetarians display low category width by looking down on meat eaters as inferior and less informed. Richard Rohr says, "I'm not against vegetarianism, but if it's used as our new way to be in control and morally superior, we are not enlightened. While crunching organic carrots, some assure their egos bite by bite, 'I am right.' Health can become the new name of salvation. . . . How can we be fully present to another human being if all we see is their eating habits so we can judge them accordingly?"[15]

Rohr goes on to describe the egocentric tendency among North American Christians to always seek a way to be right, while wanting to label the viewpoint of the Other as wrong or inferior. To a large extent, this impulse also exists in other cultures because of the fallen nature we all share as humans. But this tendency plays out in especially harmful ways with people who have narrow category width. There's a great deal of talk in Christian churches about belonging. I think there's something really right about that. We were created to live and belong together in community. The problem is, our attempts to bring about belonging and community often mean getting people into groups where everyone conforms to a similar set of norms. Homogeneous, affinity groups of belonging are found in churches as much as anywhere else, and there develops an unspoken call for group members to conform to similar taste in fashion, music, schooling, and other areas that aren't necessarily issues of right versus wrong. *To what degree do the people in your small group, church, or neighborhood all dress the same, like the same music, have the same political views, and enjoy the same forms of recreation?* Beware the ways homogeneity can hinder cultural intelligence.

A narrow-category-width approach makes us susceptible to elbowing ourselves into the morally superior position of being right, which of course means we look down on the Other as being "wrong." This is one of my fears for my church. Our church has a bent toward activism, one of the many things I love about it. We're not simply interested in pontificating about theological truth; we want to live it. We're committed to being a different kind of church in the world and responding to the injustices of oppression in our own city and in places around the world. If we're not careful, the very activist nature that energizes us to make a difference in the world can too quickly move us toward arrogantly viewing other churches in town as being morally inferior because they don't go about the gospel in quite the same way we do. The very thing we defend—the need to be a new kind of church in the world that wrestles with what the gospel looks like for this time and place—can be the very issue by which we're guilty of wrongly judging others. Apart from God transforming us, we could become one more church that thinks we have it figured out and everyone else doesn't "get it." "*Overly* zealous reforms tend to corrupt the reformers, while they remain incapable of seeing themselves as unreformed. We need less reformation and more transformation."[16]

Rohr says one of the reasons most social revolutions fail is that they self-destruct from within. People working for a revolution, whether they be the left, the right, liberals, conservatives, Emergent folks, or megachurch people, too quickly move from having the answer to thinking they themselves are the answer. Jesus emphasized transformation of our souls. Unless that happens, there is no revolution. This is at the heart of why category width matters. Transformation of the soul is ultimately what we're seeking with interpretive CQ, because as we become transformed, we inevitably love and serve in culturally intelligent ways. Going to these depths is hard work and at times painful and even scary. Perhaps you've already been feeling the widening of your category width, but you're afraid to admit it because it feels like you're going soft on Christianity.

> Stop and think about things you once had in your right-versus-wrong categories that aren't so clear to you anymore. Think about with whom you can discuss the shifts that have occurred in your way of seeing what's right, what's wrong, and what's gray, or grey.

Conclusion

By the end of a semester with me, my students often start counting the number of times they hear me say, "We have to embrace the tension." I make no apologies for being so redundant with that theme. It's countercultural for many of my students to see tension as something to embrace rather than to avoid and eradicate. It goes against the grain of narrow category width to embrace tension. Narrow categorizers want to lump as many things as possible into right-versus-wrong categories, pitting one pole against the other. But as we learn to widen our categories of difference, not carelessly but in community as the Spirit guides us along to understand what's truly right and wrong, we find ourselves freed by the discoveries that come in the midst of tension, difference, and paradox.

The journey into interpretive CQ requires an ability to grasp paradox rather than forced choice. As we learn to go deep, tolerate ambiguity, and explore the complex patterns elicited by the issues we've raised in this chapter, we can make great strides in deepening our interpretive CQ.

Leading with cultural intelligence doesn't mean there is no room for categories of right versus wrong. We've repeated that several times, but that point shouldn't be missed. It does mean that we should make more room for the category of difference and that we embrace the tension of two categories that might appear to be on opposite sides of an issue. This kind of complex thinking is "evoked by situations where two contradictory statements may be both true or where a statement may be true and not true at the same time, or when formal logic remains insufficient."[17] The culturally intelligent leader begins to see the assets and liabilities of love marriages and the assets and liabilities of arranged marriages. The same kind of tension is sought in viewing various schooling models or church models or approaches to diet or leadership. This is at the core of living with the tension of kingdom values that become incarnationally present in particular cultures.

Few things have tempted me to abort my participation in the journey toward cultural intelligence as much as the tiring, painful process of questioning the assumptions on which my faith is based. But persevering through that disorienting course has led me to an intensified passion and pursuit of Jesus. The times of wrestling with your faith and doctrine are part of what moves you along the pathway toward better loving God and the Other. Don't lose heart. Our doubts, questions, and probes into the mysterious waters beneath the tip of the iceberg are often what God uses most to change us so that we can be part of changing the world.

There's one more important stop we need to make in the deep probing that comes with interpretive CQ. It relates to the essential roles of theory and praxis to the development of cultural intelligence. We'll explore a very practical model for moving toward a theory-based approach to nurturing interpretive CQ in ourselves and others.

Recommended Resources

Elmer, Duane. *Cross-Cultural Servanthood: Serving the World in Christlike Humility.* Downers Grove, IL: InterVarsity, 2006.

12

theory gets a bum rap

A Model for Going Deep

Okay. So you'd expect a guy with a PhD working for a seminary, writing a book on cultural intelligence, to defend theory as something worthy of attention. Not to fear. I have no tolerance for theory that never gets cashed out into reality. I'm forever returning students' papers with comments such as, "But what does this look like for you? What does this mean for real-life ministry?" So I'm not interested in promoting theory for theory's sake. But neither am I interested in theory bashing or the similar current that often surfaces in ministry circles, that says, "Theology is impractical and irrelevant."

If you've followed me this far through the part on interpretive CQ, you must have some appreciation for the value of theory. The whole experience of going deep as we've done in the last three chapters can sound highly theoretical, but it's accomplished best in the midst of practice and social interaction. Theoretical frameworks such as logic sets and category width help us enrich future interactions. In this chapter, we'll synthesize what we've been examining throughout this part on interpretive CQ by considering the skill of critical reflection or praxis, a skill explored by educational theorists and practitioners. Just as cultural intelligence draws from the varied disciplines of anthropology, sociology, psychology, and business, it is also enhanced when combined with some of the work by educational researchers on transformative learning. There's a great deal of synergy between the discussion of praxis in transformative learning theories and interpretive CQ. We'll begin by examining an overview of praxis and its connection to cultural intelligence, and then we'll explore a model to help us become more intentional about facilitating praxis in ourselves and others.

Going Deep Takes Praxis

In the real world, learning and thinking are social activities, not academic amusements. My friend Steve Argue often says, "The classroom is the real world!" Some of you might be wincing, thinking, "No way! The real world of ministry is standing alongside a grieving parent or arbitrating a messy divorce." But Steve's point is that classrooms are filled with real people with real needs that aren't checked at the door. Our thinking is profoundly structured by our interaction with other people.

Paulo Freire, a Brazilian revolutionary who evolved a theory of education for oppressed people, said the ability to think abstractly and generate themes and reflect on them is what makes us human. Freire opposed grand schemes of liberation in which the rich and powerful come up with great ideas for helping impoverished, undereducated individuals. Instead, he argued that one of the most powerful ways to liberate oppressed people is to help them discover the skills to generate their own ideas and themes and to act on them.[1] Freire's work has all kinds of implications for how we engage in cross-cultural ministry, especially given that we're often entering cultural contexts from the position of the dominant, privileged culture working with underprivileged people in oppressed situations. In case you aren't familiar with Freire, let me briefly summarize his theory of education as a way of explaining praxis.

Freire positions his view of praxis in opposition to the "banking" concept of education, wherein knowledge lies solely with the teacher and the purpose of education is purely to deposit that knowledge into the minds of the students. He argues that a banking concept of education involves subordinating the students by making it seem as though there were no other way to see the world than the way the teacher has presented it. Any questioning of that system is wrong or sinful. You can see that the banking concept of education fits well with bounded-set logic and narrow category width.

In contrast, the emancipatory model of education presented and embodied by Freire is embedded in the process of humanizing people who have been oppressed. It focuses on empowering people to question their lives and position in society. As they become aware of their position in society, they begin to struggle against that reality. This struggle is at the core of praxis. It involves questioning what one knows and making a conscious decision to see the reasons for the reality one lives in. Freedom from oppression can only come when the oppressed struggle to see the world and become aware of how they see the world as compared to the way others do—interpretive CQ.

Praxis is the practice of becoming critically aware of how the values and assumptions of our cultural background shape the way we perceive, understand, and feel about our world. Through this awareness, we're freed to act on those reflections and change those assumptions that no longer seem valid when viewed against new readings, events, situations, and questions. Herein lies the freedom that comes from praxis. It creates a symbiotic loop between theory and experience. This is why praxis is a critical element for growing in interpretive CQ. It allows us to go deep and see what lies beneath the tip of the iceberg—the quest we've been on throughout the journey into interpretive CQ.

Donald Schön provides a model of praxis that needs to be explored as a crucial element for interpretive CQ. Schön looked at how professionals think in the course of their everyday work. In his study of the way architects, psychotherapists, engineers, town planners, and managers operated on the job, he describes the process as reflection in action. Inherent in the way professionals work is not just problem solving but problem setting, an activity that clearly has a theoretical component. The goal lies not in just finding answers but in formulating hypotheses, a highly theoretical activity. Schön argues that alongside reflection-in-action there is also a place for ancillary, outside-of-practice learning that enhances a practitioner's capacity to think in doing.[2] Ministry leaders need to learn praxis, reflection both behind and within their actions, particularly as they engage cross-culturally. We must learn to reflect in the midst of action and create space to step aside from our constant movement in order to contemplate, reflect, and prepare for future action.

Praxis is a valuable skill for everyone. It allows for a holistic approach to education that empowers people to perceive critically the ways they exist in their worlds. Praxis enables us to see ourselves, which potentially equips us to consciously move beyond cognitive patterns such as bounded-set logic and narrow category width and into creative tensions such as the kingdom-culture axis (fig. 3) or the paradoxical discussion we had about "average Americans" having some key points of difference from other Americans.

The ability to theorize fosters functional self-awareness, the very place we began in discussing interpretive CQ. As we noted in chapter 9, awareness enables us to step back and think about thinking. Animals can't do that. So theory helps us more fully be who God intended us to be as humans. I wonder to what extent we have dehumanized people in the church by not freeing them to think. I cannot think for others, nor can others think for me. But together, we can come to think and know more fully. This straddles the strengths of individualism and collectivism, a paradox possible as we widen our category width.

But theory continues to be bashed by many ministry practitioners at the expense of real-world experience. This is not a new phenomenon. The evangelical subculture has valued practice over theory for several decades.[3] Surely to know something experientially is a central component to cultural intelligence. Empathetic awareness with the Other is unlikely without a strong measure of experiential interaction with the Other. But that interaction doesn't happen disjoined from learning and generating ideas and themes. We come to know something theoretically while also coming to know it experientially, and vice versa. Theory allows us to enhance an experience and to take it further. And when theory is fundamentally linked to the process of awareness and to cross-cultural immersion, there is no gap between theory and practice.[4]

In the midst of my fourth study examining the cultural intelligence of ministry leaders in various cultural domains, I hit the wall. The limited demonstration of critical reflection by ministry leaders wasn't new to me. It was one of the primary findings from my study of North American pastors who trained overseas. But I had hoped to discover that it wasn't a finding that could be generalized to other cultural domains where American ministry leaders serve. Notice my journal midway through this fourth study.

> I listened to the conversation in the focus group today, and I started to feel hopeless. This is the focus group I convened to better understand how pastors and their key leaders think about developing more culturally diverse ministries. These aren't clueless men and women who have no understanding of the issues involved. I'm learning a ton from several of them.
>
> But when it comes to getting them to reflect on how culture shapes their own understanding of the faith, it just doesn't go anywhere. Randy kept harping on the issue of innovating methodology but not messing with the message. "We're committed to really thinking out of the box in how we present the gospel, how we worship, and how I do my teaching. But the gospel itself isn't up for grabs. Black, white, red, green, I don't care what color you are. The gospel remains the same." He said that. He actually said that. And the worst part is, he received tons of hearty affirmation from the rest of the group.
>
> Todd was the only dissident voice. He gives me hope. He said something like, "But that's what we're really up against, isn't it? Our understanding of the message is so embedded in a white, Eurocentric, post-Reformation view of the gospel. I'm not saying it's wrong. But I think we have to rethink it." To which Randy replied, "Boy, Todd, you sound like you need to be teaching in a seminary. Those are really big words." Insert lots of laughter from the rest of the group here! I managed a courtesy chuckle.

Here I am again, staring at the infatuation we evangelicals have for being anti-intellectual and antitheoretical. So what hope is there for a framework like cultural intelligence that is so deeply committed to getting people to engage in theoretical reflection in order to improve cross-cultural behavior?

You have to understand. Randy isn't an uneducated, backward pastor. He's a well-respected leader of a sizable church. But he exemplified the sentiments of most of the subjects in the group by arguing that programs and methods are the area in which culturally enriched ministry should occur rather than rethinking theology and ministry philosophy in light of culture.

This journal entry was frighteningly similar to what I had written in my journal five years earlier, while in the midst of doing my dissertation research among the pastors who trained overseas:

> I'm more than disheartened. These leaders did not prepare for these experiences personally, educationally, etc. I try to get them to reflect on what they anticipated or what they experienced, but there is little substance to their responses.
>
> How do you get the pastors to think about the software of the culture and not just the hardware? Everyone seems to cite the obvious differences and observations that come from a surface-level analysis. How can more in-depth analysis be stimulated?
>
> Does evangelicalism breed such superficial thinking? Is there a causal link between my sample being pastors and their limited critical thinking, or would I find similar kinds of responses from a different group of trainers? Is it related more to them being practitioners or to being evangelicals? Or neither? In fairness, these trainers aren't a whole lot unlike the corporate trainers I meet "on the road" who train internationally. They don't seem very reflective either. But I would hope for something more in church leaders.
>
> How do I foster this kind of critical self-reflection?

Earlier I noted how even the subjects who demonstrated a greater degree of critical self-reflection usually relegated discussion about personal transformation from cross-cultural encounters to conclusions already predominant in the evangelical community. For example, they described increased prayer lives, reflection about materialism vis-à-vis the poverty of people in developing countries or minority communities, the need to trust God more, and similar conclusions that permeate evangelical presuppositions. Their reflections fit neatly into bounded-set categories. My concern was not with the nature of those reflections but that the reflective thinking did not go further. With such limited praxis occurring, are not their congregants being deprived of a more robust experience of the faith?

Meanwhile, as I go back and read my journal entries, I'm struck by the thought again that the uncritically, reflective ministry leader may be the Other for me. Some of my words represent an attitude in me that seems dangerously close to the very sentiments I'm concerned about in them. What does it look like for me to apply cultural intelligence and grace to my own subjects and people like them? How do I engage in praxis as I view myself as well as in the ways I view the Other?

Praxis is a skill that helps us structure meaning around experience. As human beings, we cannot stop thinking. Every moment is filled with all kinds of impressions. As we sort through the barrage of impressions that come our way daily, we order some into the background and bring others into sharper focus. The practice of reflecting through dialogue with others and ourselves, such as through journal writing, is one of the most important ways to create meaning out of our many impressions. More than simply recording information that comes along, it is paying attention to how that information integrates with what we already think and value.

Educator and writer Parker Palmer describes the angst he has felt as a teacher watching students take copious notes on what he's saying without taking any notes about what's going on inside them as they interact with the content of his teaching. I observed this same phenomenon in many of the journals I read by the subjects studied. Journals were often little more than a chronicling of events rather than reflective descriptions of how the subject was processing the cross-cultural experiences being faced. The subjects seemed to fear being too honest with themselves. Knowing I would be reading their journals may have been a limitation, but if anything, I would have expected that to cause the subjects to be more intentional about deeper observation and reflection. But then many of my own journal entries seem oriented more toward deeper reflection about what's going on in the Other rather than toward looking within myself.

How do we move toward a heightened use of praxis in our lives? How do we help others in our ministry do so? What does it look like to remain equally committed to active service and thoughtful reflection? We want to explore some of the existing models that enhance our ability to be ethnographers of our own souls and experiences. These kinds of tools have the potential of helping us become contemplative activists so that we can more fully engage the reality of encountering the Other and ourselves with all the wonder, joy, and conflict that comes with those encounters.

Kolb's Model

David Kolb's theory of experiential learning[5] is one of the most pervasive theories used to explain how adults learn in the midst of experience. The theory has been broadly applied in several professional areas, including education, psychology, medicine, nursing, general management, computer science, accounting, law, and ministry. Over the last thirty years, more than 1,800 studies have either directly used or been influenced by Kolb's theory.[6]

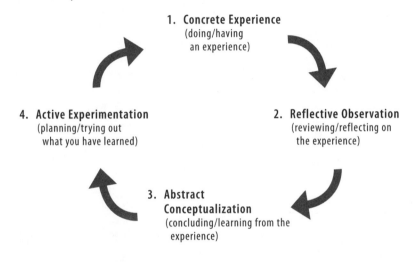

1. Concrete Experience
(doing/having
an experience)

4. Active Experimentation
(planning/trying out
what you have learned)

2. Reflective Observation
(reviewing/reflecting on
the experience)

**3. Abstract
Conceptualization**
(concluding/learning from the
experience)

Figure 8. Kolb's Model of Experiential Learning. (Adapted from David Kolb, *Experiential Learning: Experience as the Source of Learning and Development* [Englewood Cliffs, NJ: Prentice-Hall, 1984]).

Kolb's praxis-based model draws on the works of John Dewey, Kurt Lewin, Jean Piaget, William James, and Paulo Freire and in so doing, suggests that experience creates the foundation for four modes of learning: feeling, reflecting, thinking, and acting. These modes then represent a four-phase learning cycle (see fig. 8).

The first step is concrete experience. Concrete experiences may be as significant as the trauma of losing a loved one, as life-changing as the adventure of traveling to another part of the world, or as "small" and everyday as a jarring interchange with someone from a different generation over lunch. The second stage of Kolb's model is reflection, in which the individual steps back to think about and observe what has happened in the concrete experience. Here awareness largely comes into play. Intentional awareness enhances effective reflection in the midst of the experience and creates the space and time after the experience to reflect

on it. The individual moves into the third step, abstract conceptualization, as he or she begins to generate ideas and themes related to what was
observed. Here drawing on things such as logic sets and category width
can help the individual conceptualize the nature of what occurred in
the initial experience. How does the experience fit with the individual's
existing categories? Does it fit? If not, how does that affect the way the
individual views the experience? How might others from different cultural contexts view this experience? Is a new category needed? Which
assumptions need to be deconstructed? Asking these kinds of questions
and beginning to hypothesize responses to them are both part of the
abstract conceptualization that occurs. This is why theory is extremely
practical. Finally, the initial concrete experience is formed into active
experimentation through future, ongoing experiences and encounters.
This allows the individual to draw on theories generated in the reflective
mode as he or she reengages in action.

Whether conscious or not, this is the cycle I moved through when using
my bottom-line, direct-communication approach in Liberia. The concrete
experience (step 1) occurred when I asked the Liberian pastor whether the
concerns raised by Moses about Dr. Jones were accurate. The pastor's indirect responses and my subsequent interaction with Moses were all part of
the experience, during which I was certainly engaging in some reflective
thinking. But only as I later spent time journaling about it did I more fully
enter the stage of reflection (step 2). As I began to recount the experience
in my journal and think about all the varying dynamics, I moved into
abstract conceptualization (step 3). I began positing reasons why the episode unfolded the way it did. I wrestled with how kingdom values should
interface with the differing cultural values about direct versus indirect
communication. The next day, Moses and I were with another individual
who also knew Dr. Jones well. Having moved through the praxis cycle, I
engaged in the final stage of Kolb's model (step 4), active experimentation
with a different approach. This interaction went much better.

Some preliminary research has explored the relationship between Kolb's
model of experiential learning and cultural intelligence.[7] There are several
connections between the two frameworks. Interpretive CQ begins with
awareness of ourselves, of others, and of the environments in which we
find ourselves. In the process of becoming more mindful, we encounter
varying ways of seeing and hence describing the world. That's why it was
important for us to explore different ways of categorizing the world, namely,
bounded sets versus centered sets. And then we examined the degree to
which we're comfortable with things and situations that don't neatly fit
into any of our existing sets but instead fall into a category of difference.

Kolb expands his theoretical framework to include different learning
styles that align with the four steps in the learning cycle. These are less

helpful to the process of cultural intelligence and seem a bit forced. But Kolb's learning cycle is a helpful way to think about the process of interpretive CQ.

Joplin's Model

Even more helpful is the adaptive work that Laura Joplin has done based on Kolb's model. Joplin created a five-stage model based on Kolb's work to provide an extremely relevant and transferable way of using it in many different active learning contexts. I find Joplin's model more helpful because it's simple and transferable to many different settings. It's something that I've taught a number of times to youth workers, pastors, and laypeople. And I even use it regularly in processing experiences with my children.

I've been collaborating with a group of other research practitioners to integrate Joplin's model of experiential learning with cultural intelligence. Initially, we conducted focus-group research by convening leaders and ministries deemed as positive examples in their short-term missions practice. This was called the Short-Term Missions Effectiveness Project. Joplin's model and cultural intelligence were the theoretical frameworks that guided the data collection.[8] Joplin's model is also helpful in enhancing interpretive CQ in other kinds of cross-cultural ministry opportunities. I've provided a brief overview of Joplin's model and how we might think about it in relationship to interpretive CQ. We can use this model personally as we engage cross-culturally, and it's especially helpful in facilitating the cross-cultural encounters of others in our ministries (see fig. 9).

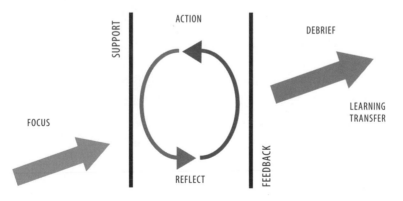

Figure 9. The Joplin Model, Modified by Linhart. (Adapted from Laura Joplin, "On Defining Experiential Education," in *The Theory of Experiential Education*, ed. K. Warren, M. Sakofs, and J. S. Hunt Jr. [Dubuque, IA: Kendall/Hunt, 1995], 15–22; and Terrence Linhart, "Planting Seeds: The Curricular Hope of Short-Term Mission Experiences in Youth Ministry," *Christian Education Journal*, 3rd series: 256–72.)

Stage 1: Focus

In the first stage we focus on what it is we hope to learn. Our lives are filled with many unexpected experiences that we have little chance to anticipate ahead of time. But many more of our cross-cultural experiences occur with some advance warning. Before we head to the meeting with the seniors' group or to the denominational convention or before we visit the local mosque, a culturally intelligent approach begins with focus. I couldn't have fully anticipated how the Liberian pastor would respond to my query about Dr. Jones, but I did know ahead of time that we were going to meet, and I did make a mental note to talk with the pastor about Dr. Jones. A greater effort to focus in my thinking about how to most appropriately raise this conflict-laden issue might have yielded different results.

A period of focus might include anticipating the answers to questions such as, What do you anticipate happening? What is it you hope to learn? What are your hopes and fears? What assumptions do you have about the Other in this context? Which judgments do you need to suspend? Write them down. Talk about them with others. Given the barrage of cross-cultural encounters many of us have daily, focus might not always be something we can sit down and write or discuss. But at the very least, while traveling to the upcoming meeting, we can turn down the music, shut off the cell phone, and make it a time of prayerfully anticipating what is likely to occur.

If you're leading others on a short-term missions experience or into some other kind of cross-cultural pilgrimage, an important starting point for enhancing the transformative nature of these experiences lies in helping participants focus on the experience and the challenging actions they will experience. Preparation and planning are consistent themes in Joplin's model and in the metacognitive factor of cultural intelligence. The focus stage is designed to help us anticipate areas where we need to be *aware*.

Some focus questions you might want to use with a team you lead include:

- What is our motivation for reaching into this cultural context?
- What is God already doing there?
- What would it look like for this experience to be a success? A failure?
- How do the people perceive us? How do they think we perceive them? How do we perceive them?

Stage 2: Action—Reflection

The second stage is the part that relates most directly to the praxis material we're examining in this chapter. This is the most critical component in nurturing interpretive CQ through the experience. It's the action and reflection loop, when both during the interaction and afterward we reflect on what has occurred.

Kolb's four-stage cycle is helpful for thinking about the process of reflection, but the simplicity of Joplin's model is something we can immediately enact in all kinds of cross-cultural experiences. It seems to fit more realistically with our full, busy lives. When watching a movie with different cross-cultural episodes, we can engage in the action and reflection loop. When we're driving through an ethnic neighborhood or attending an event that consists largely of an age group other than our own, we have a perfect opportunity to go through the action and reflection loop.

As we grow in praxis, an element of this action and reflection cycle occurs continually, whatever the experience. But it's most germane to situations that particularly stretch us. The action is a chance to engage with familiar skills in an unfamiliar environment.

Most short-term missions trips are filled with varied activities and experiences, whether by eating local foods, mixing cement by hand, or attending a church service in another language. Consciously or not, participants are continually reflecting and drawing meaning from these events and the ensuing interactions. They are constantly engaged in a highly personal, ongoing "conversation" in their own minds about who they are in relation to what they are encountering. Since the reflection usually occurs internally, participants may draw conclusions from their experiences that do not reflect reality. And more often than not, participants aren't even aware of the internal dialogue they're having with themselves.

The constant barrage of experiences during a typical short-term missions trip comes at participants so quickly that it resembles the experience of walking through a museum and encountering entire civilizations in a single hallway.[9] Ralph Winter says short-term missionaries can be like dogs running through an art museum. They see everything and appreciate nothing. Not all short-term experiences are like this, however. Granted, the brevity of these kinds of cross-cultural encounters makes it difficult for participants to make sense of the experiences. But when facilitators share and process provocative encounters, like these with participants, those experiences can be profoundly transformative opportunities. Facilitators need to ask questions that help participants decipher the meaning behind what they experience. I'll suggest some examples of those kinds of questions in the next stage: support and feedback.

The same kinds of challenges exist for each of us, whatever the nature of the cross-cultural encounter. A brief interaction with a neighbor from another cultural background and a counseling session with parents who come from a different generational culture include many of the same internal dialogues. There is an action and reflection loop taking place internally. We hear and see certain things as we encounter the Other, and unless we make a conscious choice otherwise, the observations and subsequent interpretations further reinforce what we already thought about the Other. And the cycle continues in ongoing iterations.

Sandy is a thirty-eight-year-old American missionary working with Albanian refugees in Greece. That alone gives her ample need for cultural intelligence. But add to that her marriage to Alek, a thirty-five-year-old Albanian man. Sandy and Alek have been married ten years. They both speak fluent English, Greek, and Albanian. I asked Sandy to describe her level of confidence in feeling that she understands Albanian culture. She said,

> We've been married for ten years. And I've been working among Albanian people for twelve years. Just about the time I start to think I understand the Albanian perspective, something unexpected happens that throws me off. I mull it over for a while, talk about it with Alek and some friends, and I start to see how much I have yet to understand the Albanian world. But each one of those encounters gives me a more complex view of their culture. . . . Things go pretty well for a while, but then it happens all over again. I've decided this is going to be our life together. I wouldn't trade it for anything. We'll see how badly we mess up our kids though!

Sandy provides such a positive, realistic picture of what interpretive CQ looks like. *It's an ongoing process of understanding and reflection in the midst of everyday interactions and experiences.* And I'm encouraged that she doesn't move through the action-reflection loop individualistically. Alek and other people process her experiences with her. That leads us to stage three.

Stage 3: Support—Feedback

The reinforcing nature of the action-reflection cycle makes the third stage, support and feedback, vitally important. As demonstrated in figure 9, these are the walls that provide support to the process of praxis and oftentimes challenge what's occurring in the internal dialogue.

The support in the midst of a cross-cultural encounter usually comes from other people with whom you're sharing the experience—whether it be the group of elders or youth leaders from your church, your family members, your fellow short-term missionaries, or those who come from the different cultural context you're encountering. Research shows a strong correlation between an individual's success in a cross-cultural experience and the emotional and tangible support that person has from his or her friends and family members.

According to information gathered in the Short-Term Missions Effectiveness Project, most leaders guiding short-term missions trips overlook the importance of high-quality, ongoing feedback. As the action and reflection cycle continues throughout the learning process, the facilitators must intervene with participants and help them talk about their reflections. Many groups share daily during short "debriefing" times, but the size of the group and the brief time often limits feedback to simply reviewing the activities of the day rather than effectively directing reflection that stimulates transformation.

Planned reflection times during cross-cultural experiences, either short-term missions trips or any of the other varied examples we've described in the book, usually mirror the preconceived categories of Christian reflection we've described elsewhere. And the questions asked by participants and facilitators both tend to be fairly generic, such as, "What did you learn today?" "What was the best/worst part of the day?" and "Where did you see God today?"

Questions that better prompt reflection that leads to transformation might be as simple as using the "Gracie approach." My daughter Grace has never outgrown the "Why, Why, Why?" mode of questioning often used by kids younger than she. But I'm really grateful. Linda and I have a few Singlish (the vernacular form of English spoken throughout Singapore) phrases we've taken on as our own. One example is the Singlish use of "Can?" an example I shared earlier. "Can?" is a one-word question that can be used in myriad ways, such as, "Are you comfortable with what I suggest?" "Would you be able to pick that up?" "Is it okay if we spend that much money for that repair?" So the other day I used "Can?" when asking Linda if an appointment I scheduled for both of us would work. Watch the interchange that ensued between Grace and me as she overheard my "Can?" to Linda.

Grace: Why did you ask mom "Can?"

Me: It's easier than asking the whole question. They do it that way in Singapore.

Grace: Why?

Me: Because they abbreviate a lot of their words.

Grace: Why?

Me: Because they're obsessed with efficiency.

Grace: Why?

Okay. By this point she had stumped me. I have some ideas of why Singaporeans do things in a speedy, truncated way, but now I was moving into conjecture. But Grace's constant level of questioning holds a great deal of promise for the way we provide feedback to people's interactions. One need not have an advanced degree in intercultural communication to help nurture cultural intelligence in others. It can be as simple as asking, Why, Why, Why? The practice of asking why several times is an approach often advocated in business literature. "By repeatedly asking the question 'Why' (five is a good rule of thumb), you can peel away the layers of symptoms which can lead to the root cause of a problem."[10] This is a very practical tool for getting down into the deeper layers of the iceberg. It is something all of us can do. In seeking to increase our awareness and empathy, we can ask why people label things the way they do (logic sets). And why do we? Why are the driving patterns the way they are? Why does that church organize its staff and ministry around those departments? The people in those cultural contexts might not even know, so we have to learn how to creatively dig deep to explore the answers to these "why" questions. And what about these people is most different from us? Is it right, wrong, or just different (category width)? *Why? Why? Why?*

Cross-cultural encounters often bring about so many new experiences in a short, rapid period of time that participants feel pressured to label or make sense of each moment too quickly. In doing so, they revert to the superficial responses described throughout the book. Surrounding ourselves with people who can offer support and feedback and looking for ways to offer that to others is a promising way to move toward a heightened degree of cultural intelligence. The most consistent finding among the exemplary leaders and ministries convened for the Short-Term Missions Effectiveness Project was the integral role that trip leaders and facilitators played in determining whether the trip was effective for the locals and the participants alike. There was a wide range of divergence in the selection process of participants, the kinds of projects done, and the type of training and debriefing used. But the exemplary groups all placed a similar value on having leaders who could help participants critically reflect on their experiences. This process forces people to think deeply about their assumptions rather than reinforcing unchecked assumptions.

Stage 4: Debrief

When the action component is completed, participants begin the process of leaving the experience and enter into a stage described as the "debrief." Different from the reflection process, the debrief stage, according to Joplin, is the organized process of identifying learning that has happened, discussing it with others, and evaluating it. This debriefing process can be done individually but is most effectively done with others. The most helpful debriefings on short-term trips often include having participants reread their journals, where each day's reflections have been recorded before and during the trip. This practice doesn't have to be limited to short-term missions trips though. And if you already journal, you don't have to create a whole new journaling discipline for cross-cultural encounters. It can simply be incorporated into your usual journal-writing rhythm.

I find it helpful to note in my journal those entries that relate to my cross-cultural experiences. I periodically schedule a time to go back and read through those entries. This is a helpful way of debriefing, especially as I then enlist the community with whom I share life to help me process some of the things about which I've been thinking and reflecting.

Stage 5: Learning Transfer

The final stage of Joplin's model of experiential learning is learning transfer. Most of us invest little time in transferring the learning from a cross-cultural experience to the rest of our lives. Two realities make effective learning transfer challenging. First, most of the significant learning in cross-cultural encounters takes place in environments very different from our home environments. Second, we often don't know how to transfer the learning to life back home. Examples abound of ministry leaders attending forums and conferences on how to reach the younger generation but walking by the young people helping with registration at the event and not even taking time to talk with them. Far too many missions teams travel to Mexico to lavish love on the people in a village there, only to come back home and lock their car doors when driving through the Hispanic neighborhoods nearby.

The subjects studied in the Short-Term Missions Effectiveness Project all emphasized the importance of weaving short-term missions into the year-round life of the parish and the individual. This correlates positively with the cultural intelligence literature that refers to cultural intelligence as a malleable, ongoing growth process.[11]

Learning transfer can occur if we find a mentor who can help us think about how to translate our interpretations by going deeper into our everyday practice. The best mentors for learning transfer know what kinds of questions to ask. Questions like the ones we explored in the action and reflection loop are helpful, especially because they move us toward applying what we learn to life in our everyday routine and rhythms. Learning transfer might come from looking for the similarities and differences that exist in how we relate to the Other in various cultural domains. And it means we'll ultimately incorporate our deeper awareness through interpretive CQ to part of our holistic development as followers of Christ.

Conclusion

People at higher levels of cultural intelligence have a more complex perception of the environments in which they find themselves. That doesn't mean you have to be highly intellectual or have graduate degrees to be effective cross-culturally. I've traveled with high school students whose curiosity led them to mindfulness, empathy, and metacognition in ways that demonstrated a great deal of interpretive CQ, even though they had never heard of the term. They had sufficient appreciation for the process of reflection alongside action and learning to engage in that process with others. That kind of process is what begins to translate interpretive CQ into service that is respectful and loving to the Other.

Mindfulness in the midst of our social experiences allows us to be fully present while simultaneously relating what we're observing to our knowledge CQ. As we compare our observations with our cognitive understanding and engage in reflective praxis, we become more adept at transferring our learning from one situation to another. Although we've talked a great deal in this book about the endless barrage of cross-cultural encounters facing most twenty-first-century ministry leaders, those varied encounters in diverse cultures needn't be unrelated to one another. Through praxis, we become attentive to each situation, retain the knowledge gained from it, learn to reproduce some of the behaviors observed, and receive feedback about the effectiveness of our adapted behavior for use in another cross-cultural encounter.[12]

Throughout this part on interpretive CQ, I've argued that interpretive CQ is the key linking process between knowledge CQ and behavioral CQ. It's what makes the difference between understanding cultural difference and being able to effectively interact with cultural difference in ways that reflect the love of Jesus. But how does interpretive CQ actually lead us to the destination of culturally intelligent behavior? David Thomas, an expert in international management, draws on the work of Piaget and Lawrence Kohlberg to demonstrate how interpretive CQ moves us from abysmal cultural intelligence to the point of moving seamlessly in and out of various cultural contexts. Notice the progression as we move from interpretive CQ into the final part of the book, where we actually apply CQ to our lives and relationships. I render Thomas's five stages on the following scale: CQ1 describes an individual with almost no interpretive CQ present, and CQ5 describes an individual with an unusual presence of interpretive CQ.[13]

CQ1: We view the world in light of what is "normal" in our cultural context, and as a result, we resolve simply to treat everyone the same.

CQ2: We recognize that different cultural norms exist, and we become motivated to learn about them.

CQ3: We begin to grow in category width and might even learn to adapt to different cultural norms and behaviors, but it takes a great deal of thinking and planning to do so.

CQ4: We begin to assimilate different cultural norms and behaviors into our repertoire such that we can quite freely slip into different gears as appropriate.

CQ5: We proactively recognize cultural cues that others typically miss, and we often tune into what's going on even before people from the other cultural context do so.

Notice how the transition between theoretical processing and behavior becomes almost seamless by the time you get to CQ5. I'm not sure that any of us consistently relates at level 5. But surely we can move in that direction by incorporating praxis into our daily interactions. That brings us to the final two legs of our journey together: perseverance and behavioral CQ.

Go deep. It might feel as if we're a long way from getting to the extremely practical expressions of loving the Other. But we're making progress. By diving into the deep waters through awareness and empathy, by looking at how culture shapes the way we label things and tolerate difference, and by learning how to do all this while continuing our busy lives, we've gone below the tip of the iceberg. It's time to turn the corner for the final leg of our journey together. Love. Understand. Go deep.

Recommended Resources

Klug, Ron. *How to Keep a Spiritual Journal: A Guide to Journal Keeping for Inner Growth and Personal Discovery.* Minneapolis: Augsburg, 2002.

Palmer, Parker. *The Active Life: A Spirituality of Work, Creativity, and Caring.* San Francisco: Jossey-Bass, 1999.

Schön, Donald. *The Reflective Practitioner: How Professionals Think in Action.* New York: Basic Books, 1983.

part 4

express: perseverance
and behavioral CQ

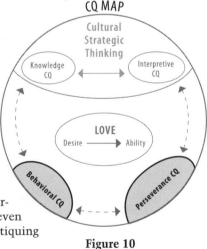

Figure 10

From my journal:

It's unusual for me to feel that I'm the most positive person in the room talking about short-term missions. I'm usually the one raising the cautions and challenging the dogmatic claims about what these trips accomplish. But I'm so uncomfortable with the dehumanizing, patronizing tones some of these researchers are using to talk about short-term participants and local church leaders. It feels even more toxic than the paternalism we're critiquing in the short-termers themselves.

Maybe the most unnerving part about this is that I see how quickly I can go there. The very ethnocentric, "my way is best" attitude that I'm trying to awaken ministry leaders to see just might be the way I sometimes approach them! May the time we're investing in theorizing and researching these issues of cross-cultural engagement go beyond theory and research to actually changing the way we engage in mission.

—March 23, 2007. Chicago, Illinois

Express. *Maitri* is translating our desire and capacity to love into effective expressions of love. We're back nearly full circle to where we began—love. The ways in which we understand, think about, and reflect on cultural issues are integral to actually interacting with the Other in ways that are loving and respectful. That's been demonstrated in numerous ways throughout the last several chapters. But eventually we have to move beyond understanding and interpretation to live, serve, and lead in culturally diverse contexts. We have to move from the *intention* to love to *expressing* our love to the Other. In some regards, this part is the most important because it's the final factor determining whether all our hard work from knowledge and interpretive CQ actually translates into behavior that's respectful and loving to the Other. On the other hand, the most helpful ways of manipulating our motivation to be culturally intelligent and our actual behavior is to focus on knowledge and interpretive CQ.

This last part of our journey together begins with the third of the four factors of cultural intelligence—perseverance CQ. Perseverance, or motivational, CQ is our level of interest, drive, and motivation to adapt cross-culturally. The material in this chapter looks at some of the challenges we face individually when attempting to translate our understanding and awareness into action.

The next chapter examines behavioral CQ, which is the extent to which we appropriately change our verbal and nonverbal actions when we interact cross-culturally. This is the factor of cultural intelligence by which we're most often judged. Do we behave in ways that are culturally intelligent? We'll look at when we should and shouldn't flex our behavior while keeping in view the importance of being ourselves.

The final chapter provides a long list of practical ways to move forward in the journey of cultural intelligence. The entire book is oriented to that goal, but this final chapter suggests some everyday practices for building on the overall perspective and understanding I hope to enhance in the rest of the book. It suggests directions for continuing on in the journey with our respective communities.

I've intentionally devoted only one chapter each to the perseverance and behavioral factors of cultural intelligence. That's not because this part of the journey is less important, but my research finds that most of us as ministry leaders are weakest in knowledge and interpretive CQ. We have much zeal, and we have no trouble staying busy. But our zealous activity can be more effective and loving when informed by good understanding and depth. As we grow in knowledge and interpretive CQ, we acquire the raw materials needed to express love to the Other.

Understand. Go deep. And express God-given love for the Other through perseverance and action. Serving and interacting with the Other in ways that are respectful and loving *are* possible. The hard work you've done to understand culture and the ways it shapes life and the efforts you've made to submerge deeply into thinking about thinking will pay off. With time and discipline, more culturally intelligent love and service can be a reality for all of us and, more importantly, for those we encounter.

13

when the goin' gets tough

Perseverance CQ

You might be completely aware of your own cultural context and how it shapes who you are and what you do. And perhaps you're fluent in the language of another culture not only literally but also in your understanding of the values and assumptions that shape the way people in that culture think and live. And you might continuously go deep through prolific journal writing and meaningful dialogue with yourself and others about how you categorize the world. But what if you just don't feel like behaving in the ways you know you should to be effective? How do we deal with the very real motivational issues involved in cross-cultural interaction?

Our motivation is what we want to explore in this chapter on perseverance CQ. Perseverance CQ refers to our level of interest, drive, and motivation to adapt cross-culturally. Effective cross-cultural service goes beyond simply understanding what is occurring and often involves an emotional response that surfaces for us as we reach across the chasm of cultural difference. This response is an important aspect of the cultural intelligence framework that is not included in many other theories of cross-cultural competency. You and I could go through identical training for a cross-cultural assignment, but we're likely to experience it differently because we're different. The individualized emotions experienced in different cultural situations are an essential consideration for understanding the dynamic nature of cross-cultural interactions. Although a great deal of the material we've explored throughout this journey has focused primarily on cultural norms, here we particularly turn the focus to the deepest level of mental conditioning: our individual selves. What are the things that personally motivate us, and when are we reluctant to persevere cross-culturally?

Consider these questions and ask yourself if they apply to you; respond as truthfully as possible. Nobody is going to test you on them, so avoid saying what you think you should say to be culturally intelligent and think about your honest responses.

- Do I like cross-cultural interactions that are new to me?
- Do I prefer to stay with locals when I travel cross-culturally rather than in a hotel by myself?
- Do I prefer eating local foods when I go to a new place?
- Do I enjoy spending time with people who don't embrace Christianity as their worldview?
- Am I confident I would be effective in cross-cultural ministry?[1]

These are the kinds of motivations measured when we test perseverance CQ.

Honestly exploring these kinds of issues is our goal in this chapter. We'll begin by looking at the relevance of self-efficacy to perseverance CQ. Next we'll explore some of the power issues endemic to cross-cultural work, we'll consider how an American orientation toward "doing" over "being" shapes our perseverance CQ, and we'll conclude with looking at being brutally honest with ourselves about what drives us, what scares us, and when to say, "Enough is enough!"

Up for the Challenge

Self-efficacy, the perception we have of our ability to reach a goal, is the first important consideration in thinking about perseverance CQ. It is the central aspect of how we engage the world and the circumstances and people we encounter. It's our confidence in our ability to accomplish a specific action. Self-efficacy helps us coherently organize our skills, emotions, and frame of mind as we tackle a new challenge. It results in a proactive approach to life rather than a reactive one.

There's a positive relationship between self-efficacy and cultural intelligence. "Without a strong sense of self-efficacy, a person will avoid challenges and give up easily when confronted with setbacks. The motivational aspect of cultural intelligence requires a personal sense of efficacy and desire for enactive mastery."[2]

A value of the cultural intelligence framework is the symbiotic relationship among all four factors—knowledge, interpretive, perseverance, and behavioral CQ. And the self-efficacy needed for perseverance CQ draws on all four factors, though it fits most squarely in the motivational one. Planning and anticipating what's going to occur in a cross-cultural encounter is a value we talked about when describing interpretive CQ. As one begins to focus, the individual draws on knowledge CQ for a frame of reference about what is likely to occur in another context. The belief the individual has in his or her ability to effectively engage in the experience relates to perseverance CQ, while the actual encounter itself is behavioral CQ.

Robert Merton, a renowned American sociologist in the twentieth century, developed the theory of anticipatory socialization. Anticipatory socialization provides a helpful perspective for thinking about the role of self-efficacy and agency in perseverance CQ. In describing the phenomenon of anticipatory socialization, Merton wrote, "For the individual who adopts the values of a group to which he aspires but does not belong, the orientation may serve the twin functions of aiding his rise into that group and of easing his adjustment after he has become part of it."[3]

In his initial research, Merton looked at the increased likelihood of promotions within the US Army for privates who accepted the official values of the army's hierarchy. Merton argued that those individuals who accurately anticipated the army's subculture took on the values of the positions to which they aspired.

Merton's anticipatory socialization has been used as a framework for analyzing the preparation processes of multiple kinds of groups and contexts. Anticipatory socialization is not always viewed positively. When Leo Spitzer examined how three different families from various ethnic backgrounds struggled to blend into dominant European cultures, he found that some of their expectations negatively influenced their assimilation into the respective cultures. Spitzer challenged the idea that accurately anticipating cross-cultural engagement leads to a successful encounter. For most individuals, the motivation to understand another culture is affected by how similar that culture is to their own as well as how much it has to offer them. They reason, *If I think this other culture is very different from my own and doesn't have much to offer me, then I won't feel as motivated to learn and adapt to it.* Of course, the selfless call of following Jesus and serving the Other ought to mitigate against that reality. Regardless, Spitzer's research further validates that the way one anticipates a cross-cultural experience influences his or her experience in that culture.[4]

Merton's work on anticipatory socialization has been used extensively by John Van Maanen, an organizational theorist interested in how individuals anticipated a professional work culture. He has studied how new employees' anticipatory thoughts influenced their adjustment to the work culture. Although Van Maanen's use of anticipatory socialization was limited to the domain of organizational culture, some of the concepts he developed have relevance to other cultural domains.[5] Van Maanen describes three distinct yet interrelated phases experienced as people encounter new cultural contexts: anticipatory socialization, encounter, and metamorphosis.[6]

Anticipatory Socialization

The first phase, anticipatory socialization, emphasizes the degree to which one is prepared, before entry, for what occurs in the new cultural context. The way one anticipates what will occur can either aid or hinder the individual's adjustment, but either way, it will in some way shape what occurs. Missionaries going to serve in English-speaking contexts in the developed world often struggle more than those who go to very different environments where English isn't spoken. The missionaries going to the cultures that appear more similar to home are often caught off guard by the profound differences. The same phenomenon has been seen among other expatriate professionals.

Fear is another important dimension of how one anticipates entering a new culture. In reflecting on her first role as a youth pastor, Vicki said, "I remember feeling like I was a teenager myself all over again. I felt so insecure. How should I dress? What music do they like? How am I going to communicate God's Word in a way that makes sense to them?"

The way a person responds to novelty and uncertainty is a key factor in cross-cultural adjustment. An individual's level of fear in preparing for a cross-cultural experience influences the engagement that follows. The fear can be powerful because many people feel threatened by the idea of abandoning the identity and culture that has signified them for so long.[7]

Essentially, the more completely and accurately one anticipates an experience in a different culture, the greater the ease and speed of adjustment to that new culture. This is why the focus stage of Joplin's model (chapter 12) can enhance cultural intelligence. What is not so simple is determining what accurate anticipation and focus entail. Here perseverance CQ depends strongly on knowledge and interpretive CQ.

Encounter

The second phase of socialization into a new cultural context is the encounter stage, when we actually enter the new cultural setting. Culture shock often sets in as we encounter the new environment, particularly if what we experience is unexpected or unpleasant. "Culture shock" is a term used to describe the anxiety felt when we lose all "familiar signs and symbols of social intercourse. These signs or cues include the thousand and one ways we orient ourselves to the situations of daily life."[8] When those cues are suddenly missing, culture shock often ensues.

The term "culture shock" is used most often to refer to people moving for extended periods of time across national borders, but I've observed culture shock in myself and others when entering a new organizational culture, moving to a new neighborhood, or sitting in an uncomfortable style of worship in a church service. And I, like many others, have undergone culture shock when entering the very strong cultures found in academic institutions. Many new faculty members are jarred by the culture shock they face when they are hired for the first time by a college or university. They learn to adapt to many organizational challenges within the academy through a process of trial and error. "For many new faculty, the first two years are characterized by loneliness and intellectual isolation, lack of collegial support, and heavy work loads and time constraints."[9] Thankfully my culture shock when coming to our seminary wasn't nearly that severe. But it was a disorienting experience learning where the power lies, what is valued, and how communication is expected to occur.

Culture shock is a necessary process if we are to function effectively in a setting that doesn't recognize all or part of the assumptions and behavioral patterns that we've previously taken for granted. Some of the material we examined with interpretive CQ can ease the emotional and intellectual upheaval of culture shock. Becoming consciously aware of our emotions and of how we classify the world provides a framework for what we're thinking and feeling. Without that kind of framework, culture shock often leads to loneliness, an inability to reason clearly, a poor self-image, depression, and a threat to one's security. Stress and anxiety in these kinds of situations are normal. "Indeed, it would be unusual, and a cause for some concern, if we didn't feel anxious in our situation. We should be careful not to deny that we may be feeling frustrated, lonely, or inadequate. Admitting these feelings to ourselves, and especially to others, helps reduce them."[10]

Culture shock is a highly individualized process that is ongoing, and in the end, the process typically leads to a change both in the individual and to some degree in the context in which the individual works. The extent to which culture shock affects the overall process of interacting in culturally intelligent ways depends largely on the degree to which we've correctly anticipated what will occur in a cross-cultural interaction.[11] It helps immensely to know what stresses are coming. If we expect something of a rough ride, we aren't entirely caught off guard when it happens. This leads back to the importance of the focus stage of Joplin's model explained in the last chapter. And it's why knowledge CQ is important. It helps us better anticipate how to function in a new cultural context.

Metamorphosis

Van Maanen's final phase of socialization into a new cultural context is called metamorphosis, the personal transformation necessary to continue in a new setting. Metamorphosis occurs when the individual moves toward becoming a fully accepted member in the new culture. It is largely connected to an individual's desire to belong and to one's motivation for success, so it comes back to the issue of self-efficacy. Many situations require us to undergo change whereby we take on new perspectives toward the world. If we're unwilling to reconsider how we classify the world and how things fit into categories, it's unlikely we'll experience the transformation necessary to be culturally intelligent leaders. The disorienting influence of the kinds of adjustments we must experience in culture shock are often the very things the Holy Spirit uses to bring about transformation in our lives.

This threefold process of socialization into a new cultural context helps us in thinking about the day-to-day experiences of ministry leaders. The more particularized and intimate the nature of the cross-cultural encounter, the more self-efficacy needed to persevere. For example, getting through an encounter with someone from a different cultural context who is waiting on you at the coffee shop doesn't require too much self-efficacy. On the other extreme, marrying someone who comes from a vastly different cultural background—whatever the cultural domain—brings about the greatest set of challenges. Most of our cross-cultural ministry encounters fall somewhere between these extremes. Given the personal nature of ministry, they fall closer to the side of particularized, intimate interaction with people than merely functional, business transactions. Ministry inevitably involves counseling, teaching about issues of the heart, and other deeply personal activities. That we want to do these things well, with love and respect that reflects the person of Jesus, ultimately motivates us to become more culturally intelligent ministers of the gospel.

It's unlikely we'll move through Van Maanen's threefold process—anticipatory socialization, encounter, and metamorphosis—in any single cross-cultural encounter. Significant metamorphosis or transformation as a result of any single short-term missions trip or from one jarring encounter with an individual from a starkly different generational context is unrealistic. But our transformation doesn't depend on isolated experiences.

Our varied experiences across many cross-cultural domains when entered with awareness and intentionality can bring about transformation.

Despite my critiques of short-term missions, this is one of the areas where I differ with some researchers who write off any transformative impact purportedly resulting from short-term missions trips. The change that results from a trip cannot always be quantified on a Likert scale assessment given six weeks or even six months after a trip. I think about it this way. My dad died pretty unexpectedly a few years ago. It was the very same day that my daughter Grace was born. Nothing could have prepared me for the range of emotions I felt on June 5, 1999. Several years later, I can't quantify for you exactly how his death occurring simultaneously with Grace's life transformed me. But I know it has affected me deeply, especially when combined with the other things that have been part of my life in the intervening years. Something as traumatic as death or divorce is the number one predictor of metamorphosis in the life of an adult. Cross-cultural encounters are among the top three predictors as well.[12] When a series of sojourns and cross-cultural encounters are wed together in our experience, the third step of Van Maanen's process, metamorphosis, is not only possible but quite likely when these encounters are engaged with the kind of reflection and deep introspection we explored in the part on interpretive CQ.

The self-awareness gained through interpretive CQ is vitally important here. On the whole, self-efficacy is positively related to perseverance CQ. There is an important limitation, however. Just because one knows how to proactively pursue a goal in a familiar cultural context doesn't mean the same approach will work as well in a new context. The tendency can be to learn how to achieve self-efficacy in one context and assume we can carry it with us. We might know just how to schmooze the older people or how to lighten up a conversation with a group of high school students, but applying those same strategies in a new cultural context might not be at all successful. The same result may or may not happen there. Here we're reliant on knowledge CQ to understand the role of culture in shaping the environments in which we find ourselves. And interpretive CQ helps us more accurately plan how to enact the same goals in different cultures.

My refusal to ignore the elephant-in-the-room is a direct approach to conflict that bodes well for me in most of the cultural contexts in which I interact in the US. I've learned how to finesse the edge of directness with diplomacy and grace. But that approach got me nowhere in trying to get to the bottom of the controversy regarding Dr. Jones in Liberia.

Sometimes those who have had the greatest measure of success in reaching goals in one context are challenged the most in a new context. Success can breed an unhealthy measure of confidence that leads such people to keep pushing themselves to survive in a new context as they would back home. But when self-efficacy is combined with interpretive CQ, a healthy measure of confidence usually aids in the process of effectively interacting across various cultural divides.

The "Power" of Generosity

When applying cultural intelligence to ministry and service, we need to consider another important motivational factor. We must ask why we're interested in cross-cultural service in the first place. Businesses are interested in cross-cultural work as a way to open up new markets and to tap into a more cost-effective workforce. Many business leaders study cultural intelligence so that their companies can become more profitable. Governments, the medical sector, and educational institutions also have varied reasons for being interested in work across various cultures and in using cultural intelligence to fulfill their overriding agendas.

Ministry leaders see cross-cultural work as connected to our God-given calling as the people of God. We want to serve the needs of others in unselfish ways. We want to use things such as cultural intelligence as a way to relevantly live out the presence of Jesus. It's easy to assume a smug attitude about the finite purposes of the business world and other sectors in doing cross-cultural work intelligently. But we're wise to pay attention to the ways even ministry and service can become more about serving the self than serving the Other.

Service is sexy these days. Brangelina. The Red Campaign. Bono. Oprah. Everywhere you look, the causes of Hollywood and many churches seem to be synonymous when it comes to serving the Other. I thank God for entertainers who invest in something that really counts. Some would say these are the newest ways to gain publicity in Hollywood, but I'm not ready to be that suspicious. I'm grateful for anything that is a catalyst toward ending poverty, hunger, and HIV/AIDS.

But perhaps we can step back and think about our own motivation and the reasons we serve by looking through the window of Hollywood's "service" to the Other. Consider Oprah's Leadership Academy for Girls in South Africa. I'm really grateful for Oprah's investment in something that counts, both the investment of her fame and her finances. And she isn't simply sending "leftovers" to South African girls. The 152 high school girls live and study in a state-of-the-art facility. The living quarters include oversize rooms with five-star-hotel-quality linens, a yoga studio, a beauty salon, indoor and outdoor theaters, hundreds of pieces of original artwork, and other lavish amenities. It seems a bit over the top, but I celebrate her generosity.

I do have a concern, however. There are aspects of Oprah's approach that seem to mimic our tendency in our service projects and missions trips. We love to go in with our programs and ideas to help people. And whether we realize it or not, to many of those we're serving, it comes off as if we're the "Great American Saviors" who have come in to save them from themselves. And we want to make sure the cameras are running while we do it.

What if Oprah had gone in with a commitment to help *existing* schools in townships throughout the country rather than developing her own school with her name on it? What if her specials were less focused on the Oprah Winfrey Leadership Academy and more about how through additional resources, the local schools in townships across the country are thriving and empowering all kinds of young people across the country?

Are our faith-based service projects really all that different? Pictures that portray us in the midst of down-and-out people lavishing us with praise run the risk of appearing to be our own version of trying to pull off a blockbuster service project. Can we be more excited about partnering with a group of local people, never getting any attention for it, but instead talking about the great things *they're* doing? Can we come home with stories that speak honorably about the good things going on in the places we visit rather than all the horror stories and what we did to fix those atrocities?[13]

Generosity has power, and it isn't all good power. Power, a term used to describe the ability an individual has to make choices or influence outcomes, is an important consideration that relates to perseverance CQ. This is especially relevant when we interact as people from the dominant culture with people in more subordinate cultures. To say an individual is from the dominant culture means that his or her cultural context aligns closely with those who hold the greatest degree of authority, control, and resources within the broader cultural context. We can't necessarily choose to be with or without power, so it's prudent to use the power we have in ways that are empowering to others. But do we do so in ways that lift up and share the power with the Other, or do we use the Other to further validate ourselves and further reinforce our positions of power?

Let me share an example closer to home than Oprah's academy in South Africa. Jamar, one of the pastors at Our Father's Blessing Church (OFBC), an inner-city church, described what happened when he was contacted by Alan, a leader from Grace Community Church (GCC), a church from a nearby suburb. Alan called Jamar to see if OFBC would be interested in being the recipient of GCC's Gifts of Grace program at Christmas. Alan explained that each year the men and their sons purchase gifts for underresourced kids and hand deliver them to kids living in the inner city. GCC works with a different church every year, and this year, they wanted to work with OFBC. Jamar told Alan, "Thanks for thinking of us. The way this might be most helpful is if your men buy the gifts; then we'll open up a temporary store at the church for a couple weeks. We'll let the fathers in the community know it's here. And we'll offer the gifts you purchased at really reduced prices. But we'll still charge them something. That way the dads can enjoy the dignity and joy of picking out gifts and handing them to their kids themselves." Alan responded, "Oh, I don't think we're interested in that. Every year the highlight of this program has been watching the look on our kids' faces as they hand that gift to a kid who otherwise wouldn't receive one. This is such a great bonding experience for our fathers and sons."

In recounting this experience, Jamar said to me,

> I really wasn't interested in exploiting the men in our community so the guys over at GCC could have a nice bonding experience with their kids. All I need is one more message to the kids in our community that says, *Guess what! This six-year-old white kid got you a better gift than your schmuck of a father did.*
>
> I even told Alan they could come run the store for us. But it was a deal breaker for them. I'm not sure who got the "Gifts of Grace." Hah! Did you get that? "Gifts of *grace*?!"

How might generosity turn into something that's not very generous and pretty self-serving? How do good intentions such as GCC's end up objectifying people as a way to make the "servants" feel good at the expense of those being served?

Much of my work on short-term missions has described the way many of these projects are oriented more for the benefit of the missionaries than for the benefit of the local communities and people who receive them. But instead of continuing to point the finger, I must admit that I'm not immune from these self-serving approaches to "generosity."

Our seminary president and I recently traveled to North India to spend time with a partnering college there. One hot afternoon, we needed to get from one side of town to the other, and an aggressive rickshaw driver earned our business. This was a bicycle rickshaw, so he had his work cut out for him to taxi two American men across town. He quoted me 40 rupees, just under US$1, to take us on our fifteen-minute taxi commute. I knew he was overcharging us in a big way compared to what he would charge two locals. But I was feeling generous, so I said sure.

When we arrived at our destination, I pulled out a 100-rupee bill (nearly US$2.50). I handed it to him, and he started to get me change. But I motioned to him that he could keep the whole thing. He appeared to be a Dalit, the lowest caste in India, so he proceeded to bow profusely. I presume he was thanking me for my generosity.

I walked away feeling pretty good about the fact that not only did I not barter him down, but I paid him two and a half times what he had quoted me. As I walked back to my hotel room, I felt a bounce in my step. I felt a sense of power and arrogance. "Look what I just did for that poor taxi man. I must have at least doubled his daily wage." Committed to living out the interpretive CQ that I talk about with others, I sat down to journal a bit about the day. As I began writing about the encounter that had just occurred with the rickshaw driver, my good feelings about my generosity began to dissipate. I started to think about the dehumanizing, power-oriented position I had felt over this driver. To him, $2.50 was a gold mine. To me, it wasn't even the cost of my daily cup of coffee. I had the option to use these resources however I liked, and today I had decided to be generous with them. I'm not suggesting I should have given him exactly what he quoted, much less bartered him lower. But I am saying that we have to view honestly the way our motivation can quickly become skewed toward a position of dominance and control.

For those of you thinking, *Lighten up, Livermore. You just gave the guy a generous tip and felt good about it,* I didn't lose sleep over it that night. There are far worse things I could confess to you. And we have to beware of analysis paralysis, in which we keep from doing anything compassionate for fear of doing it for the wrong reasons. But I do know that when these kinds of experiences continually build on one another, they lead to a toxic, dehumanizing way of viewing and hence relating to the Other. That's why I jumped in when I recently overheard my girls describing the Rwandan girl we support through one of the large relief organizations. I heard them saying to a friend, "Angelique wouldn't have anything to eat if it weren't for us. She gets a good meal, gets to go to school, and gets medical care because we give her money every month." I love hearing my girls pray daily for Angelique and putting together their change so we can play a small part in helping her. But I interrupted their conversation about Angelique to talk with them about the subtle issues of power that can come with our thinking more highly about how we're helping Angelique than might be true.

Henri Nouwen points to power as one of the great causes of so many people having left the church. He writes, "One of the greatest ironies of the history of Christianity is that its leaders constantly gave in to the temptation of power—political power, military power, economic power, or moral and spiritual power—even though they continued to speak in the name of Jesus, who did not cling to his divine power but emptied himself and became as we are."[14]

May we beware of the potential that exists to wield our acts of service as yet another way of using power to build our own kingdoms. One of the ways to turn this upside down is to look for ways to pursue mutual relationship and service rather than one-way service. How can we serve and learn together? Every church, whatever the context, has *gifts*. Every church, whatever the context, has *needs*. We must develop cross-cultural partnerships with churches that are mutually enriching and beneficial. When asked how American churches should develop relationships with churches in Africa, Bishop David Zac Niringiye said, "It's very simple. Just come be with us, with no agenda other than to be with us. Together, we'll discover what God might have us do."[15]

Mutuality means finding ways to truly engage in reciprocal learning. And it can't be just lip service. One time I told my Indian friend Ashish, "I've learned as much or more from you in our conversations together as you've learned from me in the workshops I've taught here." He put me on the spot. "Like what?" he asked. He went on, "You've been coming to Chandigarh for years, and I always sit and listen to your workshops and all. So it's easy for me to spout off the things I've learned from what you've taught, Dave. But what have you learned from me?"

Ashish and I had shared many wonderful meals and conversations together, so I thought it would be easy to answer his question. But I found myself tongue-tied. I responded with some very generic things that could have been said about most any Christian living in the developing world. Ashish called me on it. He said, "You haven't really learned those things from me personally. Or if so, you could easily have learned them from someone else. But what is it you've really learned from our friendship?"

It wasn't that I hadn't truly learned from him. Ashish has taught me all kinds of interesting things about postmodernity in a South Asian context, about what Indian Christianity might look like if it had been more authentically contextualized when it first entered India, and about why Gandhi's role in the world was even greater than I had previously understood. That's just the beginning. But when Ashish first asked me what I had learned from him, I was in a mode of what I had come to teach, not what I had come to learn. When we make our motivation to be colearners rather than the sole givers and teachers, it better reflects the essence of the gospel.

Oscar Muiri, the pastor of Nairobi Chapel, offers words of caution in this regard to those of us who are Americans. His counsel helps us think about how to enter the culture as learners and how to be aware of the power we represent when interacting with people in places such as Kenya. Pastor Muiri says,

> I tell Americans: "We're going into this meeting. Don't say anything! Sit there and hold your tongue." When you sit around a table, the people speaking always glance at the person they believe is the most powerful figure at the table. They will do that with you when you're the only American. And at some point, they will ask you, "What do you think?"
>
> Don't say anything. If you say anything, reflect back with something like, "I have heard such wisdom from this table. I am very impressed." And leave it at that. Affirm them for the contribution they have made. Don't give your own opinion.
>
> Americans find that almost impossible. They do not know how to hold their tongue. They sit there squirming, because they're conditioned to express their opinions.[16]

What fuels our motivation? Why are we reaching into a new cultural context in the first place? We have to honestly face the motives behind our service, travel, and work. And we have to bear in mind that *we* are the Other to billions of other people.

Eat to Live or Live to Eat

One of the cultural values we explored in chapter 8 was a being-versus-doing orientation to life. We noted how American culture is extremely skewed toward the "doing" side of the continuum. Tasks, accomplishments, and efficiency are the standards for success in the American world.

This shapes the way we often go about doing cross-cultural service. People are highly motivated to serve well by building the house for Habitat for Humanity, organizing the sale to support the city schools, participating in the HIV/AIDS walk, and teaching English to the newly arrived immigrants. We've seen how even with the individual variance that occurs among different personalities, an American who scores high on the "being" scale will still appear to have a "doing" orientation among most people who come from a "being" culture.

As "doers" we're usually highly motivated to work hard on tasks involved in cross-cultural work. But our motivation often dissipates when it comes to the hard perseverance needed to interact with those unlike us. Eating unfamiliar foods, straining to know what to talk about, and adjusting to standards of living that are unfamiliar to us take a lot of drive for most of us. There are ways our doing orientation can be a value-added contribution among those we serve. Houses need to be built for

Habitat, something must be done about HIV/AIDS, and immigrants are looking for competency in English. But there are aspects of our "doing" orientation that need to be tempered.

Add to this challenge the fact that cultural differences often become more pronounced in social settings than in work settings. Web designers interacting cross-culturally with other Web designers talk in code and know how to relate to one another professionally. Sociologists from Germany find a common language with sociologists in Brazil by drawing on their shared discipline. And to a certain extent, pastors have a shared professional literacy with other pastors, regardless of the cultural context. Professionals can relate more easily with their cross-cultural peers in the work environment than they can in the social environment. There are some cultural norms within their work contexts according to which they can naturally operate. But many of those norms are absent once those same individuals move from the work context into the social one. Many of the greatest cross-cultural challenges experienced by business executives, academics, and ministry leaders occur over dinner after work.[17]

Another way our doing orientation affects our perseverance CQ is the way we approach the experience of eating unfamiliar foods. The other day Grace blurted out, "This tastes like another country!" How many times have you felt that way when biting into something unfamiliar? Eating food with people from other socioethnic cultures is an ideal way to reveal how our doing orientation shapes our perseverance CQ. If you come to my house and you don't like some of the dishes we've prepared for you, I'd prefer you eat what you like and leave the rest. It's fine with me if you don't like everything we've made. Perhaps you feel the same way. And without interpretive CQ, it's easy to assume people in other cultures will feel similarly when they serve us something we don't like.

Food has a primarily utilitarian function for Americans. We eat to have energy. We eat so we can "do" more. Sure, we're accused of being obese and obsessed with junk food, but food primarily serves utilitarian ends for us. In contrast, for many cultures food is a direct expression of who the people are. There are people in India who use spices that come from plants that have been growing on their homestead for multiple generations. The best Indian meals take days to prepare. So to pass on eating dishes prepared for you in that context could be far more than passing on a dish you just don't care for. It can be seen as an all-out rejection of the Other. And as for eating with utensils versus eating with our hands, one of my Indian friends puts it this way: "Eating with utensils is like making love through an interpreter!" They want direct contact with their food.

Here the complexity of perseverance CQ comes into play with the understanding gained from knowledge and interpretive CQ. When is it okay to pass on eating something that turns your stomach, and when must we eat it and say, "Dear God, help me keep it down"? As we broaden our repertoire of cultural understanding and behavior, we'll become more attuned to knowing which response is appropriate. We'll address the issue of when to adapt and when not to adapt in the next chapter. But first we need to look at one more important consideration related to perseverance CQ.

> What are some of the cross-cultural dynamics you experience that make you uncomfortable? How do you react to this discomfort? What's behind your discomfort? Why? Why? Why? What does it look like for you to persevere through this discomfort?

Don't Kid Yourself

I began this chapter by asking us to honestly face some of the things that keep us from persevering in what we know we need to do to be more culturally intelligent. Some of us will thrive on the chance to stay with locals; others among us will pray to God that we get to stay in a hotel. Some of us love trying new foods. Others hope to sneak a taste from home when traveling abroad. I thrive on being in new cultures—whether it's observing the way a different denomination works through a highly volatile issue, seeing the way youth express their identity, or observing the practices of a tribal group in Southwest China. Part of me really comes to life with these kinds of opportunities. But I regularly have my share of moments when I hit the wall. They don't have to be all out meltdowns, and they usually aren't. Take this one for example:

I'm tired. My internal clock still hasn't adjusted to the time here in Kuala Lumpur. And Em is sick at home. Is what I'm doing even making any difference? I wish I could jump on a plane and go home.

On top of all that, the teaching didn't go very well yesterday. I should know better than to think I can pose questions to the large group and expect I'll get meaningful responses, but I didn't want to use smaller discussion groups. We're already a relatively small group, so I wanted us to benefit from the collective conversation. But Esther was the only one who would speak up. I know I need to use a different approach today.

But there's no time to prepare right now. I need to get downstairs and have breakfast with the group. I'd love to run around the corner to Starbucks, but I don't think that's appropriate.

I'm learning to be more honest with myself about my motivation level when I'm engaged in cross-cultural work. Honestly facing our lack of motivation is integral to all the other dimensions of cultural intelligence that we've talked about. And sometimes our lack of motivation to think and act in culturally intelligent ways doesn't look very flattering or politically correct. But if we can't be honest with ourselves, there's little promise of persevering through cross-cultural challenges. Notice the frank, raw musings written by Sharise, a ministry leader in Portland.

> Am I the only one who owns up to being racist? Yesterday when I stopped to get my blood drawn, a black man walked in. I just assumed he was the lab tech. Only later did it become evident that he's a physician. . . . Why did I so quickly assume he must be the lab tech? If he had been a white guy, I probably would have guessed him to be the doctor.
>
> My next stop was at the seminary where I'm starting classes this fall. They told me my advisor is Dr. Pratt. I don't know the guy, but I just looked up his picture. He's overweight, looks like he's sixty years old, and white as they come. . . .
>
> I hate that I thought these things! I'm doing the same things so many white folks do to me. I'm just assuming things about Dr. Pratt based on what I've experienced for the last forty-three years of my life.

I actually find great hope in the honesty of Sharise's reflections. And it's not that I'm just extending more grace to her because she's an African American woman. I'm also encouraged by the honesty of Mindy, a thirty-six-year-old blonde mother in the suburbs. She said,

> Our ladies' group has been building friendships with a group of women who are from a church in the city. Many of them are from different ethnic backgrounds, but every one of us from our group are as white as they come. We look like total soccer moms.
>
> But it's been so rich to see how differently our two groups talk about our families, our walk with God, and even things like getting ready for the holidays.
>
> But I have to admit. There are days when I wish it could be just our group. It's easier. And, okay, now I'm going to be really vulnerable. It scares me to drive there and leave my car there. I know that sounds so awful. But last night's news reported another shooting right on the block where we meet when we go there.

The combination of her self-description as a soccer mom with her fear of driving in the city during broad daylight might make you wonder why I say I'm encouraged by Mindy's comments. But I have far more hope in our moving toward culturally intelligent service when we can get beyond the benign statements of how much we view everyone the same and start speaking honestly about our fears and discriminatory views as Sharise and Mindy do. The whole process begins with honesty.

Few movies have elicited as much internal conflict for me as *Crash*, a film with several interweaving stories involving different cultures over a two-day period in Los Angeles. Every time I would get irate about the ways people in one subculture were negatively stereotyping people in the other subculture, something would happen that reinforced the negative stereotype. These are the very real challenges that come with actually living out cultural intelligence.

A familiar comment I've heard from people as I share some of the issues related to cultural intelligence is "Great! Now I feel paralyzed to do anything for fear of messing up." Given the importance of efficacy to effective perseverance in cross-cultural work, feeling paralyzed isn't a great place to be. With some measure of caution, I often tell people, "The very fact that you're concerned and now a bit tentative is a great starting point!" At the same time, we have to move beyond our fear, be willing to take risks, and trust that a heart undergoing transformation will allow us to serve the Other in ways that are respectful and loving. Most importantly, we want to believe God will work through our culturally intelligent ministry and service rather than in spite of us, though surely we realize both will occur.

To what degree should we try to enter new cultural contexts together with others from our familiar context? There's a safety that comes with experiencing another culture with others from home. Suburban church planters feel more comfortable if they bring other suburbanites with them to plant a church in the inner city. Southern Baptists checking out an emergent gathering feel less exposed if they go together. But we're much less likely to succeed in a cross-cultural setting when we encounter it with a large group of companions from our familiar context. Large, short-term missions teams who stay together in hotels or dorms are at a great disadvantage to smaller groups of short-termers who stay with locals. Members of the large groups will tend to gravitate toward staying with the familiar group, or at the very least, they will share their most significant encounters with the group from home rather than with the local hosts.

There is also the temptation to put on our best behavior when we're in front of the Other but to let down our guard when we're with those from home. But if I speak respectfully to the group of Honduran believers, only to rant and make fun of some of their customs when alone with my short-term team, it will inevitably shape how I view the Hondurans when I reconnect with them tomorrow. Outsiders who come into a new environment as a large group "have a fully functioning reference group, support group, and the like, so they are not as motivated to integrate themselves into the local setting."[18]

At the same time, there are occasions, especially when we're immersed in ongoing, extended work cross-culturally, that we need to withdraw for a while, either to spend time with people coming from a more familiar cultural context or to have time alone with some of the comforts of our cultural environment. I think any short-term missions team can survive without rooming together for a couple weeks, not to mention that they can get along without a McDonald's fix (okay—and without Starbucks!). And I think any mature believer ought to be able to endure a different genre of worship music for a season. But there may be times when it is not only appropriate but even healthy to steal away to eat some trail mix or to listen to your favorite bands on your iPod.

In talking about this need for expatriates working in a different national culture, Storti says,

> As long as we don't shrink from further contact, there's nothing wrong with retreating from time to time to recharge our batteries. But we must be careful lest we begin trusting our instincts entirely in this matter, for they will invariably draw us deeper into the expatriate web, and before we know it, a little innocent contact with fellow sojourners has become an exclusive way of life. In the end, the time and effort spent befriending other sojourners must necessarily come at the expense of reaching out to the local culture.[19]

I'm probably going to regret this confession, but I have to come clean here. I'm known for my great love for good coffee. My girls gave me a personal-size French press last year for my birthday so I could take it with me when I travel to places where only weak instant coffee is available. Now you might see this as an addict's grand scheme at rationalization. But given the frequency with which I travel, I often take along my French press to enjoy a good cup of coffee when I'm alone. I do use discrimination about where and when I use it. I don't haul it out and carry it into the dining area of a place where I'm staying. But if I can get some hot water in the privacy of my room, I make myself a cup of good brew as a small comfort from home and then fully engage with the people in the culture where I'm spending the rest of the day.

Conclusion

Perseverance CQ relies on honesty about what we like and dislike about another culture. We can't expect to like everything about another culture any more than we like everything about our own. "If we genuinely respect another culture, we must allow ourselves to be appalled by it."[20]

We need honesty about where our greatest points of resistance lie in making the adjustments necessary to sincerely express the love of Jesus to the Other. There will be times when we must learn to adjust despite the discomfort it causes, but we must beware of walking the fine line between respectful adjustment and altering who we genuinely are. "If we are not at ease with ourselves, can we ever be truly at ease with another culture?"[21] Maybe we're never fully at ease with ourselves, but the goal is to become at ease with embracing the tension that comes with going below the surface in ourselves and others. This is at the crux of looking in as we reach out—knowing how to sacrificially love the Other while still authentically being who God made us to be.

We've explored four crucial parts to persevering across the chasm of cultural difference—self-efficacy, considering the motivation behind why we serve, looking at how our orientation toward doing influences our cultural intelligence, and honestly facing where we find the greatest internal resistance to adjust to the Other. This leads us to the final factor of cultural intelligence, behavioral CQ.

Recommended Resources

Easterly, William. *The White Man's Burden: Why the West's Efforts to Aid the Rest Have Done So Much Ill and So Little Good.* New York: Penguin, 2006.

Nhat Hanh, Thich. *The Art of Power.* New York: HarperOne, 2007.

Rolheiser, Ronald. *The Holy Longing: The Search for a Christian Spirituality.* New York: Doubleday, 1999.

14

kiss, bow, or shake

Behavioral CQ

mpirical studies suggest that more than half of American adults can be described as conformists. That is, they make choices about where to live, how to dress, what car to drive, and where to vacation based on the norms of the dominant group(s) to which they belong. Conformists are characterized by stereotypical thinking, clichés, all-or-nothing statements, and concrete thinking. Conformists want what "their" group values. They feel trust and warmth with people like themselves and feel uncomfortable and suspicious of people who are different. Conformists living alternative lifestyles (notice the irony!) are uncomfortable with "straight" people, and conformists living as "straight" people are uncomfortable around people living alternative lifestyles. Baptists seek out Baptists. White-collar professionals seek out white-collar professionals. Emergent church leaders hang out with emergent church leaders. Mexican Americans look for Mexican Americans. Thirty-somethings look for thirty-somethings. This is what it means to be a conformist.

The identity of the conformist is scarcely derived from an internal sense of self but mostly from the various groups to which the individual belongs. How do they perceive me? How do I present myself as successful in this context? For the conformist, knowing how to behave when encountering the Other is often disorienting and frustrating. And even service to the Other is usually used to form one's self-identity rather than as a true act of selfless love for the Other. Most adults around us are preoccupied with appearance, reputation, social acceptance, and belonging.[1]

We all struggle with these insecurities. To desire love, acceptance, and belonging is not a bad thing. It's part of what it means to be human. We long for community and a secure sense of identity and belonging. But remaining in a state of conformity throughout adulthood runs against the Christian call to surrender control and power and to love God through our selfless service to the Other. The way we serve the Other is reflected in our behavior, which is nothing more than a symptom of what lies deep within.

At the end of the day, our love for the Other is judged based on how we behave. Can we move from the intention and desire to love to effectively expressing our love to the Other? This is where the rubber meets the road. Do we know what someone is talking about? Are we able to communicate effectively? Can we greet people appropriately and adjust our behavior as needed while still remaining true to who we are? Behavioral CQ is the extent to which we *appropriately* change our verbal and nonverbal actions when we interact cross-culturally. The real challenge here is knowing when it's appropriate to flex our behavior from how we would act in our own cultural context and when it isn't. When will not flexing our behavior become a roadblock, and when will doing so appear inauthentic?

Those are the questions we want to explore as we look at this final dimension of cultural intelligence, behavioral CQ. The goal is to be yourself, while figuring out which behaviors need to change in order to lovingly express who you are and who Jesus is. This is not unlike what I have to learn as a father. My two girls are very different from each other. Emily is a homebody who loves to hang out and snuggle together while reading a book, and she loves to share a long meal together. Grace, on the other hand, is constantly moving. She's happiest when there is a lot going on. She wants to walk to the store, throw a Frisbee, or work on an art project all in the same hour.

I want my girls to experience love in their own language, so I work hard to relate to them differently. I express my love for both of my girls in ways that are authentically me, but I express it uniquely to each of them because of their personalities. It's not that I'm trying to be a chameleon and change who I am. I simply want them to experience my love for them in ways that are meaningful to each of them. We can't possibly learn the love languages of all the people we encounter in ministry. But learning the cultural norms of different groups of people helps us more effectively communicate love in ways they will understand. That's why cultural intelligence is so important to me.[2] It's an essential competency for me as a ministry leader in order to effectively and authentically become a living picture of Christ to the Other.

Our cultural intelligence is ultimately judged based on how we behave. How do you fare based on these measurements?

- Do I use pause and silence differently to suit different cross-cultural situations?
- Do I alter my verbal behavior (e.g., accent, tone) according to the culture that I am in?
- Do I display different behaviors based on specifics of the local culture?
- Do I change the manner in which I greet others (shake hands, bow, nod, etc.) when in different cultures?
- Do I change the amount of warmth and enthusiasm I express when talking to others to suit the cultural setting?[3]

These are the kinds of actions measured when we test behavioral CQ.

Ironically, the most effective way to manipulate our behavior is through the other three factors of cultural intelligence. Behavioral CQ is primarily the outcome of our understanding, thinking, and motivation, so there's less information here about behavioral CQ than in the chapters devoted to the other three factors. In one sense, this whole book is about behavioral CQ. Moving from the desire to love to actually expressing love in respectful, meaningful ways is manifested in our behavior. Understanding, going deep, and persevering translate into behavioral CQ. Notice how knowledge, interpretive, and perseverance CQ influence the behavior of the individuals involved in this scenario:

Habib is an immigration official in a Middle Eastern country. One of his jobs is to review applications for trading permits issued to overseas visitors. He has to ensure that all the appropriate criteria are met. If they are, he will normally grant the permit.

Habib's salary for this job is extremely low. Relying on his salary alone, Habib would find it very difficult to provide even the bare essentials for his family. Fortunately, there is relief for him in the system. He is good at his job, and it is customary for applicants to show their appreciation for his service by giving him small sums of money. Some of these applicants are Americans and Europeans, who can easily afford these additional costs. The arrangement is well understood by nearly everyone in Habib's country and works to the advantage of all.

Recently however, Habib has had some difficulty working with a man named Tom Wight, who recently arrived as the director of a Christian relief organization. Tom is well dressed and formal. When he presented his application, it was impeccable. However, he showed no signs of offering a financial accommodation. Perhaps, Habib thought, this was just an oversight. Perhaps Mr. Wight did not realize how much authority Habib had in this situation. He told him there was some further paperwork to be done and that he should come back in a few days.

Tom has been back twice. On each occasion, he has become more irritated at the delays, but despite some broad hints dropped by Habib, he still has not offered any cash. So Habib persists in his approach: If Mr. Wight will not play the game according to the established rules, he will have to accept the consequences.

Back at his office, Tom calls an old friend back in the States, a man with experience in the country in question. The friend immediately realizes what the problem is and advises Tom how much he should offer and how he should make the offer. Tom becomes angry.

"But that's bribery!" he exclaims. "Pure corruption."

"No, it's just the way people do things," says the friend. "Think of it as a tip."[4]

Knowledge CQ would help Tom grow in his understanding of why bribery occurs in this cultural context as well as learn how to deal with delays. It would serve Habib in realizing why Tom might not be picking up on the cues being sent. Interpretive CQ serves people such as Tom and Habib by helping them step back from the immediate frustrations and behaviors to ask, "What's really going on here? Why isn't Habib cooperating even though everything was filled out correctly? Why doesn't Tom offer the appropriate remuneration?" Interpretive CQ will lead both parties to go deep and ask, "Why am I feeling so irritated by all this?" Such introspective honesty leads to perseverance CQ. Both Tom and Habib are motivated to resolve this problem, Tom so that he gets his necessary permit and Habib so that he gets paid. This leads Tom to call his friend back home. He's determined to get this sorted out. In question is whether either Tom or Habib have much motivation to truly understand the Other beyond getting their needs met. For now, the primary point is for us to notice how all these dimensions influence how Tom and Habib actually behave.

For Tom, presumably a man seeking to follow Jesus, the question becomes how might he flex his behavior in a way to accomplish what needs to get done while still remaining true to his sense of ethics. How do kingdom values intersect with cultural values? How does a realization that Habib's income depends on extra payment from foreigners shape the ethics of the situation? And the ethics aside for a minute, when it is an issue of neither right nor wrong but simply different, when is it appropriate to flex our behavior to mirror that of the Other and when isn't it? We pick up where we left off with perseverance CQ: to flex or not to flex? These are the two aspects of behavioral CQ that we need to consider.

Flexing

Learning if and when it is appropriate to adapt our behavior to the culture of the Other is a complex question. That's why cultural intelligence includes the various dimensions that it does. It's more than simply adapting behavior to the culture of the Other. It also requires that we in turn consider what the Other expects of us. How do people expect us to act based on our cultural context? And how should that affect our behavior? What misconceptions are likely to be present in their assumptions about me? These are all critical considerations for how we interact with the Other.

Actually, though we speak of behavioral CQ as cultural adjustment, we really adjust not to culture but to people's behavior. Behavior is the principal manifestation and most significant consequence of culture that we actually experience. "It is culture as encountered in behavior that we must learn to live with."[5] For example, it isn't hyper-fundamentalism itself that really annoys us. It's the actions of the hypocritical deacon who challenges our patience and grace. If our neighbors are Muslims, we don't need to adapt to Islam per se. Rather we must learn how we as Christians lovingly and respectfully interact with Aatif and Ghadir next door. An understanding of fundamentalist culture and Islamic norms will help us down that road, but ultimately it's person to person interaction that we must effectively accomplish. We love the Other up close.

Craig Storti describes two types of adjustments that invariably must occur as we interact cross-culturally. We have to adjust to behaviors of the Other that annoy or confuse us. And we have to adjust our own behavior so that it doesn't needlessly annoy or confuse the Other. This is a helpful contribution to the study of behavioral CQ. Storti describes these two adjustments as type 1 and type 2 behaviors.[6]

Type 1 behaviors, those actions of people in the other culture that annoy us, are the kinds of behavior to which we must learn to appropriately adapt. This might be everything from the way a Chinese taxi driver belches loudly to the frustration felt by a black preacher speaking to a staid, verbally unresponsive white congregation. Failure to adapt to these kinds of incidents seriously undermines the effectiveness and fulfillment of a ministry leader working cross-culturally.

Type 2 behaviors are the things we do that are offensive to others. Culture shock is not only something we experience. It's also something we inflict. Eating while walking down a street in Tokyo, wearing shorts while leading worship, and handing a passport to someone with the left hand are but a few of our behaviors that can offend people from other cultural contexts.

Suddenly we can see how our own willingness to change certain habits and behaviors can make the world a better place. It involves a reciprocal relationship. As I encounter other parts and people of the world, it changes me. A changed me allows me to be part of changing the world. And together, we're part of how God is restoring all of creation to be as he intended it to be.

> Think about a time when you were offended by someone's type 1 behavior. What happened? How about a time when you caused a type 2 offense? What did you do? What did you learn?

The cultures with which we have ongoing, extended contact are settings where we must diligently learn which behaviors to adjust. "Most of us are capable of handling an occasional encounter with unexpected, unfamiliar behavior; we do it all the time. It's the constant onslaught that takes some getting used to."[7]

One of my own learning curves in behavioral CQ has involved the realization that cultural intelligence is a two-way street. One day I was ranting to Soon Ang, my CQ mentor in Singapore, about having just come from West Africa, where I was with a group of Americans who brought along bottled water and antibacterial wash everywhere they went. It just seemed incredibly insensitive and obnoxious to me. Soon started to chuckle. She thinks I get too worked up over some things like this. She asked me, "So why do you expect them to have the cultural intelligence to not carry around their water bottles, but you don't expect the Sierra Leoneans to have the cultural intelligence to know Americans can't handle drinking the unfiltered water?"

I argued that when we enter a culture as the guests, we can't expect the hosts, in this case Sierra Leoneans, to change their behavior to suit our expectations. So it is up to us to change our behavior to conform to theirs. "We are the ones, after all, who have gone abroad; as guests we can't very well demand that our hosts adjust to us."[8] At the same time, many of our cross-cultural encounters don't involve clear distinctions of guest and host. So we need to explore ways to make cultural intelligence something we encourage in both directions. Soon's point is well taken. The richest cross-cultural relationships involve cultural intelligence flowing both ways.

There are some basic behaviors we simply need to hone before interacting with people in certain contexts. Slowing our rate of speech, knowing when or if it's appropriate to take pictures, learning how to appropriately greet people, eating with chopsticks—these are some of the rudimentary behaviors that we need to add to our repertoire for interacting in many cultures. But although these habits are often heavily emphasized in cross-cultural training, their importance pales in comparison to the most significant internal transformation that comes about through the other three factors of cultural intelligence. God in community brings about redemption in us, often through these elements of thinking, reflection, and motivation, so that we might more lovingly express his redemption to others.

Behavior is ambiguous. The same action can have many different meanings. Knowledge CQ can help inform us about possible underlying causes of behavior, but we need to persevere in using interpretive CQ to identify the context of the behavior and the contingencies of action before jumping to conclusions about the meaning of a particular action.[9] As we utilize interpretive CQ to explore these dimensions, we may also discern behaviors to which we should *not* try to adapt.

Not Flexing

One of the subtle but important differences between the conceptualization of cultural intelligence and that of other theories of cross-cultural sensitivity is the acknowledgment that in some situations the best option is not to adapt at all. Adjusting to the behavior of the other culture is a double-edged sword. Some level of adapting to communication styles and patterns cross-culturally is usually viewed positively because it leads to perceptions of similarity. However, high levels of adaptation are viewed negatively. Extensive mimicry will be seen as insincere and possibly even deceptive.[10]

Youth are usually grateful for youth leaders who seek to understand and respect their reasons behind dressing the way they do and listening to the kind of music they like. But that doesn't mean they want their leaders to start dressing like them and mirroring their iPod playlists.

Likewise, if I'm invited to participate at a conference in Japan, most Japanese will be favorably impressed if I am courteous, polite, and somewhat reserved. But they don't expect me to master the intricate social skills of Japan such as bowing appropriately. In fact, if I try to mimic cultural behaviors like these too much, at best my actions will be seen as amusing, and more likely, they will be seen as offensive.

One time some Hindu friends invited my family over for dinner. They invited us to sit at the kitchen table, and then they stood around and watched us the entire time we ate. With people from our own culture, we would have insisted they join us at the table. But we didn't do that because we weren't sure if their choice to stand and watch us eat was out of respect for us as guests, if they were uncomfortable sitting at the table, or if it was because they viewed us as "unclean" and would have had to violate their religious convictions to sit and eat with us. But when we invited them to our home, we sat and ate at the table with them just as we would if we invited you to our house. We flexed our behavior, and we didn't. We made our choices based on cultural strategic thinking (knowledge and interpretive CQ).

Because I grew up in a good Baptist home, dancing in church is not exactly something that comes naturally to me. But when I worship in some African American congregations, I try to figure out how not to look like a complete fool while also being aware that standing totally motionless could communicate my disengagement or, worse yet, disapproval. I try to figure out how to flex without being inauthentic. Someone not used to youth ministry culture could feel a similar dilemma when attending a youth retreat. Again, the challenge is to be true to who we are while altering our behavior in ways that will best communicate love and respect to the Other.

To flex or not to flex? How do we know? Those questions bring home why behavioral CQ is primarily a culmination of the other three factors of cultural intelligence. Rather than our simply mimicking the behaviors we observe, our decision to adapt needs to be based on the knowledge of the other culture and the people's expectations. Using that cultural understanding, interpretive CQ will help us pay attention to the appropriate cues in order to evaluate the possible outcomes and to know which behavior is appropriate. Through a state of liminality and praxis, we can persevere and draw on a growing repertoire of cross-cultural behavior. "Over time, of course, some adaptive behavior may become so well learned that it is initiated without much active thought. This ability may be indicative of quite a high level of cultural intelligence."[11] That's the goal. We want to get to a point where this high level of thinking and consequently acting happens as naturally as the thinking and behaviors enacted in our familiar cultural contexts. But getting there might be as simple as trial and error. Try flexing a bit and see what happens. Test it in lots of different situations. Ask a trusted peer with some relevant knowledge CQ about the situation how flexing or not flexing might be perceived by the Other. Then ask someone else. Then ask another person.

Just as exclusive withdrawal into one's own cultural context is inappropriate, so is "going native." Individuals who go native try to entirely strip themselves of their own culture in a fit of enthusiasm for the culture of the Other. These individuals can be seen embracing all the values and practices of a new culture with an eagerness that perplexes even those who are part of that culture. Uncritically accepting everything in a new culture and turning one's back on one's own birth culture is not culturally intelligent behavior. "It is as illogical to prefer everything about the native culture as it is to prefer everything about one's own. And both reactions are nurtured by the same factors: an ignorance of the local culture and an even deeper indulgence in self-deception."[12] We don't want to become the bull in the china shop when it comes to trying to adjust our behavior, but neither do we want to suffer the paralysis of overanalysis that keeps us from ever trying. And while good intentions by themselves are not enough, your heart and attitude toward the Other will speak volumes.

Conclusion

The most common problems in ministry across different cultural contexts are not technical or administrative. The biggest challenges lie in miscommunication, misunderstanding, personality conflicts, poor leadership, and bad teamwork. Cultural intelligence is demonstrated through our social interactions in cross-cultural relationships. The behavioral component of cultural intelligence "is the ability to adjust behavior based on the situation and expectations of others who are culturally different."[13] As opposed to mimicry, behavioral CQ involves learning from one's cultural understanding, interpretations, and motivation.

The ability to generate *appropriate* behavior in a new cultural context is another component of cultural intelligence that distinguishes it from other related ideas. Using knowledge and interpretive CQ, people who are culturally intelligent develop a behavioral capability that allows them to become competent across a wide range of cultural situations. This ability involves choosing the appropriate behavior from a well-developed repertoire of behaviors that are correct for different intercultural situations and also extrapolating to generate new behavior.

We can enjoy and respect the norms and customs of the Other without thinking we have to conform to everything we observe. The desire to love the Other is what starts us on the pathway of cultural intelligence. Understanding (knowledge CQ) plus going deep (interpretive CQ) combined with God-honoring motivation (perseverance CQ) leads to action (behavioral CQ). And when we get to action, we've arrived at the point of reaching across the chasm of cultural difference in ways that effectively express love to the Other. The point isn't to accomplish flawless cross-cultural behavior. In fact, some of the greatest lessons to be learned happen in our cultural faux pas. But as we build on our understanding, interpretation, and attempts to persevere, we come closer to behaving in ways that more effectively reflect Jesus to the Other through culturally intelligent communication.

Recommended Resources

Kohls, L. Robert, and John M. Knight. *Developing Intercultural Awareness: A Cross-Cultural Training Handbook*. Yarmouth, ME: Intercultural Press, 1994.

Seelye, H. Ned, ed. *Experiential Activities for Intercultural Learning*. Yarmouth, ME: Intercultural Press, 1996.

Storti, Craig. *Cross-Cultural Dialogues*. Yarmouth, ME: Intercultural Press, 1994.

where do we go from here?

Twenty-four Ways to Advance Your CQ

A couple of weeks ago I was teaching a class at a university in a little town in Indiana. In between class times, I read through some drafts of the preceding chapters for this book. I needed a break from reading and writing, so I decided to go for a run before joining some other people for dinner. As I looked around me, I muttered to myself, "Oh, God, I could never live in this town." Before I even finished the sentence, I felt a bit caught off guard by my own sentiment. I can walk the streets of cities and small towns in Ecuador, India, China, and Liberia and be filled with appreciation for all that is there. But I can find myself appalled by a sleepy town so close to home. A little while later, while eating ham loaf and mushy sweet potatoes, I kept reminding myself that cultural intelligence is an ongoing journey.

Thankfully I've seen plenty of growth in my own journey of interacting with the Other compared to the patronizing, immature perspectives found in my journal entries back in 1986 on my first missions trip. But I continue on the journey toward viewing and relating to the Other in ways that are respectful and loving. Who represents the cultural group most difficult for you to appreciate? By what group do you find yourself most easily appalled? Cultural intelligence and effectively expressing love to the Other is an ongoing journey. There's no such thing as achieving perfect cultural intelligence by reading a couple of books, taking a class, or going through a set of experiences. It's a lifelong quest of becoming more Christlike in how we interact with those unlike us.

All throughout the book, we've explored various ways to enhance living in the way of Jesus with the Other. There are practical implications to what we need to understand as we grow in knowledge CQ, to how we make meaning through interpretive CQ, and to the motivation and actual behavior that results from our perseverance and behavioral CQ. In this final chapter, I want to offer a few concluding thoughts for moving along in the journey of cultural intelligence long after you put this book aside. We'll begin with exploring some core commitments as we move forward in cultural intelligence, followed by a list of some practical activities to immediately enhance our growth in cultural intelligence.

Core Commitments

Regardless of where you are in your own journey toward cultural intelligence, the following core commitments need to guide our perspective on how we think about advancing cultural intelligence in ourselves and others.

Start the Anthropological Dig in Your Own Soul

Cultural intelligence is rooted in who we are as people; it is not a mechanistic tool for changing our behavior and strategies in order to get people to do what we want. So the guiding perspective for the journey ahead toward increased cultural intelligence must be a relentless commitment to continually *look in* as we reach across the chasm to the Other. Nothing is more important than digging into our own soul to understand who we are, how we relate, and what drives us. Self-awareness about our own upbringing, our cultural heritage, and our individual personality is the core aspect of moving forward in relating to the Other in ways that reflect Jesus. As we go through this transformational process, we live with the paradox of working hard to become more Christlike in our interactions cross-culturally while also acknowledging that ultimately a supernatural process of sanctification must occur for us to become people who unselfishly relate to the Other. Looking within need not lead to navel gazing and self-obsession. Instead, with intentional effort, it becomes the pathway toward selfless service.

Root Your View of the Other in the Imago Dei

I've said plenty throughout this journey about the importance of viewing both the things we have in common with all humanity and the profound differences. But seeing every person as created in the image of

God, the *imago Dei*, will shape how we relate. Who most represents the Other for you? The intolerant fundamentalist, the colleague from another culture who sees no need for deodorant, the seminary guy writing books about cultural intelligence, the person overspending at Wal-Mart after being laid off, the Indiana housewife who has never left the Midwest, the alternative-looking youth hanging out at the skate park? Whoever they are, whatever the group, they're all created in the image of God. Seeing the Other first in light of that theological reality is essential. It's hard to be entirely appalled by someone who reflects God, no matter how dim the reflection appears. And remember, we each represent the Other to someone else.

Seek First the Kingdom of God

Cultural intelligence can't be compartmentalized from the rest of our lives. It's all part of living in the Way of Jesus. I have little hope that I'll make cultural intelligence a more regular part of the way I relate to the Other if it's a skill I develop in isolation from my ongoing formation toward reflecting Christ. We're not seeking some politically correct way of behaving nor ways to better market the gospel. We're concerned about this issue because we, the body of Christ, are the language of God today. God continues to speak in Son (Heb. 1:2) through the resurrected body of Jesus—you and me. Growing in cultural intelligence must be seamlessly connected to how we follow Jesus and represent him to others.

Live Up Close

When taken off whiteboards and applied to real-life relationships and interactions, cultural intelligence is a messy, challenging process. "The proximity of friendships is the authentic classroom. . . . Transformation occurs when we begin to do life together with those who are not like us. We change. We find new paradigms and enjoy awareness of others and of God that we never knew."[1]

We were designed to live in relationship with those who see the world differently than we do, not to merely cloister ourselves with those who look, think, and act like us. The underpinning of cultural intelligence is not cerebral understanding of different cultures; it's love. That's why love continually appears in the center of the CQ map (fig. 1). Cultural intelligence helps us express love more authentically. But love is the driving point, and ultimately, love can't be lived out in books and journals. Love is lived out up close. In our world of loneliness and broken relationships, there is an enormous need for men and women with hearts that only want to give love. "It is a heart that suffers immensely because it sees the magnitude of human pain and the great resistance to trusting the heart of God who wants to offer consolation and hope. The Christian leader of the future is the one who truly knows the heart of God as it has become flesh."[2] This is why I care about cultural intelligence. It strengthens our ability to be the language of God wherever we go. Seek out the Other in ways that allow you to interact up close. Develop and join groups that don't merely perpetuate conformity to one cultural identity.

These core commitments—digging in our own souls, viewing the other as an image bearer of God, seeking the kingdom first, and living up close—must shape everything else we do in the pursuit of living and relating in culturally intelligent ways. Cultural intelligence allows us to more fully live as God intended in relationship with those he has created from all different cultural backgrounds.

Practices for Increasing CQ

With those core commitments in mind, let's consider several practices, many of which you may already do, to enhance the development of cultural intelligence in yourself and others. Some of these practices emphasize one of the four factors more than the others, and many of them help develop two or three of the factors simultaneously. Highlight a few that you'll begin doing immediately.

Read

At the risk of making you feel as if you've wasted your time reading this book, I find what most advances my ability to understand and potentially empathize with people from other cultural perspectives is to read memoirs and novels about the Other. Even if the culture represented by the book is very different from one you encounter, the very act of stepping into another world as we're allowed to do through narrative writing plays a profound role in making us more culturally intelligent. A few suggestions include:

The Kite Runner (Riverhead, 2003) and A Thousand Splendid Suns (Riverhead, 2007), by Khaled Hosseini.

The Poisonwood Bible (Harper Collins, 1998) and The Bean Trees (Harper Torch, 1998), by Barbara Kingsolver.

The Spirit Catches You and You Fall Down: A Hmong Child, Her American Doctors, and the Collision of Two Cultures (Farrar, Straus, and Giroux, 1998), by Anne Fadiman.

A Tribe Apart: A Journey into the Heart of American Adolescence (Ballantine, 1999), by Patricia Hersch.

White Man's Grave (Picador, 1995), by Richard Dooling.

These kinds of books, when read in tandem with more theoretical books such as *Cultural Intelligence*, play a particularly powerful role in increasing our knowledge and interpretive CQ.

Go to the Movies

Films can also help transform the way we see the Other in some of the same ways that novels and memoirs do. They allow us to step outside our immediate world while simultaneously comparing our experiences with those we're viewing in the story line of the movie. A few movies to consider for the purposes of enhancing cultural intelligence include:

Crash

Fond Kiss

The Motorcycle Diaries

The Namesake

The Last King of Scotland

Some viewers might find a few of the scenes and elements in some of these films offensive, but on the whole, they offer powerful lessons for cultural intelligence. Edward McNulty's *Praying the Movies* is a helpful resource for considering how to better tap into the transformative power of film for one's inner journey, the central component of cultural intelligence.

Eat

Food provides another powerful window into culture. Go to various ethnic restaurants and seek to understand the meanings that lie beneath the foods offered. Are the foods authentic, or are they adaptations for the American pallet or whoever is the primary clientele? Better yet, share the meal with someone who comes from the same culture as the food you're eating and see if she or he can offer some perspective about various dishes. Beware. A Thai friend might not be able to offer the history behind pad thai any more than someone from northern Michigan might be able to offer the history behind pasties. Most of us Americans might have little clue as to why peanut butter is the most common American food. But at the very least, when eating foods from other places with people from those places, we can ask what memories this dish evokes for them.

Journal

Journal writing can play a transformative role in helping us become more aware of ourselves, others, and our surroundings. Don't write for an audience. Be free to rant, ask yourself tough questions, expose your insecurities, and use the pages of your journal to chronicle your look within as you encounter the Other. You might choose to keep a separate journal to record your cross-cultural experiences, but I prefer to incorporate those reflections with the rest of my journaling. It connects my cross-cultural reflections more seamlessly to the rest of my life. Do more than chronicle what has happened; delve into the hard introspective work of reflecting on how you feel about what happened, what you think might be behind what you observed, and what you need to explore further.

Learn a New Language

As described in chapter 7, learning another language is directly connected to our knowledge CQ. It allows us to begin to see the world differently. Take a class in a new language or hire someone in town from another country to teach you his or her language. And seek to understand the various subcultural languages you encounter as well. When you're with someone from another part of the country, or an individual from a different denomination, profession, or generation, ask the person what a word or an acronym means when you don't understand it.

Attend Cultural Celebrations

With the growing diversity occurring all across the United States, local ethnic celebrations are becoming more readily available. Locate an ethnic organization in a community near you and attend its cultural celebration. If at all possible, participate in the event. Ask someone to explain the significance of the event and related activities. Get a group of friends to go to a Cinco de Mayo party together or attend an outing with the seniors' group from your church to learn about their generational culture.

Go to the Pride Parade and the Mosque

It's one thing to attend a Latin festival or a Chinese New Year party and soak it in. There is value in that. But what we're seeking with this strategy is to purposely find a cultural group with a set of beliefs that conflict with your own and attend one of their gatherings or events. Go to a mosque, a gay and lesbian meeting, a rave club, or a political gathering that is least aligned with your own leanings and seek to understand what's behind the beliefs and behaviors of this group. Beware of hasty assumptions and suspend judgment for a while. The goal is not to proselytize, though we should always be ready to call people to follow Jesus. The primary objective is to seek out a cultural context that is uncomfortable for you and observe what you see and how it makes you feel. What goes on within you as you observe it? Mark Vamos of *Fast Company* magazine makes a similar suggestion by encouraging us to tap into news sources we might not otherwise seek out. He writes, "We may not like what we hear on Al Jazeera International, but if it helps us understand how the rest of the world sees us . . . it will have performed a signal service."[3]

Be Informed

Americans are notorious for an abysmal global consciousness, a crucial part of increasing our knowledge CQ. "One of the things that's fueling disdain for the United States is the sense that we know little about the world beyond our borders and that we no longer harbor the 'decent respect for the opinions of mankind' cited in the Declaration of Independence."[4] Asking questions is one way to enhance our understanding of what's going on in other places and other cultural contexts. Tapping into various news sources is another way of doing so. You might be nervous about having Al Jazeera cookies on your Web browser, so start with something like *BBC News*. Listening to *BBC News* or adding its Web page (http://news.bbc.co.uk/) to your browser's favorites and reading weekly periodicals like the *Economist* provide a much more global perspective on world happenings than most of our US-based news sources. If nothing else, it's worth reading about some of the same events from a variety of cultural perspectives.

In a global survey recently released, most countries polled believed that China would act more responsibly in the world than the United States. "How does a Leninist dictatorship come across more sympathetically than the oldest constitutional democracy in the world? . . . The problem today is not that America is too strong but that it is seen as too arrogant, uncaring, and insensitive. Countries around the world believe the United States, obsessed with its own notions of terrorism, has stopped listening to the world."[5]

Simply being better informed about the issues facing our world is a step toward regaining the respect and admiration we used to have globally. Followers of Jesus ought to be leading the way in having that understanding and posture of listening.

Look for the Invisible

Constantly look for what's behind the actions, the words, the buildings, or the art you experience when encountering the Other. Why does the skate park look the way it does? What's behind the order of the liturgy used in that church? What does the newsletter teach you about the values of this cultural group? When doing so, suspend judgment for a time, test your assumptions, and listen, listen, listen. These are the kinds of things to record during journal writing. Without making culture the one-stop explanation for everything, we can benefit from making it one of the filters we immediately put in place when observing any situation. Whenever we see or hear something, we might ask ourselves, *How is culture shaping this?*

Study the Scripture with People
from Varied Cultural Contexts

There's an unbelievable treasure that exists given the growing degree of connectivity we have around the globe. It drives me nutty when I hear from short-term missions teams who spent time sharing their testimonies abroad but never heard any testimonies from the locals. Never before have we had more opportunity to get a multicultural perspective of Christianity and the Scriptures. Find ways to study Scripture with people coming from various cultural backgrounds—different ethnic cultures, organizational cultures, and generational cultures. A growing number of commentaries are being written by people from various ethnic cultures. Read them.

I have a friend who recently led devotions for her fellow faculty at the school where she teaches. She placed the faculty in groups so that a variety of disciplines were present in each discussion group. She had them discuss a particular passage of Scripture and asked them to specifically think about it through their lens as scientists, foreign-language instructors, mathematicians, humanities teachers, and so on. This is one of many creative ways to tap into the colorful mosaic around us to enhance our understanding of one another and God.

Always Do Mission with the "Oppressed"

When joining God to bring about redemption among those who are oppressed, both spiritually and physically, we must not do mission *to* oppressed people or *for* oppressed people. We must always do mission *with* them; otherwise we're perpetuating the very oppression we're seeking to break. The groups we serve, whether they be Mexicans, teenagers, or senior adults, can't be simply objects of our good will. If we're engaged in a cause that matters, some of them will be concerned about it as well. And for that matter, we're wise to realize the way we ourselves are oppressed by sin and perhaps by other forces. If we think of only others as the oppressed ones with needs, we fall back into that unhealthy position of power rather than engaging in mutual learning and service.

Whoever the receiving community is, there is always a missional cause you can join in together. Paint the building together. Work at the AIDS clinic together. Wash the lepers' stumps together. And unabashedly call people to follow Jesus as the best possible way to live.

Beware of Culturally Embedded Language

Words are powerful, and there will be times when we choose to be intentionally provocative. But we must anticipate the impact of the words we use, even when interacting with people who speak the same national language as we do. For example, a pastor ought to think carefully before flippantly throwing out a comment such as, "I'm committed to the authority of Scriptures, but I'm not so sure about inerrancy." Among many groups a whole set of assumptions come with the idea of inerrancy. Carefully considering our language might be simply learning to translate our in-house jargon into words that make sense for people who aren't familiar with the acronyms we're using or the technical terms used by our organizational culture. Grow in cultural intelligence by thinking about whether the Other understands the language and concepts you're using as you speak.

Speak Slowly

When you speak to people from other cultural contexts, slow down. Particularly when interacting with people whose dialect is different from ours or for whom our language isn't their primary language, we need to slow our rate of speech. I'm being a total hypocrite here. It's excruciatingly painful for me to speak slowly, particularly when I'm teaching publicly. But a simple way to enhance culturally intelligent behavior is to slow one's rate of speech. Our well-prepared lessons or our caring words of interaction mean little if the Other can't understand us or keep up with us.

Observe Body Language

We're wise to pay attention to the cues that body language offers. Communication experts tell us it's much harder to lie nonverbally than verbally. We certainly have to beware of thinking we can make solid assumptions based on the ambiguous messages received from nonverbal communication, particularly when coming from someone from a different culture. But observing nonverbal language is another simple tool to aid in advancing cultural intelligence. When you begin to interpret meaning from the nonverbal cues you observe, find appropriate ways to test your interpretations and assumptions.

Try Mimicry

Actors often invest weeks and even months in researching the life of a character they're going to portray on stage. We're not interested in playacting when encountering the Other, and I've already cautioned against thinking that we should always adapt our behavior. But there will be times when learning to mimic the behaviors of another culture will enhance our ability to relate. Some people pick up cues and mimic quickly, while others may need to practice much longer. When done respectfully and thoughtfully, mimicry can be a fun way to work on identifying and empathizing with the Other.

Find a Cultural Guide

A cultural guide, sometimes referred to as a cultural broker, can be an integral part of helping us become more culturally intelligent. My friend Andrew has lived in the academic culture much longer than I have and often helps me interpret university culture, even though he teaches at another school. And our seminary dean, John, has been my lifeline in helping me understand the culture of our seminary. Judy has been guiding me through life in Southeast Asia for more than ten years, Ashish and Joel have been helping me in India, and Mark in South Africa. Steve sometimes comes to me for perspective on the subculture of fundamentalist Christianity, since I grew up in it and he didn't.

Cultural guides can be a valuable asset in any of the cultural domains we've explored. The challenge is finding one who can truly play that role. For example, sometimes outsiders, such as a missionary or another expatriate worker, can be a valuable guide because they too are bridging from another culture into this one. But I've also encountered expatriates who have very skewed, ill-informed understandings of the cultures in which they live. Locals can be good guides, but we also have to beware of assuming that the people who live in a culture make the best guides. They often lack the necessary objectivity.

Effective cultural guides will use questions to guide us and offer support and feedback. They need to be people who are careful not to oversimplify while also offering some helpful, neutral stereotypes. Whoever our guide may be, we must remember the importance of not generalizing based on the advice we receive from any one individual. "What they say may be true for people of their own age group, level of education, socioeconomic background (not to mention caste, religion, region or locality, sex, and experience) but not for other sectors of society. Ask a Montana rancher and a Manhattan banker what proper behavior or dress is at a dinner party and try to generalize from their answers!"[6]

Formal Education

I've been careful not to make cultural intelligence something that requires degrees and formal training. If it did, I'd have little hope that most ministry leaders would actually have the opportunity and resources to acquire it. But certainly formal courses and training, when done in tandem with real-life experience, can play a significant role in enhancing our cultural experiences. Any formal education in cultural intelligence or the like must include immersion in various cultural contexts. Increasing numbers of workshops, online courses, and degree programs are being offered that can be valuable tools in moving us another step forward in the journey of cultural intelligence.

Multicultural Groups and Teams

There are few things as challenging and rewarding as serving on a multicultural team to complete a project. Culturally diverse groups offer you the opportunity to observe the behavior of culturally different individuals in the same context. Diversity in age, ethnicity, socioeconomic status, or denomination are but a few of the ways to mix up the cultural perspectives on a team. Again, we have to avoid developing diverse teams simply because doing so makes us look more diverse. Instead, we do so because we truly believe we'll have a more effective team when we more closely mirror the mosaic of God's people scattered across the planet. Appendix D includes some preliminary findings of elements consistently found among churches and ministry teams that collectively serve in culturally intelligent ways.

Overseas Experience

Although overseas experience by itself doesn't guarantee cultural intelligence, when wed with the many dimensions we've explored throughout this journey, it is a valuable contributor to our becoming more aware of cultural difference. We need to seek out experiences working overseas that don't exploit the Other just to make us more culturally intelligent. But as we engage in activities abroad that allow us to serve *with* the Other, we're tapping into a primary source for growing in the journey of loving like Jesus. International travel with large groups of people from our own cultural group (e.g., short-term missions trips or study-abroad tours) do much less to increase our cultural intelligence. Such trips usually lead us to process the experience with people like ourselves rather than with the Other. But international travel done alone or with a few significant others, especially when combined with a cultural guide, is an essential part of developing cultural intelligence.

Attend the Wedding Ceremony of Someone from Another Culture

Just as cultural celebrations can aid us in becoming more culturally intelligent, religious services or special ceremonies can do so as well. Attending an unfamiliar religious service or wedding ceremony is one of the times when it's really helpful to have a cultural guide. A great deal of high-context communication occurs in these kinds of ceremonies. Much of what occurs is symbolic and assumes understanding by those involved. Having someone explain the significance of the rituals involved is extremely helpful.

Read the Local Paper, Not USA Today, When Traveling

Whether in small-town Indiana or in Chaing Mai, Thailand, read a local paper. English newspapers are available in a growing number of places around the world. If you're addicted to something like *USA Today* or the *Wall Street Journal*, at least read it alongside a local paper and compare what gets reported in one as compared to the other. Skim all of it—advertisements, classifieds, public notices. You can gain a fascinating insight into a place by reading what is reported in the local news.

Walk through the Grocery Store

Grocery stores are another fascinating way to get a glimpse into the local culture. Find where the locals shop and look at what's on the shelves. Again, I enjoy doing this in various parts of the United States as well as when I travel abroad. The products sold locally and the way they're displayed provide interesting cues about the local context. Go into other stores that target niche markets such as older people, teachers, Harley fans, or Catholics.

Seek Out the Other

Look for ways to experience life with people who don't all look like you or see the world the way you do. We're inclined to form small groups, align with accountability partners, and attend conferences with people like us. Break the constraints of conformity. Read books by people with whom you're likely to disagree. Seek a neighborhood that reflects diversity. Create a "faith club" to engage in interfaith dialogue with people from other religions.[7] Again, we must beware of exploiting the Other simply to increase our cultural intelligence or as a target of proselytizing. But diversifying the community in which we live can play a key role in moving us forward on the path toward better expressing love to the Other.

Question, Question, Question

Ask questions. Listen hard. Ask questions. Listen hard. Ask questions. Listen hard. I can't think of anything more crucial on the journey of cultural intelligence than this point. Continually ask questions of yourself. Continually ask questions of others. And listen for what's said in response (and what's *not* said). Then test what you hear by posing the questions to someone else from that cultural group, and another person, and another person. And keep asking questions of yourself. It's difficult to empathize with the Other if we merely make assumptions about ourselves and him or her without asking questions.

Questioning itself requires some measure of cultural intelligence. Earlier I mentioned Ashish, my dear friend in northern India who asked me what I've learned from him. Ashish and I have had many long, intimate conversations over the last several years. A couple of years ago Ashish and I met for dinner, and within the first few minutes of being together, I asked Ashish what I'd be inclined to ask many close single friends: "How's your love life these days?" Ashish rebutted, "Hang on awhile. Maybe we can talk about that a bit later."

Later on Ashish brought up his dating life on his own, or more literally, he shared the quandary he was facing with the marriage his parents wanted to arrange for him. As we tap into knowledge and interpretive CQ, we can learn how to appropriately learn when, how, and what to ask. I've talked with many international guests to the United States who say that the only question they're asked while here is how they like life in the States. Some say they will spend years here without being asked a single question about what life is like in their country of origin. Ask questions. Listen hard. If you don't practice anything else, do this. It's one of the most powerful ways to move toward more lovingly relating to the Other.

These are only a few of many practical, everyday ways to advance cultural intelligence. Of course, many of the things I've suggested, such as going to a local celebration or walking through a grocery store, do little more than show us the artifacts of culture that appear at the tip of the iceberg. But these strategies, when combined with the fuller journey of cultural intelligence that we've explored throughout this book, can be helpful practices for more lovingly relating to the Other.

Conclusion

The journey toward more effectively expressing love for the Other begins by looking within. Rare is the ministry leader who reaches a place of wholeness with Christ that results in surrendering power, control, and judgment over the Other. Few are the churches and organizations led by men and women who are content to make their vulnerable selves their greatest offerings to the world.[8] Yet the key to culturally intelligent spiritual leadership has much more to do with our internal lives than with our expertise, gifts, or experience.[9]

I've journeyed to many communities around the world and to many places deep within myself since my first short-term missions trip in 1986. I expect you could recount similar transformations from your own journey within and across. If I'm around in twenty years, I'll probably have a whole different measure of insight into what the journal entries I'm writing this week say about who I am and how I view the Other. That doesn't paralyze me. It propels me to continue along in the journey within that I might better express my love to the people I encounter day in and day out.

Love.   I want to relate, serve, and live with the Other in ways that better express the sacrificial, unconditional love of Jesus.

Understand. I want to understand myself and others and the ways culture shapes who we are.

Go deep.   I want to go deep into the waters of what lies beneath the behaviors of myself and others.

Express.   I want to see my desire to love the Other become more of a reality. I want to draw on my understanding and deep reflection in order to persevere through the hard work of authentically expressing my love for the Other in ways that are respectful and dignifying.

Love.   "Love the Lord your God with all your heart and with all your soul and with all your mind. . . . Love your neighbor as yourself" (Matt. 22:37–39). That is what this journey is all about. Cultural intelligence is a pathway for moving from the *desire* to live out Jesus's timeless words to *actually doing it*. This is why cultural intelligence matters. This is *maitri*. This is the essence of the gospel—selfless love that calls people to Jesus.

God, the Holy Other, loves us more than anyone else ever has or will. He reaches across every chasm of difference and meets us where we are. In the end, God is in charge. He is building his kingdom in every culture, and we get to be the living demonstrations of his work. And through us, he reaches across the chasm to others.

Every geopolitical nation of the world has some remnant of the Christian church. As the rest of humanity brushes up against us, they get pictures of what Jesus looks like. May the pictures they see reflect the sacrificial, revolutionary love of Jesus. May we look within that we might better reach across the chasm of cultural difference in ways that are loving and respectful. May we let the world change us so that we can change the world. And may we lead the way in demonstrating selfless love for the Other in the twenty-first century.

God is redeeming all of creation, including you and me and the ways we relate to the Other. He allows us to be both recipients and agents of his redemption. He is the I Am. You and I are not. *Soli deo Gloria*. God bless you as you look in and reach out.

Recommended Resources

Axtell, Roger, ed. *Do's and Taboos Around the World*. New York: Wiley, 1990.

Lingenfelter, Sherwood. *Leading Cross-Culturally: Covenant Relationships for Effective Christian Leadership*. Grand Rapids: Baker Academic, 2008.

glossary

Attribution theory: Research that explores how we name and label the world.

Bounded sets: Sets that use clear boundaries that group people and things in a category and separate them from other people and things not in the category. People and things are classified in light of their intrinsic value.

Category width: Refers to the number of events individuals place under one common label. It is the degree to which one is comfortable with things that don't clearly fit into one category or the other (e.g., right versus wrong versus different).

Centered sets: Sets in which things related to the center belong to the category, and things not related to the center or moving away from the center do not belong. People and things are classified by defining a center or reference point.

Collectivism: A cultural value that leads people to see their identity in light of a group (family, church, etc.). They prefer group decisions and working with others.

Cultural intelligence (CQ): A metaframework that measures and explains one's ability to reach across the chasm of cultural difference in ways that are loving and respectful.

Empathy: The ability to imagine ourselves in someone else's position and to intuit what that person is feeling.

Guanxi: The Chinese word for the personal relationship between people that obligates them to one another's needs and desires.

Individualism: A cultural value that leads people to see their identity as personally rather than collectively derived. Individualistically inclined people prefer to work toward personal goals and to be rewarded individually (as compared to "collectivism").

Logic sets: The way a culture shapes how an individual forms categories (e.g., bounded sets versus centered sets).

Maitri: A Sanskrit word for love rooted in the idea that compassion and generosity begin with an individual's *desire* to love, but love is expressed only when one knows how to move from *desire* to *action*.

The Other: Refers to those who are different from us as a result of our different cultural contexts.

self-assessment of CQ

The Self-Assessment of CQ[1] is intended primarily to enhance your understanding of cultural intelligence. Assessments like this one are limited without also including the feedback of others who observe you in cross-cultural contexts. Information about a multirater assessment can be found at http://www.culturalq.com. The Self-Assessment of CQ was developed by Linn Van Dyne and Soon Ang and originally appeared in *CQ: Developing Cultural Intelligence at Work*, permission granted by Van Dyne and Ang for use in this book.

A Self-Assessment of CQ

The following questions are about dealing with diverse cultures. There are no right or wrong answers. Instead, the questions simply allow you to express your preferences, desires, and habits. Thinking about these questions can help you understand your unique strengths and how you relate to people you meet in your own country and those from other societies. *In order to gain the most benefit from this assessment, be as honest and realistic as possible about what truly reflects who you are and how you think and feel.*

Read each question carefully and choose either A or B. Do not think too long about any question. If you cannot decide on a particular answer, skip the question and come back to it at the end.

Section A

Instructions

Which of the following choices *best* describes you *when you are in situations characterized by cultural diversity*? Circle either A or B (*not both*) for each question to indicate which better describes you as you are most of the time.

1. Would you rather work with someone who is from
   A the same or a similar culture, or
   B a very different culture?

2. When you are with a person from a different culture, do you
   A plan what you say, or
   B act spontaneously?

3. Do you like to
   A travel in your home country, or
   B travel to faraway places?

4. When you know you will be meeting someone from a different culture, do you
   A script what you want to say before you start, or
   B treat him or her as you would any other person from your own culture?

5. Do you typically
   A assume many roles, or
   B adopt one primary role?

6. At parties with people from diverse cultural backgrounds, do you
   A mimic other people, or
   B maintain your own style?

7. In your daily work, would you prefer a job in a culture that is
   A similar to your own, or
   B different from your own?

8. When thinking about understanding people from different cultures, are you
   A an expert, or
   B a novice?

9. Do you view yourself as
   A beginning to learn more about culture, or
   B having lots of cultural expertise?

10. When speaking to people from diverse cultures, do you use
    A a consistent speaking style, or
    B a variety of accents?

11. Would you say you are
    A not really aware when people are from other cultures, or
    B very aware when people are from other cultures?

12. Which best describes you?
    A I can read more than two languages.
    B I can read one or two languages.

13. Are you
    A alert to the possibility that someone might be from a different culture, or
    B indifferent that someone might be from a different culture?

14. When you are in groups of people who have diverse backgrounds, do you
    A usually stick to your normal way of speaking, or
    B change the way you speak depending on the group?

15. When you work on a project, do you find you prefer to work with
    A people from similar cultures, or
    B those from different cultures?

16. When you are with people who have a different cultural background, do you
    A think about the differences, or
    B forget they are different?

17. In getting a job done, which describes you better?
    A I am indifferent to working with people from other cultures.
    B I celebrate cultural differences.

18. When it comes to knowing how to cope with cultural diversity, would others say you are
    A very knowledgeable, or
    B a neophyte?

19. In your spare time, would you choose to
    A upgrade your technical skills, or
    B learn about cultural differences?

20. Given the choice, would you select working with people who are
    A not that competent technically, but from similar cultures, or
    B technically very competent, but from very different cultures?

21. In knowing how to navigate new cultures, do you see yourself as
    A highly experienced, or
    B at the entry level?

22. Do you tend to
    A be aware that people from another culture are different, or
    B pay very little attention to their difference?

23. Is it your habit
    A not to plan in advance when interacting with those from different cultures, or
    B to take charge of your interactions when you're with others from different cultures?

24. Do you typically
    A stick to your own mannerisms, or
    B modify your mannerisms when you talk with people from different cultures?

25. Would you rank working with people from different cultures as
    A one of your many interests, or
    B a top interest?

26. Do you
    A eat what is familiar to you, or
    B try what others eat when having meals with people from other cultures?

27. Are you more likely to
    A set clear goals before you start working with others from different cultures, or
    B work with them as if they were your regular colleagues?

28. When you have to meet strangers from another culture, do you
    A go with the flow and according to the situation, or
    B carefully plan your conversation in advance?

29. Would you say that you enjoy
    A striking up conversations with culturally diverse people, or
    B having conversations with those who are more similar to you?

30. In your work, do you
    A use a uniform style of interacting with everyone in the group, or
    B change the way you interact depending on the cultural backgrounds of those in the group?

31. In ministry situations that require cross-cultural negotiations, do you have
    A deep knowledge, or
    B little knowledge?

32. When visiting different cultures, do you
    A modify the way you dress, or
    B dress the way you do in your home country?

33. When conflicts arise with those from other cultures, do you
    A try to learn from failures and build on successes, or
    B pay little attention to cultural reasons for failures and successes?

34. In keeping a conversation going with someone from another culture, do you
    A find it difficult to deal with ambiguity and differences, or
    B deal successfully with ambiguity and differences?

Section B

Instructions

Imagine that you are in a situation where you are interacting with people from different cultural backgrounds. Circle the answer (A or B) that best describes you. Don't overthink your response.

35. In cross-cultural situations, you are
    A spontaneous.
    B careful to plan.

36. In cross-cultural situations, you are
    A predictable.
    B flexible.

37. In cross-cultural situations, you are
    A attracted.
    B indifferent.

38. In cross-cultural situations, you are
    A systematic.
    B casual.

39. In cross-cultural situations, you are
    A neutral.
    B engaged.

40. In cross-cultural situations, you have
    A cultural knowledge.
    B technical knowledge.

41. In cross-cultural situations, you
    A anticipate.
    B react.

42. In cross-cultural situations, you are
    A a learner.
    B a professional.

43. In cross-cultural situations, you are
    A highly interested.
    B somewhat interested.

44. In cross-cultural situations, you
    A go with the flow.
    B prepare in advance.

45. In cross-cultural situations, you are
    A reserved.
    B a good actor.

46. In cross-cultural situations, you are
    A broad.
    B narrow.

47. In cross-cultural situations, you are
    A excited.
    B neutral.

48. In cross-cultural situations, you are
    A current.
    B dated.

49. In cross-cultural situations, you are
    A unsure.
    B energized.

50. In cross-cultural situations, you are
    A confident.
    B uncertain.

51. In cross-cultural situations, you
    A speak one language.
    B speak many languages.

52. In cross-cultural situations, you are
    A experienced.
    B a novice.

53. You view cross-cultural situations as
    A an activity.
    B a priority.

54. In cross-cultural situations, you are
    A conscious.
    B unaware.

Scoring Instructions

Section A

For each question, score a 3 in the box to the right of the item if your answer corresponds to the letter shown in the answer column.

Add up the columns at the bottom of the page for your Cultural Strategic Thinking[2]—Knowledge and Interpretive CQ (CST), Perseverance CQ (PSV), and Behavioral CQ (BEH) Scores.

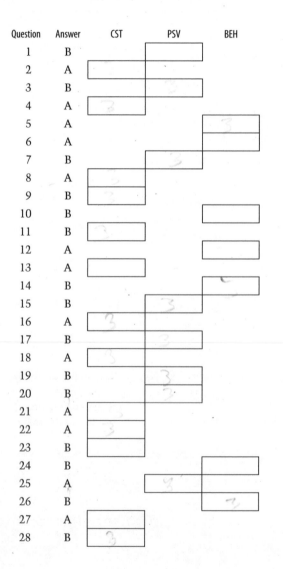

Question	Answer	CST	PSV	BEH
1	B			
2	A			
3	B			
4	A			
5	A			
6	A			
7	B			
8	A			
9	B			
10	B			
11	B			
12	A			
13	A			
14	B			
15	B			
16	A			
17	B			
18	A			
19	B			
20	B			
21	A			
22	A			
23	B			
24	B			
25	A			
26	B			
27	A			
28	B			

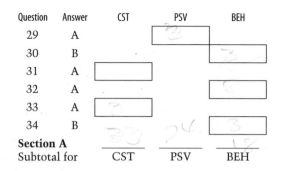

Question	Answer	CST	PSV	BEH
29	A		3	
30	B			3
31	A			
32	A			6
33	A	3		
34	B			3
Section A Subtotal for		CST	PSV	BEH

Section B

For each question, score a 3 in the box to the right of the item if your answer corresponds to the letter in the answer column.

Add up the columns at the bottom of the page for your Cultural Strategic Thinking—Knowledge and Interpretive CQ (CST), Perseverance CQ (PSV), and Behavioral CQ (BEH) Scores.

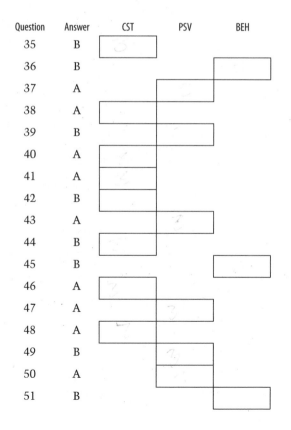

Question	Answer	CST	PSV	BEH
35	B			
36	B			
37	A			
38	A			
39	B			
40	A			
41	A			
42	B			
43	A			
44	B			
45	B			
46	A			
47	A			
48	A			
49	B			
50	A			
51	B			

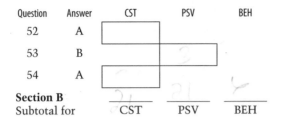

Question	Answer	CST	PSV	BEH
52	A			
53	B			
54	A			

Section B
Subtotal for   CST   PSV   BEH

Work Sheet

	Cultural Strategic Thinking[3] (CST)/Knowledge and Interpretive CQ	Perseverance CQ (PSV)	Behavioral CQ (BEH)
Subtotal from Section A			
Subtotal from Section B			
Total (Sections A + B)			

Overall Cultural Intelligence

Overall Cultural Intelligence = Total CST + Total PSV + Total BEH

Write your overall cultural intelligence score here: _____

Interpretation of Your Overall CQ Score

Your Score	Interpretation
126 and above	You perceive yourself as having *excellent* overall CQ in your ability to work in diverse cultural settings (domestic and/or international).
95–125	You perceive yourself as having *average* overall CQ in your ability to work in diverse cultural settings (domestic and/or international).
94 and below	You perceive yourself as needing to develop your overall CQ to be able to work more effectively in diverse cultural settings (domestic and/or international).

Interpretation of Your Score for Knowledge and Interpretive CQ (Cultural Strategic Thinking)

Your Score	Interpretation
51 and above	You are *excellent* in your cultural strategic thinking.
38–50	You are *moderate* in your cultural strategic thinking.
37 and below	Your cultural strategic thinking indicates a red alert, which means that you need to work on your knowledge and interpretive CQ.

Interpretation of Your Score for Perseverance CQ

Your Score	Interpretation
45 and above	You are *excellent* in your cultural motivation.
38–44	You are *moderate* in your cultural motivation.
37 and below	Your cultural motivation indicates a red alert, which means that you need to work on your cultural motivation.

Interpretation of Your Score for Behavioral CQ

Your Score	Interpretation
30 and above	You are *excellent* in your cultural behavior.
21–29	You are *moderate* in your cultural behavior.
20 and below	Your cultural behavior indicates a red alert, which means that you need to work on your cultural behavior.

Variability in Your Scores

If your scores vary across the three facets of cultural intelligence, you should think of ways that you can leverage your strong areas (high scores) and ways that you can improve in areas where your scores are lower.

Given that this is a self-assessment, keep in mind that these scores simply indicate your self-perception of your cultural intelligence in these various areas. Many individuals under- or overestimate themselves; therefore, a multirater assessment has much greater validity.

Visit http://www.davidlivermore.com for more information on how to obtain CQ-related assessment, consulting, or training for you and your ministry.

research context

The research referenced throughout the book comes from a variety of sources. The information and examples drawn directly from the research of others are cited as such. The information from research I've personally done combines data from a few different studies, all of which have been qualitative in nature though always informed by the helpful quantitative work of others. First, I've drawn from three studies I conducted that compared the experiences of North American short-term missionaries with the experiences of the locals who hosted those short-term missionaries. Samples involved 630 North American[1] subjects and 380 local subjects from 23 different countries. These studies were intended to be descriptive in nature. I used a grounded-theory approach by interviewing subjects, reading journals written by the North American subjects, administering surveys, and making firsthand observations.[2]

Also, from 2007 to 2008, as part of the Cultural Intelligence and Ministry Leadership Project I've been conducting a series of studies that test and apply cultural intelligence to the work of American ministry leaders in three cultural domains: socioethnic culture, organizational culture, and generational culture. To date, 417 subjects have been involved in this research project. The hypothesis of the Cultural Intelligence and Ministry Leadership Project is that a positive relationship exists between the acquisition of cultural intelligence and ministry leaders' effectiveness in the twenty-first century. I continue to be indebted to a small but growing community of researchers studying the emerging domain of cultural intelligence. In particular, Dr. Soon Ang at Nanyang Technological University in Singapore and Dr. Linn Van Dyne at Michigan State University have generously shared their research, insights, and time. Though their expertise is in applying cultural intelligence to organizational management contexts, their informed counsel has significantly enhanced my ability to apply cultural intelligence to ministry and faith-based contexts.

Building on my study on the short-term missions movement, the greatest amount of the research for the Cultural Intelligence and Ministry Leadership Project has been oriented toward understanding and explaining the experiences of ministry leaders crossing *socioethnic cultures*. This included studying the experiences of American ministry leaders who crossed socioethnic cultures within their own national cultures (e.g., serving an urban community, ministering among immigrants, or planting a multicultural church) and those who crossed international lines (e.g., short-term and long-term missions experiences). Like my research on short-term missions, this data was gathered through interviews, journals, surveys, and firsthand observation.

The Cultural Intelligence and Ministry Leadership Project has also included testing and applying cultural intelligence to ministry leaders' work in organizational and generational cultures. Most of this data was collected through focus-group research. A great deal of my discussion of cultural intelligence in the organizational and generational domains of culture is far more dependent on the research of others. Much more needs to be explored about how cultural intelligence influences the work of ministry leaders in these domains.

To respect and protect the confidentiality of the subjects surveyed, their names and the names of their ministries have been changed; however, other demographic information (e.g., gender, age, ethnicity) have not been altered in the reporting of the findings here and elsewhere. I'm extremely grateful for the generosity of hundreds of ministry leaders and their organizations for entrusting me with some of their thoughts, sentiments, and reflections about cross-cultural ministry.

This has been a deeply personal book for me to write because I do not write as one merely standing on the outside, objectively observing the cross-cultural interactions of others. I'm personally on a long journey toward more lovingly relating to people different from me. It seemed inauthentic to write about the inward pathway of cultural intelligence without personally interacting with what that means for me. Some quantitative researchers may cringe at the degree to which my voice and personal experience is commingled with the data I've collected from others and the presentation of my findings. But in the spirit of the qualitative designs used to gather the data reported, it seemed necessary to be explicit about my personal interaction with my subject matter.[3]

This book differs from my book *Serving with Eyes Wide Open: Doing Short-Term Missions with Cultural Intelligence* in that it more broadly applies cultural intelligence to the everyday cultural demands facing most ministry leaders. These demands might include leading a short-term missions team, but that's only one of several contexts where today's leader needs to apply cultural intelligence. In *Serving with Eyes Wide Open*, I used a popularized approach to report on a subset of my research findings regarding short-term missions. Cultural intelligence was included in the last part of that book to address some of the critiques of short-term missions. This book reports on the actual testing of cultural intelligence in the numerous contexts where it is needed by ministry leaders—socioethnic cultures at home and abroad, organizational cultures, and generational cultures.

forming a CQ ministry environment

Most of us as ministry leaders are interested not only in increasing our own cultural intelligence but also in seeing the cultural intelligence of others in our ministry increase. Some novel testing is being done on whether entire teams and organizations can have a collective measure or quotient of cultural intelligence. More needs to be understood about how to enhance the cultural intelligence of a ministry team as a whole. I've done some initial testing among churches that have become adept at drawing a more culturally diverse congregation. Initial predictors and pathways consistently found in my preliminary testing of this concept have included the following elements.

Dialogue

Churches that have wanted more ethnic minorities or more generational difference reflected in their communities have consistently started with extensive dialogue with some of the groups they hoped to engage. They asked questions such as, "What's your perception of us? What would be your fears about being part of a church like ours? How can we do this together?" They spent a great deal of time *listening*.

Community Reputation

The churches that reflected diversity throughout their congregations became known as places that valued cultural difference. They were known as churches that were serious about responding to the inequities between the dominant cultures and the more oppressed ones. Many of these churches were actively engaged in local schools and provided mentors; these cross-cultural relationships were built for the beauty of the friendships they provided rather than as goodwill projects. The churches were oriented toward using diversity in part to bless the community as a whole.

Structural

One of the most significant predictors found in churches that appeared more culturally intelligent as a whole were in the structural decisions they made involving areas such as staffing, budgeting, and program development. Cultural intelligence was made a nonnegotiable requirement in the hiring and recruiting of all paid and lay staff rather than being something done simply out of concern for the missions pastor or the community outreach pastor. These churches were as concerned about a children's director who demonstrated concern for these issues as the outreach pastor was. These churches were more likely to have people of color filling positions such as youth director or senior pastor rather than just in positions working to reach minority groups. Dollars were budgeted for training and programs that would elevate this priority.

Extended Time

The exemplary churches had a long-term orientation toward developing this priority. This orientation was a predictor in that there were both extended times of being together (full retreats with different ethnic church leadership teams) and a patient view of this effort as something that would take several years to unfold.

The Medium Is the Message

Most of the exemplary churches were in locations and had buildings that reflected the cultural diversity they were seeking to nurture. Furthermore, the style of worship, teaching, and social interaction reflected the desired diversity. Interestingly, the most effective churches seemed to be those that didn't simply try to offer a potpourri of traditional/contemporary, country/classical, or hip hop/praise and worship. The most effective churches developed their own unique style as a ministry. They created their own subculture of sorts and tapped into members who could write or at least arrange their own music, liturgy, and services.

Education

All the churches made education about these issues a regular part of their scope and sequence both implicitly and explicitly. This included everything from preaching to Sunday school curriculum to special workshops. Teachers also continually worked to make this effort a regular part of instruction. For example, one pastor in Chicago, while teaching about the Ethiopian eunuch, made it a point to emphasize the African location of this ancient Bible story. Education occurred in many kinds of implicit ways as well. Rather than simply bringing in ethnic minorities to speak to issues of race and oppression, these churches used them to speak on their areas of expertise.

Shared Calling

Not unlike the unique culture that many of these churches tried to develop through a specially tailored worship style, all the exemplary churches described a shared cause and calling that transcended the myriad of cultural differences. A relentless commitment to that cause motivated them to the ongoing hard work of dealing with the cultural collisions that continued to occur. And in that regard, they all emphasized the need for an ongoing spirit of grace with one another that did not seek out conformity or uniformity. None of them provided flawless pictures of culturally intelligent behavior. But they talked about the commitment to work through the difficult issues as a way to live out the presence of Jesus in their local communities.

More research is needed to explore the notion of cultural intelligence as a value that permeates a collective ministry rather than just an individual ministry leader. We continue to build on these preliminary findings at the Global Learning Center of Grand Rapids Theological Seminary.

notes

Series Preface

1. James W. Fowler, *Faith Development and Pastoral Care* (Minneapolis: Fortress, 1987), 17.

2. Scott Cormode, "Constructing Faithful Action," *Journal of Religious Leadership* 3 (1/2), (Spring/Fall 2004): 267.

Introduction

1. Studies examining the failure of missional efforts due to cultural differences are most often found in missiological literature. Visit http://grts .cornerstone.edu/resources/glc/research for some of the most seminal studies exposing missional failure due to cultural difference.

2. Michael Phillips, "Unanswered Prayers: In Swaziland, U.S. Preacher Sees His Dream Vanish," *Wall Street Journal*, December 19, 2005.

3. See my book *Serving with Eyes Wide Open: Doing Short-Term Missions with Cultural Intelligence* (Grand Rapids: Baker Academic, 2006) and the October 2006 issue of the journal *Missiology: An International Review*. The entire issue is devoted to social-science research conducted on short-term missions.

4. Michael Emerson and Christian Smith, *Divided by Faith: Evangelical Religion and the Problem of Race in America* (New York: Oxford University Press, 2000).

5. Many of these resources are referenced throughout this book. Note the footnotes and the recommended resources at the end of each chapter.

6. John Russon, *Reading Hegel's Phenomenology* (Bloomington: Indiana University Press, 2004), 102.

Part 1 Love: CQ Overview

1. See the explanation in the introduction for how the term "Other" is used throughout the book.

2. The Legal Reader, "Larry Flynt on Jerry Falwell: Hustler Lawsuit Revisited on Day of Rival's Death," May 15, 2007, http://www.legalreader .com/archives/003764.html.

Chapter 1 Twenty-First-Century CQ: Getting Along in the Flat World

1. Technically, the term "cross-cultural" differs from the term "intercultural." "Cross-cultural" typically refers to the interactions of a limited number of cultures (e.g., a Brazilian missionary interacting with locals in Morocco), while "intercultural" refers to the interactions among many different cultures simultaneously (Brazilians, Koreans, and Americans working together in Morocco). Increasingly, most of our encounters are "intercultural," and it is to those interactions that most of this book is devoted. However, consistent with a growing number of authors writing about intercultural relationships, I've used the more familiar term "cross-cultural" to refer to any of our interactions with individuals from another culture.

2. My research context and methodology is explained in appendix C.

3. Siobhan Roth, "World Travelers," *National Geographic*, July 2006, 25. Admittedly some individuals get more than one tourist visa in a year; therefore, one billion is a rough estimate. But there are also others who move across borders without getting a tourist visa. So one in six still seems a

fair estimate of the number of people traveling internationally each year.

4. Thomas Friedman, *The World Is Flat: A Brief History of the Twenty-First Century* (New York: Farrar, Straus, and Giroux, 2005).

5. Christian Smith, *Soul Searching: The Religious and Spiritual Lives of American Teenagers* (New York: Oxford University Press, 2005), 69.

6. M. Shaw, "Korean Short-Term Missionaries," personal e-mail, June 28, 2006.

7. David Livermore, *Serving with Eyes Wide Open: Doing Short-Term Missions with Cultural Intelligence* (Grand Rapids: Baker Academic, 2006).

8. Kurt VerBeek, "The Impact of Short-Term Missions: A Case Study of House Construction in Honduras after Hurricane Mitch," *Missiology* 34, no. 4 (October 2006): 477–95.

9. Robert Priest, Terry Dischinger, Steve Rasmussen, and C. M. Brown, "Researching the Short-Term Mission Movement," *Missiology* 34, no. 4 (October 2006): 431–50.

10. For a helpful overview of research findings on short-term missions, see the October 2006 issue of *Missiology* (34, no. 4), which is devoted to short-term missions. Also, Kurt VerBeek of Calvin College has an interactive bibliography of some of the research-based studies done on short-term missions; see http://www.calvin.edu/academic/sociology/staff/kurt.htm.

11. Mary Pipher, *The Middle of Everywhere: The World's Refugees Come to Our Town* (New York: Harcourt, 2002), 37.

12. Grand Rapids Convention and Visitors Bureau, "Diversity in Grand Rapids," http://www.visitgrandrapids.org/multicultural.php.

13. I'm sensitive to the idea that using "America" to refer exclusively to the United States and its citizens is an ethnocentric use of the term. People across North, Central, and South America are all part of the Americas. I've resisted using "America" to exclusively refer to the United States as a nation, but for ease of writing/reading in this book, I have used "American" as commonly used throughout the world, that is, to refer primarily to people from the United States. My apologies for any insensitivity that usage implies to others sharing the Americas.

14. Julie Ray, ed., "Growing Diversity Translates into Classroom Challenges," December 13, 2005, http://www.gallup.com/poll/20425/Growing-Diversity-Translates-Into-Classroom-Challenges.aspx.

15. Eddie Gibbs, "Culture since 1985," *Missiology* 35, no. 2 (April 2007): 158–59.

16. Ibid., 158.

17. Ibid.

Chapter 2 First-Century CQ: God Speaks "Jesus"

1. Steve Argue and Dave Livermore, "MTV . . . PS2 . . . Thai . . . German . . . Jesus," *Group* 29, no. 4 (2003): 57.

2. Lamin Sanneh, "Global Christianity: Challenging Modernity and the West" (paper presented at Pruit Memorial Symposium, Baylor University, November 10, 2005).

3. Eugene Peterson, *The Message: The Bible in Contemporary Language* (Colorado Springs: NavPress, 2002), 1808.

4. David Livermore, *Serving with Eyes Wide Open: Doing Short-Term Missions with Cultural Intelligence* (Grand Rapids: Baker Academic, 2006), 82.

5. I'm indebted to my friend Bill Clem of Mars Hill Church in Seattle for our collaborative effort in thinking about the dynamic relationship of these priorities as expressed in this diagram.

6. George Eldon Ladd, *The Gospel and the Kingdom: Scriptural Studies in the Kingdom of God* (Grand Rapids: Eerdmans, 1959).

7. Ibid., 41.

8. David Turner, *The Gospel of Matthew,* Cornerstone Biblical Commentary 11 (Carol Stream, IL: Tyndale, 2005), 21–22.

9. Robert Webber, personal conversation, October 3, 2003, Wheaton, IL.

10. N. T. Wright, *The New Testament and the People of God* (Minneapolis: Fortress, 1992), 224–32.

11. Bruce Chilton, *Rabbi Jesus: An Intimate Biography* (New York: Doubleday, 2000), 24.

12. Dave Livermore, "Emerge or Submerge: Is 'Cultural Relevance' an Effective and Theologically Sound Wineskin for the Emergent Church or Is It Moving Christianity toward Oblivion?" *Pneuma Review* (January 2007): 31–55.

13. Other books take us further in exploring how the gospel should live between the tension of Christ's reign and culture. Niebuhr's classic *Christ and Culture* is a widely read treatise that interacts with this complex relationship, though he is criticized for not having included the ways the church itself—for good and evil—is shaped by culture. Other important contributions to exploring this issue further include *Resident Aliens,* by Stanley Hauerwas and William Willimon; Robert Webber's Ancient-Future series; Lesslie Newbigin's *Open Secret* and *The Gospel in a Pluralist Society*; as well as resources available through the Gospel and Culture Network led by George Hunsberger.

14. N. T. Wright, *What St. Paul Really Said: Was Paul of Tarsus the Real Founder of Christianity?* (Grand Rapids: Eerdmans, 1997), 154.

15. Lesslie Newbigin, *The Gospel in a Pluralist Society* (Grand Rapids: Eerdmans, 1989), 234.

16. See Sherwood Lingenfelter and Marvin Mayers, *Ministering Cross-Culturally: An Incarnational Model for Personal Relationships* (Grand Rapids: Baker Academic, 2003) for a much fuller treatment of how the incarnation applies to cross-cultural relationships.

Chapter 3 CQ 101: The Path to Loving the Other

1. Some of the best books on this subject from a cross-cultural ministry perspective are Sherwood Lingenfelter and Marvin Mayers, *Ministering Cross-Culturally*; Duane Elmer, *Cross-Cultural Servanthood*; and Patty Lane, *A Beginner's Guide to Crossing Cultures*.

2. Howard Gardner, *Frames of Mind: The Theory of Multiple Intelligences* (New York: Basic Books, 1983).

3. James Paul Gee, *Social Linguistics and Literacies: Ideology and Discourse* (London: Routledge, 1996).

4. "Cultural strategic thinking" is an overarching label for the iterative relationship between the thinking processes of knowledge CQ and interpretive CQ. See figure 1.

5. William Kiehl, *America's Dialogue with the World* (Washington, DC: Public Diplomacy Council, 2006), 42.

6. *Baywatch*, http://en.wikipedia.org/wiki/Baywatch.

7. P. Christopher Earley, Soon Ang, and Joo-Seng Tan, *CQ: Developing Cultural Intelligence at Work* (Stanford, CA: Stanford Business Books, 2006), 49.

8. Ibid., 51 (italics added).

9. Ibid., 83.

10. Edward Stewart and Milton Bennett, *American Cultural Patterns: A Cross-Cultural Perspective* (Boston: Intercultural Press, 1991), 15.

11. Eddie Gibbs, "Culture since 1985," *Missiology* 35, no. 2 (April 2007): 164.

12. David Thomas, "Domain and Development of Cultural Intelligence: The Importance of Mindfulness," *Group & Organization Management* 31, no. 1 (February 2006): 94.

Part 2 Understand: Knowledge CQ

1. Excerpted from the "CQ for Cross-Cultural Ministry Leadership" Assessment, adapted by David Livermore, developed by Linn Van Dyne, Michigan State University, and Soon Ang, Nanyang Technological University, Singapore, http://grts.cornerstone.edu/resources/glc/cqprofile.

Chapter 4 The Average American: Understanding Our Own Culture

1. Craig Storti, *The Art of Crossing Cultures* (Yarmouth, ME: Intercultural Press, 1990), 44.

2. Kevin O'Keefe, *The Average American: The Extraordinary Search for the Nation's Most Ordinary Citizen* (New York: Public Affairs, 2005).

3. Ibid., 139.

4. First Amendment to the US Constitution.

5. John Steinbeck, *America and Americans* (New York: Viking, 2002), 32.

6. Henry Ford, interview, *Chicago Tribune*, May 25, 1916.

7. Harry Truman, source unknown.

8. Michael Emerson and Christian Smith, *Divided by Faith: Evangelical Religion and the Problem of Race in America* (New York: Oxford University Press, 2000), 79.

9. Ibid.

10. Soon Ang, personal communication, August 16, 2007.

11. Edward Stewart and Milton Bennett, *American Cultural Patterns: A Cross-Cultural Perspective* (Boston: Intercultural Press, 1991), 108.

12. Ibid., 100.

Chapter 5 Getting below the Surface: What Is Culture Anyway?

1. James Clifford, *The Predicament of Culture: Twentieth-Century Ethnography, Literature, and Art* (Cambridge, MA: Harvard University Press, 1988), 10.

2. H. Richard Niebuhr, *Christ and Culture* (New York: Harper & Row, 1951), 29–39.

3. C. Kluckhohn and A. L. Kroeber, eds., *Culture* (New York: Random House, 1952), 181.

4. Howard S. Becker, *Art World* (Berkeley: University of California Press, 1982), 133.

5. Geert Hofstede, *Cultures and Organizations: Software of the Mind* (New York: McGraw Hill, 1997), 5.

6. Edgar Schein, *Organizational Culture and Leadership* (San Francisco: Jossey-Bass, 2004), 17.

7. Clifford Geertz, *The Interpretation of Cultures* (New York: Basic Books, 1973), 5.

8. Adapted from Schein, *Organizational Culture and Leadership*, 26.

9. Edward Hall, *The Hidden Dimension* (New York: Anchor Books, 1969), 188.

10. Anthony P. Cohen, *Self Consciousness: An Alternative Anthropology of Identity* (London: Routledge, 1994), 118–19.

11. Hofstede, *Cultures and Organizations*, 5.

12. Plato, *The Republic* Book 4, trans. Benjamin Jowett. http://classics.mit.edu/Plato/republic.html.

13. L. Robert Kohl, *Survival Kit for Overseas Living* (Yarmouth, ME: Intercultural Press, 2001), 56.

14. Craig Storti, *The Art of Crossing Cultures* (Yarmouth, ME: Intercultural Press, 1990), 50.

15. Soon Ang, personal e-mail, June 26, 2007.

16. "Adolescent Fears," *Straits Times*, August 24, 2007.

17. Gert Jan Hofstede, Paul B. Pedersen, and Geert Hofstede, *Exploring Culture: Exercises, Stories and Synthetic Cultures* (Yarmouth, ME: Intercultural Press, 2002), 41.

Chapter 6 Hutus, Presbyterians, and Boomers: Cultural Domains

1. P. Christopher Earley, Soon Ang, and Joo-Seng Tan, *CQ: Developing Cultural Intelligence at Work* (Stanford, CA: Stanford Business Books, 2006), 20.

2. Adapted from Peggy McIntosh, "White Privilege and Male Privilege: A Personal Account of Coming to See Correspondences through Work in Women's Studies," in *The Social Construction of Difference and Inequality*, ed. Tracy E. Ore (Mountain View, CA: Mayfield, 2000), 475–85.

3. Michael Emerson and Christian Smith, *Divided by Faith: Evangelical Religion and the Problem of Race in America* (New York: Oxford University Press, 2000).

4. Ibid., 69.

5. Ibid., 69–70.

6. Ibid., 70.

7. Ibid., 170.

8. Jeffrey Sonnenfeld, cited in G. Sadri and B. Lees, "Developing Corporate Culture as Competitive Advantage," *Journal of Management Development* 20, no. 10 (2001): 853.

9. Rick Lawrence, "The 18 Month Myth," *Group* 20, no. 2 (January/February 2000): 24.

10. Harry Triandis, "Cultural Intelligence in Organizations," *Group & Organization Management* 31, no. 1 (February 2006): 24.

11. Chap Clark, *Hurt: Inside the World of Today's Teenagers* (Grand Rapids: Baker Academic, 2004), 25.

12. Mark Senter, *The Coming Revolution in Youth Ministry* (Wheaton: Victor Books, 1992), 39.

13. Paul H. Ray and Sherry Ruth Anderson, *The Cultural Creatives: How Fifty Million People Are Changing the World* (New York: Three Rivers Press, 2001), 30–31.

14. Ibid., 25.

15. Rick and Kathy Hicks, *Boomers, Xers, and Other Strangers: Understanding the Generational Differences That Divide Us* (Colorado Springs: Focus on the Family Press, 1999).

16. Paul Lakeland, *Postmodernity: Christian Identity in a Fragmented Age* (Minneapolis: Fortress, 1997), ix–x.

17. John Franke, *The Character of Theology: An Introduction to Its Nature, Task, and Purpose* (Grand Rapids: Baker Academic, 2005), 21.

18. Ibid., 16.

19. See Webber's Ancient-Future series (Baker Academic); Darrell L. Guder, ed., *Missional Church* (Grand Rapids: Eerdmans, 1998); and Stanley J. Grenz, *Primer on Postmodernism* (Grand Rapids: Eerdmans, 1996) as a start.

20. Richard Rohr, *Everything Belongs: The Gift of Contemplative Prayer* (New York: Crossroad, 2003), 173.

Chapter 7 When Yes Means No and No Means Yes: Language

1. Edward Stewart and Milton Bennett, *American Cultural Patterns: A Cross-Cultural Perspective* (Boston: Intercultural Press, 1991), 45.

2. P. Kay and W. Kempton, "What Is the Sapir-Whorf Hypothesis?" *American Anthropologist* 86, no. 1 (1984): 65–79.

3. Benjamin Lee Whorf, *Language, Thought, and Reality: Selected Writings of Benjamin Lee Whorf*, ed. John Carroll (Cambridge, MA: MIT Press, 1964), 212–14.

4. John Gumperz, "On Teaching Language in Its Sociocultural Context," in *Social Interaction, Social Context and Language: Essays in Honor of Susan Ervin-Tripp*, ed. D. I. Slobin et al. (Hillsdale, NJ: Lawrence Erlbaum, 1996), 469–80.

5. P. Christopher Earley, Soon Ang, and Joo-Seng Tan, *CQ: Developing Cultural Intelligence at Work* (Stanford, CA: Stanford Business Books, 2006), 33.

6. Peter C. Patrikis, *Reading between the Lines: Perspectives on Foreign Language Literacy* (New Haven: Yale University Press, 2003), 1–2.

7. Andrew Rudd, "New Cuss Words," *In the Space Between* blog, August 25, 2007, http://inthespacebetween.blogspot.com/.

8. Craig Storti, *The Art of Crossing Cultures* (Yarmouth, ME: Intercultural Press, 1990), 87.

9. Henry Widdowson, *Teaching Language as Communication* (Oxford: Oxford University Press, 1978), 148.

Chapter 8 Why We Do What We Do: Cultural Values

1. For more on this, see Gert Jan Hofstede, Paul B. Pedersen, and Geert Hofstede, *Exploring Culture: Exercises, Stories and Synthetic Cultures* (Yarmouth, ME: Intercultural Press, 2002); Talcott Parson, *Social System* (Glencoe, IL: Free

Press, 1950); and Fons Trompenaars and Charles Hampden-Turner, *Riding the Waves of Culture* (London: Brealey, 2000).

2. In addition to the CQ self-assessment available in appendix B, information about a multirater instrument is available at http://www.davidlivermore.com and http://www.culturalq.com. You can select five peers who provide you with feedback on your CQ. The instrument will also give you scores on where you personally fall along these continua of cultural values. Sherwood Lingenfelter and Marvin Mayers offer a self-assessment of many of these values as well in their book *Ministering Cross-Culturally: An Incarnational Model for Personal Relationships* (Grand Rapids: Baker Academic, 2003).

3. Geert Hofstede, *Cultures and Organizations: Software of the Mind* (New York: McGraw Hill, 1997), 79–108.

4. Harry Triandis, "Cultural Intelligence and Globalization" (paper presented at Cultural Intelligence Conference, Dallas, TX, May 4, 2006).

5. Harry Triandis, "Cultural Intelligence in Organizations," *Group & Organization Management* 31, no. 1 (February 2006): 24.

6. My experience closely mirrors a simulation referenced in Craig Storti, *Cross-Cultural Dialogues* (Yarmouth, ME: Intercultural Press, 1994), 64. Storti's analysis helped my own thinking about the role of hierarchy in this encounter.

7. For the purposes of this book, I've merged uncertainty avoidance and tight versus loose as one category of cultural value, but there is benefit in viewing them independently as well. See M. J. Gelfand, L. Nishii, and J. Raver, "On the Nature and Importance of Cultural Tightness-Looseness," *Journal of Applied Psychology* 91 (2006): 1225–44.

8. Soon Ang, personal conversation, October 26, 2005; and Gelfand, Nishii, and Raver, "On the Nature and Importance of Cultural Tightness-Looseness."

9. Patty Lane, *A Beginner's Guide to Crossing Cultures: Making Friends in a Multicultural World* (Downers Grove, IL: InterVarsity, 2002), 98.

10. Hofstede, *Cultures and Organizations*, 79–108.

11. Lane, *Beginner's Guide to Crossing Cultures*, 62.

12. Richard Tiplady, "Let X = X: Generation X and World Mission," http://postmission.com/articles/letxequalx.pdf, p. 7.

13. Edgar Schein, *Organizational Culture and Leadership* (San Francisco: Jossey-Bass, 2004), 23.

Part 3 Go Deep: Interpretive CQ

1. Excerpted from the "CQ for Cross-Cultural Ministry Leadership" Assessment, adapted by David Livermore, developed by Linn Van Dyne,

Michigan State University, and Soon Ang, Nanyang Technological University, Singapore, http://grts.cornerstone.edu/resources/glc/cqprofile.

2. David Thomas, "Domain and Development of Cultural Intelligence: The Importance of Mindfulness," *Group & Organization Management* 31, no. 1 (February 2006): 92.

Chapter 9 Cruise Control Off: Awareness and Empathy

1. Marcie Boucouvalas, "Consciousness and Learning: New and Renewed Approaches," *New Directions for Adult and Continuing Education* 57 (Spring 1993): 58.

2. Ibid., 66.

3. William Weeks, Paul Pedersen, and Richard Brislin, *A Manual for Structured Experiences for Cross-Cultural Learning* (Yarmouth, ME: Intercultural Press, 1977), xv.

4. Don Riso and Russ Hudson, *The Wisdom of the Enneagram: The Complete Guide to Psychological and Spiritual Growth for the Nine Personality Types* (New York: Bantam, 1999), 39.

5. Arnold van Gennep, *The Rites of Passage* (London: Routledge, 1960).

6. Richard Rohr, *Everything Belongs: The Gift of Contemplative Prayer* (New York: Crossroad, 2003), 49.

7. Ibid., 48.

8. Thich Nhat Hanh, *The Miracle of Mindfulness* (Boston: Beacon, 1999).

9. E. J. Langer, *Mindfulness* (Cambridge, MA: Perseus Books, 1989).

10. Regarding application to cross-cultural communication, see S. Ting-Toomey, "A Face Negotiation Theory," in *Theory in Intercultural Communication*, ed. Y. Kim and W. B. Gudykunst (Newbury Park, CA: Sage, 1988), 261–76. For application to cultural intelligence, see David Thomas and Kerr Inkson, *Cultural Intelligence: People Skills for Global Business* (San Francisco: Berrett-Koehler, 2004), 51–53.

11. David Thomas, "Domain and Development of Cultural Intelligence: The Importance of Mindfulness," *Group & Organization Management* 31, no. 1 (February 2006): 86–87.

12. Ibid., 84.

13. P. Christopher Earley, Soon Ang, and Joo-Seng Tan, *CQ: Developing Cultural Intelligence at Work* (Stanford, CA: Stanford Business Books, 2006), 11.

14. Nate Ledbetter, "Life on Paper: Discovering the Essence of Neighboring" (unpublished MS).

15. Craig Storti, *The Art of Crossing Cultures* (Yarmouth, ME: Intercultural Press, 1990), 59.

16. Rohr, *Everything Belongs*, 31.

17. Ibid.

18. Henri Nouwen, *In the Name of Jesus: Reflections on Christian Leadership* (New York: Crossroad, 2001), 29–30.

19. Storti, *Art of Crossing Cultures*, 95.

20. St. Augustine, source unknown.

21. Terrence Linhart, "They Were So Alive: The Spectacle Self and Youth Group Short-Term Mission Trips" (paper presented at the North Central Evangelical Missiological Society Meeting, Deerfield, IL, April 9, 2005).

22. Daniel H. Pink, *A Whole New Mind: Moving from the Information Age to the Conceptual Age* (New York: Riverhead, 2005), 153.

23. Howard Gardner, *Leading Minds: Anatomy of Leadership* (New York: Basic Books, 1995), 117.

24. Adapted from L. Robert Kohls and John M. Knight, *Developing Intercultural Awareness: A Cross-Cultural Training Handbook* (Yarmouth, ME: Intercultural Press, 1994), 97.

25. Harry Triandis, "Cultural Intelligence in Organizations" *Group & Organization Management* 31, no. 1 (February 2006): 21.

Chapter 10 What Makes an Apple an Apple? Labeling Our World

1. Richard Detweiler, "Culture, Category Width, and Attributions: A Model-Building Approach to Reasons for Cultural Effects," *Journal of Cross-Cultural Psychology* 9 (1978): 259–84.

2. M. A. Wallach, "The Influence of Classification Requirements on Gradients of Response," *Psychological Monographs* 73 (1959): 478.

3. Paul Hiebert, *Anthropological Reflections on Missiological Issues* (Grand Rapids: Baker Academic, 1994), 110–36.

4. Ibid.

5. Ibid., 110 (italics added).

6. Ibid., 111 (italics added).

7. Ibid., (italics added).

8. Ibid., 112.

9. Conrad Arenberg and Arthur Niehoff, *Introducing Social Change: A Manual for Community Development* (Chicago: Aldine, 1971).

10. Hiebert, *Anthropological Reflections on Missiological Issues*, 113.

11. George Marsden, *Understanding Fundamentalism and Evangelicalism* (Grand Rapids: Eerdmans, 1991), 1.

12. Hiebert, *Anthropological Reflections on Missiological Issues*, 114.

13. Ibid., 113.

14. Ibid., 116.

15. Alan Roxburgh, "Missional Leadership: Equipping God's People for Mission," in *Missional Church*, ed. Darrel Guder (Grand Rapids: Eerdmans, 1998), 205.

16. Hiebert, *Anthropological Reflections on Missiological Issues*, 117.

17. Rob Bell, *Velvet Elvis: Repainting the Christian Faith* (Grand Rapids: Zondervan, 2005), 26.

18. Roxburgh, "Missional Leadership," 205.

19. This relates to Martin Buber's I-it versus I-thou distinction in *I and Thou*, trans. R. G. Smith, 2nd ed. (New York: Scribners, 1957).

20. Bell, *Velvet Elvis*, 27.

21. Hiebert, *Anthropological Reflections on Missiological Issues*, 127.

22. Roxburgh, "Missional Leadership," 206.

23. Hiebert, *Anthropological Reflections on Missiological Issues*, 130.

24. Roxburgh, "Missional Leadership," 206.

25. Hiebert, *Anthropological Reflections on Missiological Issues*, 125.

26. Michael Frost and Alan Hirsch, *The Shaping of Things to Come: Innovation and Mission for the 21st-Century Church* (Peabody, MA: Hendrickson, 2003), 61–64.

Chapter 11 Being Okay with Gray: Category Width

1. T. F. Pettigrew, "The Measurement and Correlates of Category Width as a Cognitive Variable," *Journal of Personality* 26 (1958): 532–44.

2. T. F. Pettigrew, "The Ultimate Attribution Error: Extending Allport's Cognitive Analysis of Prejudice," *Personality and Social Psychology Bulletin* 5, no. 4 (1979): 461–76.

3. Richard Detweiler, "Culture, Category Width, and Attributions: A Model-Building Approach to Reasons for Cultural Effects," *Journal of Cross-Cultural Psychology* 9 (1978): 265.

4. Ibid., 280.

5. Lexington, "Out and Proud Parents," *The Economist*, June 30, 2007, 42.

6. Richard Detweiler, "Intercultural Interaction and the Categorization Process: A Conceptual Analysis and Behavioral Outcome," *International Journal of Intercultural Relations* 4 (1980): 275–95.

7. Duane Elmer, *Cross-Cultural Servanthood: Serving the World in Christlike Humility* (Downers Grove, IL: InterVarsity, 2006), 69–70.

8. This conflict is explained further in chapter 6, "The Bible," in David Livermore, *Serving with Eyes Wide Open: Doing Short-Term Missions with Cultural Intelligence* (Grand Rapids: Baker Academic, 2006), 77–87.

9. Mark Powell, *What Do They Hear? Bridging the Gap between Pulpit and Pew* (Nashville: Abingdon, 2007), 11–27.

10. Eddie Gibbs, "Culture since 1985," *Missiology* 35, no. 2 (April 2007): 157–68, quote on 164.

11. Richard Cunningham, "Theologizing in a Global Context: Changing Contours," *Review & Expositor* 94 (1997): 359.

12. Dean Flemming, *Contextualization in the New Testament: Patterns for Theology and Mission* (Downers Grove, IL: InterVarsity, 2005), 302–5.

13. Lesslie Newbigin, *The Gospel in a Pluralist Society* (Grand Rapids: Eerdmans, 1989), 152–53.

14. Flemming, *Contextualization in the New Testament*, 305.

15. Richard Rohr, *Everything Belongs: The Gift of Contemplative Prayer* (New York: Crossroad, 2003), 65.

16. Ibid., 74.

17. Elizabeth Liebert, *Changing Life Patterns: Adult Development in Spiritual Direction* (St. Louis: Chalice, 2000), 121–22.

Chapter 12 Theory Gets a Bum Rap: A Model for Going Deep

1. Paulo Freire, *Pedagogy of the Oppressed* (New York: Continuum, 1997), 25.

2. Donald Schön, *Educating the Reflective Practitioner* (San Francisco: Jossey-Bass, 1987).

3. Mark Noll, *The Scandal of the Evangelical Mind* (Grand Rapids: Eerdmans, 1994), 12, 246.

4. bell hooks, *Teaching to Transgress: Education as the Practice of Freedom* (New York: Routledge, 1994), 59–75.

5. David Kolb, *Experiential Learning: Experience as the Source of Learning and Development* (Englewood Cliffs, NJ: Prentice-Hall, 1984).

6. Y. Yamazaki and D. C. Kayes, "An Experiential Approach to Cross-Cultural Learning: A Review and Integration of Competencies for Successful Expatriate Adaptation," *Academy of Management Learning and Education* 3, no. 4: 362–79.

7. Ibid.

8. An overview of the findings from this study and the application of Joplin to short-term missions is described in Kara Powell, T. Linhart, D. Livermore, and B. Griffin, "If We Send Them, They Will Grow . . . Maybe," *Journal of Student Ministries* 20, no. 2 (March/April 2007): 20–24.

9. Terence Linhart, "They Were So Alive: The Spectacle Self and Youth Group Short-Term Mission Trips" (paper presented at the North Central Evangelical Missiological Society Meeting, Deerfield, IL, April 9, 2005).

10. Six Sigma Financial Services, "Determine the Root Cause: 5 Whys," http://finance.isixsigma.com/library/content/c020610a.asp.

11. Portions of this section adapted from Powell et al., "If We Send Them."

12. Albert Bandura, *Social Learning Theory* (Englewood Cliffs, NJ: Prentice-Hall, 1977).

13. David Thomas, "Domain and Development of Cultural Intelligence: The Importance of Mindfulness," *Group & Organization Management* 31, no. 1 (February 2006): 91.

Chapter 13 When the Goin' Gets Tough: Perseverance CQ

1. Excerpted from the "CQ for Cross-Cultural Ministry Leadership" Assessment, adapted by David Livermore, developed by Linn Van Dyne, Michigan State University, and Soon Ang, Nanyang Technological University, Singapore, http://grts.cornerstone.edu/resources/glc/cqprofile.

2. P. Christopher Earley, Soon Ang, and Joo-Seng Tan, *CQ: Developing Cultural Intelligence at Work* (Stanford, CA: Stanford Business Books, 2006), 69.

3. Robert Merton, *Social Theory and Social Structure* (New York: Free Press, 1968), 319.

4. L. Spitzer, *Lives In-Between: The Experience of Marginality in a Century of Assimilation* (New York: Hill & Wang, 1999).

5. John Van Maanen, "Doing New Things in Old Ways: The Chains of Socialization," in *College and University Organization: Insights from the Behavioral Sciences*, ed. J. L. Bess (New York: New York University Press, 1983), 213.

6. John Van Maanen, "Breaking In: Socialization to Work," in *Handbook of Work, Organization, and Society*, ed. R. Dubin (Chicago: Rand McNally College, 1976), 67–130.

7. P. Vila, "Constructing Social Identities in Transnational Contexts: The Case of the Mexico–United States Border," *International Social Science Journal* 159 (1999): 75–87.

8. K. Oberg, "Culture Shock: Adjustment to New Culture Environments," *Practical Anthropology* 7 (1960): 177–82.

9. W. Tierney and R. Rhoads, "Enhancing Promotion, Tenure and Beyond: Faculty Socialization as a Cultural Process," *ERIC Digest* (April 1994).

10. Craig Storti, *The Art of Crossing Cultures* (Yarmouth, ME: Intercultural Press, 1990), 9.

11. Van Maanen, "Breaking In," 84.

12. Elizabeth Liebert, *Changing Life Patterns: Adult Development in Spiritual Direction* (St. Louis: Chalice, 2000), 31.

13. A portion of this discussion originally appeared in Steve Argue and Dave Livermore, "There's No U in Missions," *Group*, July–August 2007, 32.

14. Henri Nouwen, *In the Name of Jesus: Reflections on Christian Leadership* (New York: Crossroad, 2001), 58.

15. David Zac Niringiye, personal interview, June 21, 2006.

16. "The African Planter: An Interview with Oscar Muiri," *Leadership Journal*, http://www.christianvisionproject.com/2007/05/the_african_planter-print.html.

17. Soon Ang, personal conversation, March 26, 2007.

18. Earley, Ang, and Tan, *CQ*, 67–68.

19. Storti, *Art of Crossing Cultures*, 44.

20. Ibid., 67.

21. Ibid.

Chapter 14   Kiss, Bow, or Shake: Behavioral CQ

1. Elizabeth Liebert, *Changing Life Patterns: Adult Development in Spiritual Direction* (St. Louis: Chalice, 2000), 47.

2. Gary Chapman and Ross Campbell, *The Five Love Languages of Children* (Chicago: Northfield, 1997).

3. Excerpted from the "CQ for Cross-Cultural Ministry Leadership" Assessment, adapted by David Livermore, developed by Linn Van Dyne, Michigan State University, and Soon Ang, Nanyang Technological University, Singapore, http://grts.cornerstone.edu/resources/glc/cqprofile.

4. Adapted from David Thomas and Kerr Inkson, *Cultural Intelligence: People Skills for Global Business* (San Francisco: Berrett-Koehler, 2004), 40–41.

5. Craig Storti, *The Art of Crossing Cultures* (Yarmouth, ME: Intercultural Press, 1990), 14.

6. Ibid., 15.

7. Ibid., 26.

8. Ibid., 58.

9. Edward Stewart and Milton Bennett, *American Cultural Patterns: A Cross-Cultural Perspective* (Boston: Intercultural Press, 1991), 20–21.

10. H. Giles and P. Smith, "Accommodation Theory: Optimal Levels of Convergence," in *Language and Social Psychology*, ed. H. Giles and R. N. St. Clair (Baltimore: University Park Press, 1979), 45–63.

11. David Thomas, "Domain and Development of Cultural Intelligence: The Importance of Mindfulness," *Group & Organization Management* 31, no. 1 (February 2006): 88.

12. Storti, *Art of Crossing Cultures*, 81.

13. Thomas, "Domain and Development of Cultural Intelligence," 94.

Chapter 15   Where Do We Go from Here? Twenty-four Ways to Advance Your CQ

1. Nate Ledbetter, "Life on Paper: Discovering the Essence of Neighboring" (unpublished MS).

2. Henri Nouwen, *In the Name of Jesus: Reflections on Christian Leadership* (New York: Crossroad, 2001), 24–25.

3. Mark Vamos, Letter from the Editor: "When Talk Is Better than Action," *Fast Company*, April 2006, 11.

4. Ibid.

5. Fareed Zakaria, "Beyond Bush: What the World Needs Is an Open, Confident America," *Newsweek*, June 11, 2007, 24.

6. Craig Storti, *The Art of Crossing Cultures* (Yarmouth, ME: Intercultural Press, 1990), 72.

7. See Ranya Idliby, Suzanne Oliver, and Priscilla Warner, *The Faith Club: A Muslim, A Christian, A Jew—Three Women Search for Understanding* (New York: Free Press, 2006) for a true-life account of three women who did just this.

8. Nouwen, *In the Name of Jesus*, 17.

9. Peter Scazzero, *The Emotionally Healthy Church: A Strategy for Discipleship That Actually Changes Lives* (Grand Rapids: Zondervan, 2003), 20.

Appendix B   Self-Assessment of CQ

1. Copyright Linn Van Dyne and Soon Ang, A Self-Assessment of Your CQ. Originally appeared in P. C. Earley, S. Ang, and J-S Tan, *CQ: Developing Cultural Intelligence at Work* (Stanford, CA: Stanford Business Books, 2006), 217–27. Used by permission. For more information please visit http://www.culturalq.com.

2. It's important to note that this CQ self-assessment assesses both knowledge CQ and interpretive CQ under the one category "Cultural Strategic Thinking." Cultural strategic thinking refers to the iterative thinking processes that occur between knowledge CQ and interpretive CQ. Further definition of this term is provided in chapter 3.

3. Again, note that this CQ self-assessment assesses both knowledge CQ and interpretive CQ under the one category "Cultural Strategic Thinking." Cultural strategic thinking refers to the iterative thinking processes that occur between knowledge CQ and interpretive CQ. Further definition of this term is provided in chapter 3.

Appendix C Research Context

1. Of the North American subjects, 95 percent were from the United States and 5 percent were from Canada.

2. Discussion from a subset of these findings was published in David Livermore, *Serving with Eyes Wide Open: Doing Short-Term Missions with Cultural Intelligence* (Grand Rapids: Baker Academic, 2006).

3. Clifford Geertz, *The Interpretation of Cultures* (New York: Basic Books, 1973), 111.

index